# THE STORY
# OF
# AMERICA

## HENDRIK VAN LOON

Author of:
THE STORY OF MANKIND
THE STORY OF THE BIBLE

**With Selected Illustrations**

Published by
DELL PUBLISHING COMPANY, INC.
261 Fifth Avenue
New York 16, New York

Reprinted by arrangement with
Liveright Publishing Corporation,
New York, New York

Designed and produced by
Western Printing & Lithographing Company

Cover painting by Calabrese

Printed in U. S. A.

# CONTENTS

## Chapter One

## WANTED: MORE AND CHEAPER SPICES

THE GUILD OF THE GROCERS was in dreadful straits.
Their supply of spices was well-nigh exhausted.
But the demand surpassed anything that had ever been
    seen before.
The Guild of the Grocers was in dreadful straits.
And thereby hangs a story.

. . . . . .

It is a law recognized both by the professors of political
economy and the judges of our police courts that those
who have for a considerable time dined at the Ritz will
not willingly return to Jack Mulhaly's far-famed fish
chowder and beans. Of course, in case of actual need they
will content themselves with the simple fare of the excellent John. But before they reach that point of open
and avowed defeat, they will fight tooth and nail to maintain the standard of excellence to which they have become accustomed.

The barbarians who overran the greater part of western
Europe during the first ten centuries of our era were men
of simple taste, which usually means men of no taste at all.
With them, quantity came before quality, and a continent that had lain practically unscratched since the last
great glacial epoch easily satisfied their demands for a
wooden bench, a greasy slab of beef, and unlimited ale.

Besides, there was so much to be done and there were
so few people to do what needed being done that their
surplus energy was entirely exhausted by the chores of
everyday life. Roughly speaking, it took them a thousand
years to settle down. Then the job was done. Peace and
quiet returned to this earth and with peace and quiet on
the part of the elders came the Wanderlust of the younger

generation.

Ten centuries before, that Wanderlust would have led to another outbreak of anarchy. But by now the people of the West once more recognized a single master. He laid no claim to worldly power. His spiritual weapons, however, could annihilate entire battalions of Swiss mercenaries. His paper arrows could pierce the walls of the strongest castles.

His mere displeasure was more terrible than a threat of war on the part of emperor or king.

Surrounded by the cleverest of diplomats, the most astute of politicians, he was able to divert the rising tide of unrest into the practical channels of foreign conquest and to bring about that great migration toward the East which ever since has been known as the era of the Crusades. Unfortunately this episode has been so often chosen as a subject for romantic literary rhapsodies that we are apt to forget the true if more prosaic nature of the conflict.

The ancient world was the world of the Mediterranean. He who had command of that vast tract of water could dictate his will to the rest of mankind.

It was an ambitious undertaking, and the small fry of pirates and buccaneers who infested the deep bays of the Spanish and Greek and Italian peninsulas and who lived along the shallow coast of Morocco and Tripoli and Egypt could not possibly hope for more than a trifling local success.

Nothing short of "racial groups"—vast agglomerations of people bound together by tens of thousands of years of a common social, economic, and religious development —were able to handle a problem that must be settled upon so gigantic a scale. They well knew the risk they took, for such quarrels were apt to be quite as disastrous to the victor as to the vanquished.

Only twice before had it come to an open break.

The first time in the fifth century before our era, when Greece as the champion of the West had defeated the invading hordes of the Persians and in a series of brilliant counterattacks had pursued her enemies as far as the shores of the river Indus.

The second time two hundred years later, when the Romans narrowly averted disaster by such a display of national energy that the state almost perished before the last of the Carthaginian strongholds had been reduced to ashes.

Then, for more than eight centuries, there had been peace.

But in the year 622 Asia, marching under the banner of a brand-new prophet, was once more ready for the unequal struggle. This time the campaign was planned upon a truly gigantic scale. The left wing of the Mohammedan armies took possession of Spain. The right wing meanwhile made for Constantinople by way of Syria and Asia Minor. It was at that moment that the head of the Christian Church took fright and proclaimed a holy war.

This war, from a military point of view, was a complete failure. But its social consequences were of great and lasting importance. For the first time since the disappearance of the Roman state the nations of Europe were exposed to a civilization which in almost every respect was higher than their own. They went east to slaughter the infidel and to deprive him of his pagan possessions. They returned home with a new conception of comfort and luxury and with a profound dislike for the crudities of their own barren existence.

This sudden change in the general point of view was soon reflected in the houses of the people of the western mainland, in their clothes, in their manners, in the way they spent their idle hours and in the things they ate and drank.

The older generation (after the habit of all older generations) continued to talk about the simple virtues of the ancestors. The children merely shrugged their shoulders and smiled. They had been to the "big city" and they knew better. Quietly they bided their time, but as soon as the old folks were dead they hastened to reupholster the parlor, sent for a couple of outlandish cooks, and dispatched their sons to the near-by town that there they might learn how to become bankers or manufacturers and acquire within a single lifetime that wealth which the soil would not surrender in a thousand years of heart-breaking toil.

The Church grumbled.

This was a consequence she had not quite foreseen.

Alas! The returning heroes were no longer animated with that holy and unquestioning zeal which had been so characteristic of their parents and grandfathers. Familiarity with one's friends may breed contempt. But familiarity with an enemy is apt to create mutual respect.

As a result there was a slump in the building of churches. But private palaces and richly adorned municipal buildings were arising on all sides.

I do not say that this was a good thing. I do not say that it was bad. I merely state a fact. If you want to draw any conclusions, go ahead and suit yourself.

Meanwhile on the other shore of the Mediterranean there also had been a considerable decline in the ardor of that strange religious devotion which measured its love for Allah by the number of slaughtered captives. In short, both parties had accepted a stalemate and were willing to reach a compromise which meant money in the pockets of their respective merchants.

The ancient trade routes, trampled down by millions of iron heels and hoofs, were put in a state of repair. Once more the patient camels carried their burdens from Kashgar to Damascus. Again, as in the days of old, the Venetian caravels and the Genoese galleys plied regularly between Alexandria and Famagusta.

Wherefore all was well with the world and the rate of interest upon a successful Levantine deal rose rapidly from just exactly nothing to four hundred per cent.

Then one of those insignificant incidents happened which (after the nature of insignificant occurrences) are apt to change the entire aspect of history for all time to come. It was during the middle of the thirteenth century. The dreadful Tartars had just gone on the warpath and from the Amur to the Vistula people were flying in blind panic before this flood of grinning little yellow devils.

Among the fugitives was a small group of nomads (two or three hundred families at the most) who since time immemorial had lived peacefully in the heart of Asia. They ran almost as far as the Mediterranean. Then they heard that the danger was past and decided to return home. In order to do this they must cross the river Euphrates. But an accident happened. Their leader slipped off his horse and was drowned. The others who were still on the western bank of the river took fright. They regarded this sudden calamity as a direct warning of Heaven and asked the King of Persia to let them stay where they were.

The rest is a matter of common knowledge. Within less than a hundred years these wandering shepherds had made themselves the masters of the empire that had given them hospitality and one generation afterward they were the recognized rulers of the Mohammedan world and had started upon that career of conquest which eventually was to carry their horse-tail banners to the gates of Vienna and was to make the mere name of "Turk" a byword for cruelty and bravery for all ages.

Now if this sudden revival of Moslem fury had been merely a political movement, it would not have been so bad. But a profound spiritual frenzy swept across the plains and hills of western Asia. During the six centuries which had gone by since the death of the Prophet the original ardor of his followers had considerably cooled. The "faith of the fathers" was something very fine but so was the sweet profit derived from the traffic in pepper and cinnamon and indigo. It was unfortunate that this trade forced the true believers to be on amicable terms with the infidel dogs from the other side of the Mediterranean, but you know how it is. Business is business and one cannot draw the line at Christians if one is in trade.

Not so the inhabitants of the villages and the lonely valleys! They took their religion seriously and encouraged by the military and the political success of their Turkish leaders they now decided to bring their erring brethren of the big cities back to the true faith.

Far and wide the Dervishes (the monks of the Mohammedan world) traveled through the realm of the Prophet. Some of them prayed, some of them danced, some of them whirled, some of them howled. But one and all they preached a return to the stern tenets of the original desert creed.

At first the merchants of Bagdad and Damascus laughed. But the "puritans" were in dead earnest. Soon the merchants even ceased to smile. A little later (warned by the fate of their murdered neighbors) they began to restrict their commercial operations to their own fellow religionists.

And in this way, just when the people of Europe had come to depend upon certain Asiatic goods, the supply was suddenly cut off.

Of course this did not happen in a day or a week or even a single year. But those products which for more than two hundred years had flowed westward in such complete and uninterrupted abundance now began to disappear from the European markets. The available supplies were at once cornered by the speculators. Prices began to soar. Credit was withdrawn and payment had to be made in gold. This was something new in the West. The medieval world, in its everyday transactions, had never insisted upon ready money. Everyone lived within hailing-distance of everyone else. One man's pork was as good as another man's eggs. The honey of one cloister could readily be exchanged for the vinegar of another.

It is true, foreign trade had always insisted upon a certain amount of gold and silver coin. It had been impossible to satisfy the spice dealers of Calicut with slices of bacon and barrels of salt. Before they authorized their agents in Jidda or Aden to make delivery they had demanded a deposit of Venetian doubloons and pieces-of-eight.

But now the European market began to ask for cash on delivery. That greatly complicated matters.

For gold, the mysterious yellow substance which seemed to defy the power of State and Church, was another article that had to be imported from abroad. There were a few silver mines in Europe but the small amount of gold that was found in the mountains of Austria, Saxony, and Spain

14

was by no means sufficient to finance the ever-increasing operations of the speculators and the legitimate spice dealers.

Here was as pretty a vicious circle as the world had ever seen. A public ready and eager to buy—a decreasing amount of supplies—a rapid increase in prices—a general demand for bullion—a decrease in the available supply of gold—one country of western Asia and northern Africa after another falling into the hands of the relentless heathen—one caravan road after the other closed for an indefinite space of time—and the young and lusty capitalistic system of Europe fighting for its life.

The capitalistic system (using this term in the sense in which it is understood or misunderstood by most of our contemporaries) has been accused of many and highly diversified crimes. But even its worst enemies cannot accuse it of laziness or deny that in times of a crisis it is able to develop an almost supernatural energy. It was just such a crisis which now threatened to ruin the western commercial world during the first half of the fourteenth century.

I have spoken of the plight of the grocers. They were most active and vociferous in their protestations. But the entire economic (which in the last analysis means the entire spiritual, social, literary, artistic, and scientific) fabric of Europe was in imminent danger of collapse.

It is true that Syria and Egypt (the two countries through which the principal trade routes from the East to the West had run since the beginning of time) were not captured by the Turks until a dozen years after the death of Columbus. But a merchant who knows his business does not wait for the actual day of disaster. He anticipates.

We hear a great deal of the sagacity of our modern princes of commerce and we flatter ourselves that it is our own era that has given birth to this intrepid race of men. And we are apt to think rather patronizingly of the medieval trader who sat in a stuffy little room, who counted his shekels with the help of a pair of diminutive scales, who dictated his letters to two clerks simultaneously (that he might have a carbon-copy of his correspondence) and who was obliged to wait half a year before he got an answer

15

from his agents in Viborg or Novgorod.

But that is one of the fallacies of our happy age which takes to self-flattery as a duck takes to water.

The world of the year of Grace 1927 is really very much like the world of the year of Grace 1427 or 427. It is composed of all sorts of people. Some are bright. Some are not quite so bright. Others are downright stupid.

The latter (always the vast majority) did not take any interest either one way or another. The second category felt vaguely that something must be done, then got frightened at its own boldness and did nothing. But the first (a very small minority) took off its coat and vest, rolled up its sleeves, and went forth to decide the issue then and there. The overland route to the profitable East was gradually being closed. Very well. Then they would look for a new road by way of the South or the West. The undertaking, entailing a voyage across uncharted seas, looked about as hopeless as an airplane trip to the moon in our own time. Indeed, the practical obstacles were so immense that they could only be overcome by a dreamer.

The world was full of experienced sea captains, who could foretell the approaching storm through the rheumatism in their aching bones; of highly trained astronomers who could read the book of Heaven as we consult a timetable; of adventurers eager to risk their lives for a bit of excitement or a pot full of ducats.

But it took a different sort of creature to solve this problem—a strange genius who derived his inspiration from the Apocalypse of Ezra (has anyone within the memory of man read this muddled mixture of Heaven, Hell, and prophecy?)—a professional promoter who would not budge until he had been given a duly signed contract assuring him ten per cent of all the precious metals to be discovered in the domains on the other side of the ocean—a vain peacock who insisted upon being called "Admiral of the Ocean"—a humble mystic who died in the poor garb of a Franciscan monk.

## Chapter Two

## A WORLD UNSUSPECTED

HIS NEIGHBORS IN GENOA knew him as plain Chris Pigeon. The Spaniards, who made billions out of his discovery and cheated him out of his reward, called him Don Cristobal Colon and afterward, remembering the gold land to the north of Venezuela, added the grandiloquent title of Duke of Veragua. The world at large refers to him as Christopher Columbus and as such he will play his part in our little story.

He was born in 1446 or 1447 or 1448 or 1449 or 1450. We don't know, and it does not matter very much. He saw the light of day in Genoa or Cogoleto. We do not know, and that, too, matters very little. But his poor bones were buried and reburied seven times in less than four centuries. And that tells the story. Restlessness without end, and as a reward a pair of iron handcuffs and the six boards of a wooden coffin.

The father of Columbus was in the woolen business, half weaver, half merchant, but fairly prosperous and able to send his son to a good school. Afterward the boy was to succeed him in his business and become a respectable citizen and have a family of his own—everything as it always had been and always would be.

Alas! Respectability of the ordinary sort meant very little in the life of Columbus. For he was of this world and yet not quite of this world. He wanted money—a great deal of money—for his plans, for his studies, for his books. He wanted the world to recognize the fact that he was not like the common herd, that his courage and his endurance and the brilliant speculations of his mind made him, the weaver's son, a fit companion for the mighty princes of this earth. Beyond that, it is difficult to say just exactly what he hoped to get out of his career.

17

The white man's first winter in the new world. A.D. 1003

He was exceedingly clumsy at the queer business of living. But he could sail a leaky tub across an uncharted sea with no other help than a self-devised system of navigation, he could cajole a mutinous crew of jailbirds and highwaymen into a semblance of decent behavior until he had actually found what he had set out to discover, and upon occasions he could stand more thirst and hunger and scurvy and could do with less sleep than any other mortal being. Heaven knows, these are enough claims to fame for even the most ambitious of us.

One thing Columbus did not do. He did not write. Perhaps this is a pity. On the whole, however, I think it is a distinct gain. Imagine a serialized article on "How I Discovered the New World," with exclusive photographs of the wives and daughters of the Cacique of Guanahani. Imagine signed interviews on "The Hardtack that Made Me an Explorer." No, it is much better this way. We do not know quite as much about the man as we sometimes would like. It saves us from knowing a whole lot of things which would only obscure the main point in his career; his absolute and unshakable faith in the belief that by sailing due westward one would not tumble off this earth or be broiled by the rays of the tropical sun, as most of his contemporaries thought, but that on the contrary one would reach the land of the heathen Chinese and would be able to return home by way of the Indies.

The problem did not prove to be quite as simple as he had thought. A fairly wide ridge of land separated the ocean of Europe from that of Asia. That, however, was a mere detail which no one could have foretold. Most certainly it does not dim the glory of that shabby and weather-beaten Genoese pilot who first of all said, "It can be done," and then did it.

The Middle Ages had one enormous advantage over our own time. It was considered good form, yea, an essential part of life, to learn your job and learn it well. There were no short cuts. The Greeks, a thousand years before, had said that the Gods were willing to surrender all their secrets in exchange for a certain fixed amount of honest sweat. The people of the fifteenth century substituted the Guild boss for Zeus, but rigidly adhered to the doctrine that labor alone fits a man for his job. And when young Christopher decided that he did not care to succeed his father in the wool business, but wanted to be a sailor, he was immediately apprenticed to a captain and told to learn his trade by beginning as a cabin boy and scullery assistant.

During the next four years we hear of him in every port of the eastern part of the Mediterranean. A little later we find traces of his presence in Portugal and in England and we know that he pushed as far as the newly discovered coast of Guinea. Then he married. Quite typical, however, of his serious singlemindedness he married right into the profession. The lady of his choice was not rich, but she had inherited her father's logbooks and all his notes and her father was no one else than Bartholomew Perestrello, captain in the service of Prince Henry of Portugal and the first governor general of Porto Santo, one of the recently rediscovered islands of the Madeira group.

In this way Columbus came in direct contact with the work of a man (dead these last thirty years) who in every sense of the word might be called the John the Baptist of modern exploration and discovery, the prophet who prepared the way for one greater than himself but who did not live to see the day of ultimate victory.

Prince Henry of Portugal, commonly called Henry the Navigator, was the son of a Portuguese father and an English mother. In his youth he had been a great warrior, but he was a stern man, yea, a veritable puritan, and when the fighting had come to an end, when Portugal for all time had been made safe from invasion by the heathen from across the Straits of Gibraltar, then he retired from court and near the town of Sagres, on the bleak hills of a lonely promontory of his native land, he built himself a cloistered fortress that was to become the first of all nautical schools and the most important of medieval astronomical observatories.

There, undisturbed by the noise of the outside world, the royal geographers and astronomers and mathematicians and map makers collected and sifted and classified all that strange and miscellaneous amount of information that had been an integral part of the sailors' lore ever since the day when Hanno the Carthaginian had first surprised the western world with his mysterious stories of the apes that walked like men and that were called "gorillas."

Let it be understood at once that the interests of this noble Prince were not at all commercial. The grandson of John of Gaunt and the Grand Master of the immensely rich order of Christ did not have to worry about mere dollars and stivers. Besides he was too devout a son of the Church to care much about worldly acquisitions. Provided he could have the souls of the poor heathen who dwelled in multitudinous darkness beyond the hazy dimness of Cape Bojador, the merchants and jobbers were welcome to such profits as could be derived from barter with the savage blackamoors. And if his discoveries would only bring him into contact with Prester John (the mystery man of the twelfth century who proved to be no one else than the kinky-haired King of Abyssinia) then he would gladly surrender all his claims to the gold of Ophir.

Nothing, perhaps, shows the difficulty of medieval exploration quite as clearly as the slow success of the famous Sagres institute which represented the last word in the science of navigation and did not have to worry about the expense. Often it took the ships that flew its flag years to cover a distance which a modern tramp steamer accomplishes in a couple of days. Every time a new cape had been successfully rounded there was a day of hallelujahs and Te Deums. A modern explorer who has just returned from a trip to the North Pole receives less recognition than a Portuguese captain who had charted a few hundred additional miles of the west coast of Africa.

Now the difference between really great men and just great men is that the former are never in a hurry. Henry the Navigator edited his maps as Kreisler plays the violin. He had all the time in the whole wide world. No reason to get excited or do slipshod work. And so gradually the west coast of Africa began to take shape. The long-lost Azores were rediscovered. Madeira, which somehow or other had been forgotten for almost a century, ceased to be the picturesque background for a pretty English love story and became a definite if more prosaic spot on the map. Cape Bojador ceased to be the ultimate limit of all geographical knowledge. Cape Branco went next. In the year 1445 it was the turn of Cape Verde. And before Henry died, one of his captains had actually pushed as far as Cape Sierra Leone, and the preliminary work, which afterward made it possible for Diaz to sail around the Cape of Good Hope and which enabled Vasco da Gama to sail to India, had been done.

And in many other ways (although less directly) did Prince Henry help along the cause of civilization. A few drops of science will often disinfect an entire barrel full of ignorance and prejudice. Through the influence of the Sagres institute navigation ceased to be a hodgepodge of monsters and floating islands, of submersible continents and those other thousand and one fairy stories with which the early Irish missionaries had delighted their credulous parishioners. The compass and the sextant began to be substituted for the old method of coast-bumping, known generally as "sailing by God and by guess." And the strange accounts brought back by sailors who had been blown out of their course and who in their panic had seen almighty strange things were no longer accepted as gospel truth but were carefully examined and were either rejected or put over for further examination, as the case seemed to warrant.

Among those yarns there was one with which Columbus, like all his seafaring companions, must have been familiar. That was the story of the exploration of an entirely new world which was supposed to be situated somewhere north of the Arctic circle. In how far Columbus had heard of those voyages first hand we do not know. He hinted to some of his friends that he had been as far as Ultima Thule. What he meant by "Ultima Thule" we do not know. It may have been Iceland and it may have been the Faroe Islands. But remember that when Columbus lived, there still were titulary Bishops of Greenland; that direct communication with that island had been broken off only one generation before; and that the Icelanders just then were making a formidable collection of those old sagas which told of the brave deeds of their ancestors and which spoke in detail of certain mysterious lands of the far west.

In their search for documentary evidence the historians have sometimes overlooked such small trifles as currents and winds. With a map of the Atlantic before us, we no longer ask ourselves the question, "Did the Norsemen ever reach the coast of America?" We rather say, "Why did it take them so long to get there?"

A French skipper or an English one, driven out of his course, either went to the bottom of the ocean or got back to his home port. The Gulf Stream took care of that.

But a Viking on his way from Norway to the Arctic colonies ran every risk of being picked up by the Greenland current and unless he were very lucky he would next find himself the guest of the Labrador current and after that there was no escape. He was bound to land somewhere on the eastern coast of the North American continent.

Please remember that there were direct and uninterrupted communications between Greenland and Norway for more than four centuries (983-1410); that hundreds of men and women during that period must have made the trip to the western islands; that they sailed without chart or compass, and were at the mercy of the different Arctic currents to an extent which we people who regard even the Gulf Stream as a negligible quantity cannot possibly understand; and finally that they were a highly imaginative and literary people who left us a faithful and detailed record of their explorations.

I do not mention all this to revive the ancient and silly quarrel whether it was Leif, the son of Eric, the farmer from Haukadalur, or Christopher, the son of Domenico, the weaver from Genoa, who must be regarded as the real discoverer of our own continent. I merely refer to the Norsemen episode in our history to show that in the days of Columbus it was a generally accepted fact that there was "something" on the other side of the ocean and that that "something" could be found by anyone willing to take a risk and ready to sail due westward for three or four weeks.

Unfortunately the conviction that these lands (which probably were a series of islands off the coast of India and China) could be reached by boat was not enough. Someone had to provide the boats, and boats, then as now, cost money. Which brings us to the second part of the life of Columbus, his career as a promoter.

During the latter half of the fifteenth century the only supply of ready cash worth mentioning was to be found in Italy. But suppose that the Pope or the Medici had financed his enterprise, suppose that he could have induced the government of Venice or Genoa to give him their support, what good would it have done?

Spain controlled the gateway to the ocean. And Spain was a powerful country, a highly centralized country, and more than a match for the jealous little navies of the jealous little Italian cities. Spain therefore was the logical candidate for those high honors which Columbus felt sure that he could bestow upon his future patron and it was to Spain that he turned when he began to make serious preparations for his great western voyage.

In this day and age when we think nothing of wasting a couple of million dollars in just so many hours for the sake of some slight military gain, it is difficult to understand and appreciate the utter clumsiness, yea, the helplessness of the capitalistic system before the introduction of a plentiful supply of gold bullion and the invention of credit. The French Revolution (which took place only a little over a century ago) was due to the fact that the most prosperous monarchy of the eighteenth century, and all its ministers and all its faithful members of parliament, aided by the most expert financial advice of the age, could not possibly raise a sum of money which nowadays would be taken care of by half an hour's telephonic conversation between the Minister of Finance and a couple of international bankers.

And Spain almost lost her chance at becoming the master of the New World because King Ferdinand and Queen Isabella were unable to lay their hands on ten thousand dollars in cash. After a great deal of haggling and wrangling this sum was at last found. But without the private assistance of the Pinzon brothers, honorable merchants from the forgotten little city of Palos, Columbus probably would have spent the rest of his days in Paris and Lisbon and London, trying to explain to Royal Commissioners that his plans were not the dreams of a madman and that a few dollars risked now would bring untold wealth in the near future.

However that may be, the Pinzons finally decided to join forces with the King and Queen and on the third of August of the year 1492 Columbus set sail for the Azores with three ships, the largest of which was smaller than a respectable-sized ferryboat and had been built for the coastwise trade with Flanders.

Twice more he sighted land, the Canary Islands and Teneriffe. Then he boldly pushed forth into the ultimate confines of the unknown. The voyage lasted a little over two months. On the night between the eleventh and the twelfth of October of the year 1492 a light was seen. It was a watch fire of the "Indians." The next morning the first meeting between the white man and the copper-colored Indian took place. It must have been a strange scene. There was a Jewish mariner on board Columbus's flagship who had been hired on account of his reputation as a linguist. His services during this memorable occasion must have been of a very simple nature.

The Admiral: Ask the old heathen where the Indies are.

Luis de Torres (holding up a shiny brass object and waving his arms): Huh?

The "old heathen" (pointing a very dirty finger in a western direction): Huh!

And so these brave adventurers once more hoisted anchor and once more they sailed westward and found nothing but islands, low little islands with palm trees and naked savages and howling children who shrieked their heads off when the gun of the *Santa Maria* said "boom-m-m-m." But of the Indies, of the turreted walls of Kathay, of the incense-bearing trees of Zipangu not a trace—not a trace—not a trace.

Columbus, however, refused to accept defeat.

Three times more he wearily crossed the ocean. Some day, some day, surely, he would find the gap between those miserable reefs and promontories that would lead him directly to his goal.

But he never did.

Worn out by hardships and hunger and thirst and the ills of the tropics, his own body turned traitor, as so many of his captains had done before.

Columbus died on the twentieth day of May of the year 1506. His bad luck followed him beyond the grave.

During the early part of the sixteenth century there was a very popular academy of learning in the little French town of St. Dié where a specialty was made of the study of geography. Now it happened in the year 1507 that the director of this school, an honest German by the name of Martin Waldseemüller (or Hylacomylus, as he preferred to call himself) decided to publish a handbook of cosmography. But what to do with the ever-increasing number of scraps of land which seemed to float in space

25

a few thousand miles westward of the Azores?

Wasn't it about time to group them together and give them a name?

Yes. But what name?

Someone suggested, "Call them after the man who has done most for their discovery and exploration."

A splendid idea! But who was he?

Right here we come across one of the most sublime incongruities of all history.

The people of northern Europe had probably heard of Columbus, but his exploits had by no means become popular. Here and there a carelessly printed little pamphlet with terrible woodcuts of Indian natives and wild beasts had told the European aborigines that a man by the name of Dove or something like it had been to the land of the great bird roc and had come back to tell the tale. That was about all.

But during the first five years of the sixteenth century information of a slightly more amusing character began to dribble across the Pyrenees.

The second expedition of Columbus had been subsidized by a Florentine merchant in Seville. When this personage died quite suddenly the contract was taken over by one Amerigo Vespucci, also a native of Florence and financial representative of the Medici interests in western Spain. This Amerigo (if we are to believe his own stories) accompanied several expeditions to the New World and actually found a great deal of new land in the southern part of the hemisphere. He was a clever publicist and a faithful correspondent and he used to write letters to his employer, Lorenzo de' Medici, to tell that old banker of all he had seen and heard. These letters were translated and printed and spread broadcast as soon as they had reached Florence.

When the learned Hylacomylus looked for a suitable name for the group of islands that formed a barrier between Europe and the Indies, he thought at once of the popular Florentine, whose stuff was familiar to every European who could read and write. Then and there he suggested that the new land be called "the land of Amerigo" or "Terra America" because Americus, it seemed, knew more about it than anyone else. No one said no. Anyway, what did it matter? One name was as good as another and now the question had been decided and people could stop worrying.

But let us not be too hard on poor Hylacomylus. He meant no harm. He was just a simple schoolmaster and allowed himself to be taken in by a clever publicity man.

## Chapter Three

## FAITH, GOLD, AND THE INDIAN

In the year of Grace 1732, General Jeffrey Amherst (who bestowed his name upon a well-known village and college in northern Massachusetts) had reason to instruct one of his subordinates in regard to the treatment of certain native tribes which recognized His Majesty the King of England as their Lord and Master.

*You will do well,* so wrote His Excellency, *to try to inoculate the Indians by means of blankets in which small-pox patients have slept, as well as by every other method that can serve to extirpate this execrable race. I should be very glad if your scheme of hunting them down by dogs could take effect.*

If such sentiments could be publicly expressed by a distinguished and not unfriendly British general during the first half of the eighteenth century (when the world had begun to take a sincere interest in the welfare of the less enlightened races of men) then what of the poor savages who three hundred years before had suddenly found themselves placed at the mercy of the soldiers and the friars of His Most Catholic Majesty, the King of Spain? Perhaps the less said, the better.

For the Spaniard, who as a child had learned to hate and despise the dusky Moors (who for five centuries had been the rulers of his fatherland) regarded the copper-colored inhabitants of his new possessions as a species of animal that had nothing whatsoever in common with the rest of the human race.

In one respect this proved to be of great advantage to the Indians. It made them exempt from the laws and regulations of the Inquisition which were supposed to deal exclusively with "reasonable beings." Therefore whenever in Mexico City or in Cuzco a fresh batch of English heretics and Jewish backsliders was solemnly marched to the funeral pyre, the natives were allowed to come to the Quemadero and take a cheerful part in the festivities without running the risk of being molested for their own heathenish opinions. But except upon such rare occasions the fate of the Indian was not a happy one and what made it all the worse was the conviction (hidden in some obscure corner of his poor pagan brain) that he was really the rightful owner of the soil and that the foreigner who had reduced him and his neighbors to slavery was merely an intruder and only survived because he was possessed of such large quantities of blunderbusses and ten-pounders.

The native village

The question of the origin of our Indians has never yet been settled. Whether the redskins were Asiatics who had reached the American mainland by way of the frozen Bering Strait or by way of a ridge of land which since then has disappeared, or whether they were descended from a primitive people who had wandered from Europe to Labrador via Iceland and Greenland is something which no one can decide at the hand of the available materials. This much seems certain—that the American continent was not settled until thousands of years after the appear-

28

ance of true human beings in Asia, Africa, and Europe, and that the ancestors of the Indians, once they had reached these shores, were cut off from communication with the rest of the world for perhaps fifteen or twenty thousand years. Mentally the American aborigines were in no way inferior to the races that lived in other parts of the planet. But they had been left so absolutely to themselves that in most respects they were thousands of years behind those Europeans who now descended upon them with their arquebuses and escopets.

But there was another reason why the Indians should so easily have fallen victim to foreign conquest. There were so very few of them. The entire continent (both South and North America and the densely populated part known as Central America) probably did not contain more than ten million souls, as many as there are today in New York and Chicago alone. This small number was due to their wandering habits and to the fact that most of them were practically unfamiliar with agriculture.

Of course I am dealing in dangerous generalities. There were all sorts of Indians, from the highly civilized Mayas and Peruvians to the cannibalistic tribes of southern Patagonia. But by and large they were no match for the highly organized and well-armed groups of European invaders, and their territories were overrun and occupied in an incredibly short space of time.

Most unfortunately for them the discovery of Columbus came at the very moment when the Spaniards, after about six hundred years of uninterrupted warfare, had just driven the last of the Mohammedan caliphs out of their own country. Spain was still full of that strange crusading spirit which is ready to commit the most hideous of crimes in the name of the most exalted of religions. Men like Cortez and Pizarro, who with a handful of highly drilled cutthroats destroyed Indian empires as large as France, Spain, and England combined, could never have accomplished this had they not felt themselves to be the lineal descendants of the Cid and those other chosen messengers of the All Highest.

The Conquistadores, of course, were highly picturesque

fellows. Their tales of heroism and sacrifice lost nothing in the telling and when we read of their exploits, their marches across swamps and mountains, their profound and bloodthirsty devotion, we are very apt to forget that this piety was strangely interwoven with a ruthless greed for gold. A desire to serve God and the heathen may have carried a few simple friars across the much feared ocean. But the mass of the newcomers merely wanted to get rich and wanted to get rich quick. What became of the people whose houses they plundered, the peasants whose irrigation canals they destroyed, the families whose daughters they stole, all that did not interest them in the least. And as for the people at home, they were just as rapacious and indifferent. Provided the annual "Silver Fleet" carried a sufficient amount of gold and silver to finance the endless campaigns of the Philips and Charleses and Alfonsos who succeeded each other in dull succession upon the Spanish throne, very few questions were asked and none were answered.

How disastrously this system reacted upon the Spanish people has become common history. Less than twenty years after the discovery of the first American islands, such a large percentage of the native Mexican population had died that it was necessary to import laborers from elsewhere. At first these were found among the Indians of Florida and Venezuela. But the American Indians never made good slaves. As soon as they were held in captivity, they began to die like flies and so great became the scandal that a certain Bartolomeo de las Casas (the son of a man who had accompanied Columbus on his first voyage) proposed that no further natives should be forced to work in the mines and on the plantations and that their place should be taken by the hardier blackamoors from Africa.

Las Casas made this suggestion with the best of intentions, but his plan did not work as well as he had hoped. For soon all the scoundrels in Christendom (and there were a good many in those days, nor were they restricted to a single century) were hunting slaves along the Senegal River and the Congo, and this scandalous trade, once started, could not be stopped until centuries afterward.

There was, however, one other prominent reason why the colonies in the new world were doomed to failure. I refer to the innate love of the Spanish crown for centralization. Everything in that unfortunate country had to be referred to Madrid. Not a single colony ever enjoyed a vestige of self-government. The officials, all of them, must be recruited in the mother country, and not a single person born overseas could ever hope to be entrusted with a position of honor or responsibility.

Under those circumstances the colonists shrugged their shoulders, said, "What is the use?" (or words to that effect), kept away from all forms of municipal or state government, and spent their time either enriching themselves at the expense of their white neighbors or lording it over their slaves, with the exception of those who entered the Church and made such excellent use of their advantageous position in society that soon more than eighty per cent of all real estate was in the hands of the clerics and their dependents.

But the economic error which definitely killed all progress was the system of monopolies which Spain introduced into the new world as part of her general policy of colonization. Private enterprise was ruthlessly stamped out. The individual trader, when caught, was immediately handed over to the hangman and every ounce of gold and every pound of cinnamon that was exported from Buenos Aires or Havana had to be accounted for in Cadiz. Such a Paradise of stuffy clerks and bureaucrats offered no room for the development of an independent class of merchants. A small number of Jews (who by a strange coincidence were expelled from Spain on the very day when Columbus sailed from Palos) tried to get a foothold in Mexico and Peru and Venezuela. But as soon as they had accumulated a few thousand dollars by their personal thrift and energy the Inquisition invariably accused them of backsliding, burned them at the stake and confiscated their money. Whereupon the others moved to London or Amsterdam, put their brains and their credit at the disposal of Spain's archenemies, and in this roundabout way helped to destroy the nation that had been such a cruel taskmaster to their ancestors.

It would be easy to increase this chapter by several pages of duly enumerated grievances and errors of judgment. But enough has been said to show why a "Story of America" does not this day mean a history of that vast region where Spanish and Portuguese and not the English tongue happen to be the language of everyday life.

Spain, it is true, discovered and conquered a new continent. But as soon as this had been accomplished, the country made a mistake which doomed all her future efforts to failure—she tried to turn the new world into an exact copy of the old one.

The gods that shape man's destinies are of exceeding patience.

But they draw the line at some things.

## Chapter Four

### TIERRAS DE NINGUN PROVECHO

THE BARRIER—that thrice damnable barrier—that endless chain of islands that cut off the road from Europe to the Indies—was getting to be a terrible reality.

In the beginning those who undertook the perilous voyage were full of hope.

Columbus had failed.

Others might be more successful.

Besides, the reward that awaited the man who solved the problem was so great that it paid to take a little trouble. Wherefore they set to work with a will.

They explored every bay and inlet. Their ships followed every estuary and river until the unwelcome sight of a sandy shore or a broken ridge of mountains told them that once more their quest had been in vain. Even brooks and gullies were duly investigated. For one never could tell! And somewhere or other there must be an opening, a narrow channel between two islands, a .crack between the rocks just wide enough for a single caravel, but nevertheless a direct gateway to the coveted islands of cinnamon, pepper and nutmeg.

Often it appeared that this wish was about to be fulfilled. In the year 1500 Vincente Pinzon, survivor of the famous expedition of 1492, found a broad expanse of water which seemed to lead in a western direction. After fifty miles, a tangle of islands and shoals forced him to return. Forty years later it was definitely established that the Amazon was just a plain, everyday river, perhaps a little larger and wider and bigger and muddier than most other rivers, but a river just the same.

Again in the year 1513 a rumor rapidly spread through the European shipyards that the problem had been solved; that a direct water route to China had been found. True enough, but the glittering waves of which Balboa had just taken possession in the name of the King of Spain were separated from the Atlantic Ocean by several hundred miles of insurmountable rock and volcanoes. And Balboa on the scaffold (he received the usual Spanish reward for his courageous independence) must have known that he had been a failure, that nothing had been solved and the problem had been made more complicated than ever.

Meanwhile Vasco da Gama had at last discovered the direct eastern route to Calicut. The long and dangerous voyage from Cadiz and Palos to San Domingo and Cuba, with the uncertain prospect of "finding something," seemed thereafter an absurd and superfluous adventure. By going due southward and following the road laid down a quarter of a century before by Prince Henry one could (with the exception of a few short stretches of water) remain entirely within sight of land and could go on shore for fresh supplies at least once every three or four days. "Terra America" therefore lost most of its interest as a geographical problem with a practical economic future.

Remained the question: "What can we do with it for the present?"

The answer to this was very simple.

"We can despoil the natives to enrich ourselves and leave the rest to the wolves and the hyenas."

Whereupon the gentlemen adventurers, the highwaymen, the highbinders, and all the other lazzarone of the Iberian peninsula heaved one great cry of joy and chanted, "Let's go!"

How they accomplished their noble task, how they shot and hacked and hung and burned and robbed and lied and cheated and reduced half a dozen interesting experiments in statecraft to agglomerations of mud hovels and cemeteries, all this has been often and beautifully told by those writers who regard murder and arson on the part of their own ancestors as something quite different from the murder and arson committed by everybody else's grandparents. Within an incredibly short space of time those parts of the new continent which contained something of value that could be acquired by theft and did not have to be produced by honest labor were in the hands of the Spanish conquerors.

First it was the turn of Mexico. Then of Peru. Next Chili was added to the New Castille. While along the east coast the ambitions of Spaniards and Portuguese were only kept within certain reasonable bounds by the little red line which Pope Alexander VI had drawn across the flat map of the world that his faithful children should be able to divide the spoils of America without the shedding of too much Christian blood.

But the story is best told by the geographical handbooks of that day.

The sixteenth and seventeenth centuries were a golden age for the professional map makers. A great many of the cartographers of that day were first-rate artists and they took no mean rank as scientists. But the "image" which they have left us of America is a very curious one. When they undertook to depict South America and Central America, they were almost perfect in the detail of their coast lines and in the course of their rivers. Mexico, too, and part of South America they could describe with a fair degree of accuracy. Beyond that, however, they lost interest. And across the northern expanse of wilderness they printed this simple legend: *Tierras de Ningun Provecho,* or *Land that is not of the slightest possible value to anybody.*

*Chapter Five*

## SAMUEL DE CHAMPLAIN DE BROUAGE LEARNS THE NOBLE ART OF CANOEING

THE NUMBER OF PEOPLE sufficiently intelligent to think for themselves has always been exceedingly small. It is doubtful whether the percentage today is very much higher than it was in paleolithic times. It probably is slightly lower than during the third century before our èra in Greece and Asia Minor. But such things are hard to prove with any degree of scientific accuracy.

Meanwhile, we know this much—that the average mind, in times past as well as today, prefers to live on a diet of easily digestible formulas, liberally seasoned with tincture of flattery, and one of the commonest of dishes upon the tables of those who live in the northern hemisphere is the belief that the Latin race (and all other southern people) are no earthly good as sailors and that the true secrets of navigation and seamanship are the exclusive possession of the "Anglo-Saxons" to whom (for good measure) are sometimes added the Dutch and the Norwegians.

And yet, at a time when our ancestors still painted their faces green and dined on raw bear steak, a Phoenician captain with a Semitic crew had already visited the neighborhood of the Cape of Good Hope.

A little later, when the Germanic tribes gaped in utter astonishment at that startling innovation called a "wheel," the Semitic Carthaginians were dickering with the natives of the Congo, the Romans and Greeks had explored every nook and corner of the Mediterranean and certain bold mariners from Tyre and Sidon paid regular visits to the tin mines of Cornwall.

Still later the Portuguese wandered all over the face of the earth, an Italian discovered the New World, and the Spanish language was spoken in every port from Tierra del Fuego to Florida.

We may not like the idea, but the truth of the matter is that our own ancestors learned their trade from the Spaniards and the Frenchmen and that they did not appear upon the scene until the greater part of the map of the world had been carefully filled in with names of French and Spanish origin. This was not only due to the superior seamanship of the Latin sailors, but also to a difference in the technique of exploration.

Frobisher and Drake made repeated attempts to discover a passage that should lead them from the Atlantic to the Pacific. But they were sailors and stuck to their ship. When it was proved that their quest for open water had led them to the source of still another river or the dim coastline of still another bay, so much the worse. They swore, they turned their rudder, hoisted their sails and tried their luck elsewhere. But as for going on shore, no, that they would not do! Walking was a fit pastime for the peasants of Yorkshire. A true son of Devonshire, however, belonged on the wooden planks of the quarterdeck and kept away from grass and trees.

Far different the Spaniard and the Frenchman. They were great at footwork and encased in heavy armor they marched incredible distances under a tropical sun which makes a modern army shout lustily for motor lorries and ice water. But whereas the Spaniard went through the regions he visited like a Juggernaut, destroying all that came before him, the Frenchman, who could not expect his own country to back him up, gradually learned to accomplish his ends by a very different method. Upon occasions he could be quite as ruthless as all other nations who, provided with gunpowder, have come into contact with savages armed only with bows and arrows. But the Frenchman was apt first to reason and then to shoot, whereas the Spaniard invariably began by firing a couple of volleys and left the business of arguing to the friars who hastened to baptize the survivors.

The first (and therefore the most interesting) of those indefatigable French voyageurs was a certain Champlain or Samuel de Champlain de Brouage, as he proudly called himself on the title page of that remarkable book in which he suggested the digging of an early Panama canal. When he reached the northern part of the continent the existence of a big river which penetrated far inland had been known for half a century. But nothing very definite was as yet known of the land that lay beyond the fog-infested shores of the Bay of St. Lawrence. Only a man who believed desperately in his own cause would have undertaken the task of trying to find the route to India by way of the Canadian wilderness. Yet that is exactly what Champlain and some of his successors did.

They were a brave lot. They did not bother to take a large retinue of soldiers with them. As a rule they were accompanied by one or two other white men and depended upon the natives through whose territory they passed to provide them with the necessary number of porters and paddlers. For soon it became evident that the road westward ran through a territory where travel by water was much easier than travel by land.

The Indians, who for the greater part still lived as hunters and fishermen, had invented a small boat, sufficiently strong to pass through the rapids of the big rivers but light enough to be carried overland when the rivers became absolutely unnavigable. With the help of these so-called "canoes" Champlain pushed as far westward as Lake Huron, charted the lower part of the St. Lawrence River, visited Lake Ontario and Lake Oneida and by making clever use of a warfare between the Algonquins and Hurons and Iroquois was able to explore the shores of the lake that is called after him. And finally, at Port Royal, at Quebec and at Montreal he founded settlements which in later centuries were to become the nucleus for that "New France" which was expected to reach from Davis Strait to the Gulf of Mexico.

But alas! Even the enthusiasm of such men as Champlain and his equally famous successors, Marquette, Joliet, Hennepin, and La Salle, who traveled overland from the Straits of Belle Isle to the Gulf of Mobile (via the St. Lawrence, the Great Lakes, the Ohio and Mississippi rivers) failed to convince the French monarchy that an

investment in American real estate would be more profitable to them in the long run than the dreary wars of dynastic aggrandizement upon which they wasted all their
money and all their men.

The Bourbons, after all, were first cousins of the Habsburgs, and the Habsburgs derived their name from an
ancient fortress called the "Hawk's Nest." The hawk is
exceedingly brave in a fight but is not famous for his foresight.

As long as those dynasties which shaped the fate of
Europe could live upon the docile quarry found within
the territory of their peaceful neighbors, they refused to
bother about the frozen wastes of a distant northern continent.

And so, even after the exploits of the great French pioneers, everything remained as it had been before.

A few dots and lines appeared upon that part of the
map which half a thousand years before had first been
seen by Leif the Norseman. For the rest, a vast blank
space, embellished with the familiar legend of *terre in-
connue*.

Unknown it was and unknown it remained—a gigantic
geographical joke—something to be funny about after a
good supper in the Palace of Versailles—a fairy story for
the good little children who wanted to hear about the
funny king of Hochelaga who wore feathers on his head
and a ring through his nose.

## Chapter Six

## DR. CALVIN SURVEYS THIS WORLD
## AND THE NEXT

IN FLORENCE, in the church of San Lorenzo, there stands
a monument which by the general consent of fifteen generations of critical spectators is one of the most stupen-
dous bits of sculpture that the hand of man has ever hacked

out of an unwilling piece of marble. It commemorates the utterly futile life of a sixth-rate princeling who never during his entire existence did anything that was worth remembering.

Meanwhile the shrewd old pawnbroker who turned a sleepy little village on the banks of the Arno into the center of the civilized world of six centuries ago lies buried in a plain wooden coffin somewhere in a forgotten vault of the same sacred edifice.

Posthumous glory is like lightning. No one can foretell where it will strike.

Columbus added a couple of million square miles to the possessions of Spain and a simple German schoolmaster, writing an elementary geography for use in the common schools, deprived him of the honor of having his name bestowed upon that new world which he had just revealed to his contemporaries.

Afterward many attempts were made to rectify the mistake and in this question no people have showed themselves more generous than the citizens of our republic. Our map is one gigantic paean of praise to the glory of the Genoese navigator. The laws of the land are made in a reclaimed swamp called the District of Columbia. The first object that strikes the eye of the visitor to our seat of government is a gigantic statue of Columbus. Let him travel eastward or westward, let him go as far south as Florida or as far north as Vermont, and everywhere his car will speed along Columbian highways, it will be parked in Columbian garages, and he himself will be entertained in the hospitable apartment house of diverse Columbus Heights.

In short, the proverbial visitor from the planet Mars would soon be under the impression that Don Cristobal had been the silent partner in the great venture called the United States, and that he had played an enormous part in the development of our country. Whereas, if I may slightly mix my metaphors, Columbus was merely the midwife of our national existence. He was present when the territory which we now inhabit first saw the light of civilized day. But the austere genius who during the impressionable years of the lusty young infant succeeded in stamping his own character upon the boy in such a thorough-going fashion that the child, grown into manhood, would never forget his early training, that man has been so completely neglected that his name is quite unfamiliar to most of our contemporaries.

Geneva

And yet, if posterity had a true appreciation of its duty, every city and hamlet in these United States would have one or a dozen statues erected to the memory of Doctor John Calvin, who was born in Noyon in France in 1509 and who departed this life in Geneva in Switzerland in the year of Grace 1564.

Because his ruthless system of theology has grown almost as much out of date as that propounded once upon a time by the prophet of Mount Horeb, the people who write books in the year of enlightenment 1927 are apt to dismiss this antiquated French reformer with an expression of irritation and not infrequently they overlook the enormous services which this tired and sickly theologian rendered to the cause of human progress. For if it be conceded that the reasonable freedom and happiness of the average individual is the goal toward which all civilization is striving, then Calvin deserves a special and prominent niche in that hall of fame which every sensible man erects in some secret corner of his brain.

Calvin himself, if he were to read this statement, would violently deny that he had ever tried to do anything of the sort. Of course he wanted full liberty of conscience for his own people (who were right because they believed as he did). But as soon as he should have set his bailiwick free from Popish influence, he fully intended to turn Geneva into a second Rome, a town where discipline should be discipline and where the word of the Elders was to be accepted and respected as the supreme law of the land.

In this noble ambition he failed most lamentably, but his open defiance of the Papal authority caused a war during which Calvin was able to join all the heterogeneous elements of discontented reformers and Protestants into an invincible army of opposition.

Why it was John Calvin who performed this miracle and not Martin Luther, who first of all had hoisted the banner of rebellion, a glance at the map will show you.

Luther lived in Wittenberg, a small town in the northern part of Germany. A wide barrier of friendly territory separated his own country from the territory of the enemy and as a result he enjoyed a comparative amount of safety. Calvin, on the other hand, in his little mountain-locked city in southern Switzerland, was within earshot of the Catholic forces. He commanded the advance post of Protestantism. He lived all his life in an armed camp and the sort of men who do that sort of work, whether they be pioneers of the body or pioneers of the soul, are apt to develop a strange philosophy of life, the like of which is not found anywhere else.

"Be hard or perish," was the warning that was carried to Geneva from the funeral pyres in Dijon and Grenoble. And from being hard on the field of battle to being hard in the realm of the Church and State was but a short step. But it was a step which led away from the lovingkindness of the New Testament and brought the faithful back to the uncompromising cruelty which forms so large a part of the old one. It was a step which made men turn their backs upon the smiling fields of Nazareth and regard the forbidding walls of Jerusalem as the true home of the spirit.

41

It is useless to regret that this ever happened.

Within the domain of history it is useless to regret anything.

The most one can do is to try and understand.

From our point of view (no, that is too vague; from my own point of view) it was a highly desirable thing that the power of Rome as an international super-state should be definitely broken, and this could only be done by men of iron who recognized no principle except the dictates of their own rigid conscience. In due time their religious convictions, borrowed directly from the Prophets and Judges (whose terrible deeds disgrace so many of the pages of the ancient Jewish chronicles) will no doubt disappear from the face of our planet.

Meanwhile the good work they did remains. And of this I feel sure, that they never would have been able to accomplish their task if they had not been inspired and carried on by the harsh idealism of the lonely fighter on the banks of the Lake of Geneva.

*Chapter Seven*

## THE HERETIC TURNS HIGHJACKER

FOR THE BENEFIT OF THOSE who have never been newspapermen or police matrons and are not familiar with the nomenclature of crime, let me explain the word "highjacker." A highjacker is not a common thief or robber. A common thief is a low scoundrel who deprives an honest man of his possessions. In such a case the person who suffers a loss can loudly holler for help. At once the brave policemen hurry to the scene, arrest the culprit, and drag him to the courts of law where stern judges condemn him to years of suffering and repentance in the dark dungeons of our prisons.

A highjacker, on the other hand, is a depraved creature who makes it his business to attack bootleggers and no one else. Now a bootlegger (a term applied to people engaged in the illicit business of manufacturing, transporting, and selling whisky, wine, champagne, beer, and other alcoholic beverages) is by the very nature of his trade a person "outside the law." He cannot shout, "Murder!" and ask the cops to come to his assistance. For the gendarmes would ask him, "What, if you please, is the nature of your occupation, my dear sir?" and if he were to speak the truth and answer, "I am a bootlegger," he would be immediately cast into jail. He therefore is at the mercy of any highjacker possessed of determination, pistols, and a high-powered car and he thinks that the highjacker is something so low that there is not a word to express just exactly how low he is. But the highjacker goes his way and worries not, unless the bootlegger has the drop on him, and then he never has to worry about anything else as long as he lives, which usually is about thirty seconds.

Of course there is and always has been a conspiracy among grown-ups to make the younger generation believe that their grandfathers were really very nice and estimable people and that they should be regarded by all good children with that awe and reverence which the Greeks felt when they were in the presence of the mountain-dwelling gods.

The buccaneer's cook who was hanged in the year 1600 has become the "intrepid privateer" of the year 1700, has been promoted to the status of "that brave seadog" of the campaign of 1812 and gets a monument in the year 1900 as one of the founders of a glorious colonial empire.

The boy who ran away at the age of twelve because he had stolen his grandmother's purse, and who with the help of a few fellow cutthroats deprived an Indian rajah of all his jewels, may live to see the day when the countryside shall welcome him as one of the most brilliant representatives of the local squirearchy.

For in history as in life it is success that counts. Start a political upheaval and let yourself be caught, and you will hang as a traitor. But place yourself at the head of a rebellion and gain your point, and all future generations will worship you as the Father of their Country.

These things may be good and they may be bad. I don't

know and, as I have said before, the historian should not turn moralist. It is his duty to try and tell what actually happened, what actually "was" as accurately as he possibly can, and with the help of all available evidence. As for the final judgment upon the acts of his ancestors, he had better leave that to Jehovah, for that ancient Deity alone possesses that true perspective against which all the acts of mortal man can be judged with a fair degree of accuracy.

Therefore if I state that many of the great heroes of our national history (and American national history means the national history of two-score countries) were high-jackers, I am not revealing a new and startling secret. I am merely repeating what all their contemporaries knew and what several of them said as soon as they had accumulated enough wealth to retire from the profitable if dangerous profession of buccaneer.

On the other hand it would be utterly unfair if we, of the year of Grace 1927, should regard such episodes in the warfare between Geneva and Rome in the light of our own time. Today business holds the place in men's minds which formerly was occupied by religion. We are worried when our neighbors differ from us in their views upon the subject of political economy. If they confess themselves socialists, we intend that our children shall no longer play with theirs. (They might get queer ideas.) If they are suspected of a secret liking for the idea of a soviet form of government, we write to Washington and ask the Department of Justice to look into the case. But we neither know nor care whether they go to mass or to a prayer-meeting and unless they also be our most dangerous trade rivals, they may celebrate the feast of Hanukkah to their hearts' content and never mind about Christmas.

Four hundred years ago such tolerance was impossible. A Catholic in the eyes of all good Protestants was an idolater who spiritually at least recognized himself the subject of a foreign master and who by every means at his disposal, both fair and foul, was trying to recapture northern Europe for the benefit of an Italian despot. While all

The heretic turns highjacker

Protestants, in the eyes of the Catholics, were dangerous Bolshevists, bold, bad revolutionists, who had willfully destroyed the beautiful harmony of a world-wide spiritual empire and who had done this that their abominable priests might contract matrimony and that their greedy kings might enrich themselves at the expense of inoffensive monks and nuns.

Of course all these people were wrong, but there was no one to tell them so. While there were thousands of others whose personal interest it was to tell them that they were right.

As a result, whenever they caught each other upon the high seas, they threw their captives overboard with as little mercy as if they had been wild animals. And whenever they met on dry land, they hanged each other, which in the end was very much the same thing.

This being the case (and this bestial form of warfare lasted for a period of almost two centuries) it need cause no surprise that the struggle between the two parties should inevitably lead the contending forces far beyond the confines of old Europe. Already in the year 1555 the French Admiral de Coligny (afterward murdered during the massacre of St. Bartholomew) had tried to establish a Protestant colony at the mouth of the Rio de Janeiro, but the Portuguese had destroyed it. Nine years later he had tried to found a colony in Florida where his people might have expected to be safe from Spanish interference. After two months, the little Huguenot community had been attacked by a Spanish fleet and every man, woman, and child had been killed. "Not," as the Spanish commander explained, "because they were Frenchmen, but because they were Protestants."

Three years later this misdeed was avenged when the French (with the help of an Indian chieftain) attacked the fort of San Mateo in Florida and executed all the Spaniards—"not as Spaniards, but as traitors, robbers, and murderers."

An effort made two decades later by Sir Humphrey Gilbert to found a trading-post on the coast of Newfoundland for the convenience and the benefit of the English sailors who went there every year to fish for cod also failed and Sir Humphrey was lost in the attempt.

It seemed that De Coligny had gone too far south and Sir Humphrey too far north. Fortunately at that moment Sir Walter Raleigh returned from an expedition to the West and reported that the ideal territory for a prosperous colony was to be found midway between Florida and Canada, a true earthly Paradise which he had called Virginia after the Virgin Queen, for whose glory he had sent so many Spaniards to Kingdom Come.

A couple of unseaworthy tubs were duly loaded with prospective settlers and under command of Sir Walter's cousin, Sir Richard Grenville, this fleet safely crossed the ocean and deposited its cargo upon an island at the mouth of the Roanoke River.

This time it seemed that success was to be certain.

But the colony disappeared.

It disappeared utterly and absolutely.

It disappeared as mysteriously as a ship lost at sea.

Such events—murder, starvation, and banishment into deep, dark forests—were not the sort of thing to attract desirable prospective immigrants. For a long time thereafter no further attempts were made to get a foothold in the North American wilderness. Meanwhile, however, it was decided to derive as much revenue from America as possible and for greater convenience the plunder was acquired secondhand by the "highjacking" method.

The Spanish and Portuguese colonial methods greatly facilitated such proceedings. The world of the sixteenth century was still a world of monopolies. The idea of free trade and of harbors open to the commerce of all nations would have seemed as absurd to a merchant of the year 1525 as the communist system of conducting business appears to the American businessman of the year 1927. And in order to retain complete control upon their monopolies, both the Spaniards and the Portuguese gave as little publicity as possible to their discoveries and shipped the products of their colonies to the mother country at very rare intervals. That is to say, they waited until they had gathered an enormous cargo of gold and silver and then hurried these treasures across the ocean at the greatest possible speed. Of course, from a strictly legal point of view, all these riches belonged to the Indians from whom the Spaniards had stolen them. And by attacking such squadrons and sailing away with tons and tons of golden bars, the English and Dutch privateers really deprived the Spaniards of something to which they had no right. If they had been entirely logical, and had been truly actuated by those Christian principles upon which they loved to pride themselves, they ought to have returned the goods to the original owners, but I ask you, how could one ever hope to find the address of a naked savage who lived somewhere in a dark valley of distant Yucatan and who had no documents by which to prove his claims?

The relentless guerilla warfare which then commenced between the fast little clipper ships of the Protestant North and the slow-moving galleons of the Catholic South has provided both England and Holland with material for at least half a dozen Eddas, Songs of Roland, and Stories of the Round Table.

Incredible and foolhardy adventures became an everyday occurrence. Not a Spanish ship or warehouse was safe. The islands of the West Indies were forever being plundered and despoiled and with a brazen disregard for the fate that awaited all Calvinist prisoners (the stake or the gallows of His Majesty's Inquisition) the privateers from London and Flushing extended their operations as far as the eastern shores of the Pacific Ocean.

In this way a great deal of bullion found its way to the Netherlands and to England and it allowed the natives of those obstreperous countries to bring about great improvements in the construction of their ships. But more than that, the risky business of privateering taught the young men of the North a technique of sailing and fighting which, a short time afterward, was to be of great practical use.

For in the year 1588 Spain decided to make an end to all further heresies by a crusade that should for all time destroy the power of England and Holland. A fleet of one hundred and thirty-two vessels was assembled in the harbor of Lisbon and an army of sixty thousand men was collected in the seaports of Flanders. The plan was to send the fleet to Dunkirk, there to provide it with pilots and war material, and then begin a systematic invasion of the countries on both sides of the North Sea.

All Europe knew that this was to be the final struggle between two philosophies of life that would allow of no compromise. Never before was an expedition launched with such high hopes of success. Every Spaniard worthy of the name hoped to be allowed to share in the triumph of the True Faith. But in the North, too, the excitement was intense. Privateers, highjackers, patriots, call them whatever you like, they dropped everything in hand to join the hastily improvised navy that was to protect their homeland from the touch of the Beast. They were first in the field. Part of their forces blockaded Dunkirk and prevented the Spanish admiral from making a connection with his pilots and his landing troops. The rest of the Protestant fleet followed the Armada as a pack of hounds follows a couple of wounded bears.

Then nature came to the rescue of the heretics. A series of unprecedented gales blew the Armada out of its course and caused such havoc among the Spanish galleons that less than half of them ever reached the ports of departure.

In this way the last of the crusades came to a miserable end. It bore no direct influence upon the subsequent history of America. But the defeat of the Armada taught the people of the North a very valuable lesson. They learned that the Spaniards were not invincible. The Spanish colonies of the New World were no longer out of bounds. America at last was freely at the disposal of all those who thought it worth their while to cross the ocean.

## Chapter Eight

## HERBA SANCTA INDORUM

THE NATIVES of the great American continent were savages and if we are to believe the early historians of those far-off shores, they were so completely lacking in civilization that they had not even discovered the use of the wheel.

We people of the twentieth century who could not live a day without the help of millions and millions of wheels, are apt to make a mistake when we try and measure man's intelligence by his aptitude for mechanical contrivances. For those poor heathen who carried everything upon their backs (or preferably upon the backs of their wives) and never thought of building a cart, had certain other virtues which showed that they were by no means the intellectual inferiors of our own ancestors.

To mention a single item, they domesticated more plants than any other race of men. And they domesticated certain plants without which the permanent settlement of the continent would have been infinitely more difficult, to wit: corn, potatoes, coffee, cotton (a highly superior type to that which since time immemorial had been grown in Egypt and Mesopotamia), rubber, quinine, and tobacco. The rubber and the coffee and the cotton came into their own at a later date. The potatoes moved to Europe and kept whole generations from starvation. But the tobacco played an immediate and most important rôle. It saved the northern part of the American continent for the cause of Protestantism. That is glory enough for any dumb weed.

Already Columbus on his first voyage had returned with a strange story of "smoking Indians." Some of his men had gone on a little expedition of their own to one of the near-by islands, and when they returned they told how the natives used to sit around a fire made of the dried leaves of a certain plant and how they used to inhale the smoke of that fire through a queerly shaped wooden instrument which they stuck in their nostrils and how they seemed to derive great pleasure from the aftereffects. The name of the wooden contrivance through which the fumes were carried to the nose according to the sailors was "tabaco." Further research showed that the use of the "tabaco" was general among all the Indians who lived under the tropical sun.

Sixty years later a Spanish scientist who had been sent to the new colonies to report upon their agricultural possibilities brought some of the mysterious plants which were burned by the savages back to Spain. Whether the plant itself was called "tabaco" by the savages, or whether the Spaniards (who were guilty of strange philological blunders in their profound contempt for everything native) bestowed the name of the pipe also upon the nefarious weed, that we do not know. But this much is certain, that "tobacco" (to use the English version of the word) made a tremendous stir in the world. It had been rumored that the "sucking" or "drinking" of tobacco was a solemn ceremony with the Indians, that there was something sacred and holy about a "tobacco party." But in Europe the apothecaries were the first to see the possibilities of the new drug. They proclaimed it to be possessed of marvelous healing powers and as "herba sancta Indorum," a tincture of the stuff, boiled for five or six hours, was prescribed to the sufferers from several complaints. And it was not without certain pharmaceutical virtues. For it either made the patients so terribly sick that they died on the spot or it encouraged them to get better at once and avoid a second dose.

The further fact that during the first year after its arrival on the European markets it was worth its weight in gold greatly enhanced its prestige. Even Catherine de' Medici stopped long enough in her religious meditations to take an interest in this new charm and to examine the specimen leaves which Jean Nicot (see the article on "Nicotine, $C_{10} H_{14} N_2$," in any of the current encyclopedias), the French ambassador in Lisbon, had been able to procure for her from a returning sailor.

The savage and his sacred weed

But the plant did not gain its tremendous popularity until it was discovered that the fumes, when inhaled through a clay pipe, produced a feeling of contentment which left the smoker at peace with the entire universe and caused no feeling of distress except in the case of very small children who should leave such things alone anyway.

Thereafter the "herba sancta" moved from the apothecary shop to the alehouse and before another dozen years the whole masculine world (and a considerable part of the feminine world) was indulging in the agreeable pastime of lighting the "holy herb" and filling the universe with clouds of pale-blue smoke.

Of course, the older generation frowned. Older generations always frown. And they said that something must be done about it. At first people who smoked were punished with a small fine. Then imprisonment was added to the fine. The Little Father in faraway Moscow decreed that all those caught with a pipe be condemned to twenty-five lashes with the knout. The Grand Padishah in Constantinople went a step further and said, "Off with their heads!"

But the craze could not be stopped. Europe intended to smoke, and Europe did smoke.

From smoking tobacco to the foundation of a large British commonwealth on the North American continent seems a far cry. But history often moves in strange ways her purposes to fulfill and upon this occasion she outdid herself.

It is a well-known fact that both Calvin and Luther (and most of the great Protestant leaders) in anticipation of the joys of Heaven laid great stress upon the duty of going through this vale of tears with as large a modicum of physical comfort (dollars and cents, if you want to be vulgar) as possible. The Catholic Church, on the other hand (under the influence of several of the Oriental Church fathers), had always regarded the making of money as something not quite nice. Not strictly unmoral, perhaps, but the sort of thing about which a true Christian ought not to worry overmuch, lest he lose his imperishable soul in the pursuit of more perishable lucre.

Indeed, the clerical opposition to the idea of taking interest had so greatly interfered with the development of credit that business in our modern sense of the word had been almost impossible during the Middle Ages.

The Reformation changed all this. The doctrine of predestination, by which Calvin had revived the idea of a small body of "chosen people," peacefully floating amidst a turbulent ocean of others who were "eternally damned," this somewhat obscure but profoundly impressive point of theology was just the sort of thing to appeal to close-fisted traders who loved to see a secret promise of salvation in the fact that they grew continually more prosperous whereas their less deserving neighbors remained forever poor. They were therefore "ready for business" in the most ample sense of the words.

But that was not all. The holy war upon the idolatrous Papists had swamped the Protestant world with ready cash. In England alone it is estimated that the national wealth of the country had increased threefold between 1500 and 1600. Gold and silver, however, cannot be eaten. In themselves, these precious metals are of no value. They are only important in so far as they allow someone to buy himself a loaf of bread or a couple of diamonds. We know this, but only a few people in the sixteenth century suspected it. To their great surprise they discovered that the mere possession of large quantities of bullion was really a very mixed blessing, that often it looked more like a curse than a benefit.

Now it is a well-known fact that the people who live through a revolution rarely understand what is happening to them. And so one cannot blame the contemporaries of Queen Bess if they failed to comprehend that the voyage of Columbus had made a definite end to the rule of the Middle Ages and had absolutely destroyed the feudal system which had ruled supreme in this world for almost ten centuries, because he had discovered a new world which the old world could eventually use as a gigantic boarding-house for its surplus population. This did not come true until hundreds of years afterward. But the sudden and unexpected deluge of gold and silver which by way of Spain and Portugal had begun to flood all of western and southern Europe did away completely with the old system of barter which had made the landlord (the man who actually raised the beef and the honey and the eggs and the other exchangeable products) the dominant figure of medieval society.

Quite suddenly it placed millions of dollars of actual cash at the disposal of merchants who heretofore had been little better than peddlers with a pack on their back. They began to do business on a scale the like of which the world had not seen since the days of the Roman emperors. And because they were now rich and "prominent" (or were rich and therefore tried to make themselves prominent) they must at once go to live in better houses and they must send their boys to more expensive schools and they must waste a king's ransom upon their daughter's marriage.

The old landed gentry, when they saw this happen, showed no desire to lag behind. Their rustic Paradise had been rudely upset by the plentiful introduction of nicely coined shillings and pennies and pounds. But they still held the land and this land could raise grain and grain could be sold for cash.

That was unpleasant news for the men of business. They could not grow wheat in their little city gardens. They were obliged to buy it from their titled neighbors and the titled neighbors charged all the traffic would bear.

In the end (as seems inevitable) the laboring man was the victim of this economic upheaval. Nowadays, when such an occasion arises, as it did after the great interracial war of 1914-1918 (the second greatest economic revolution after the discovery of the American gold fields), the honest son of toil (who also has learned a thing or two) packs the kids in his flivver and leaves word that he will return when his wages have been sufficiently raised to pay for his bacon and his gas. But the hewers of wood and the drawers of water of the year 1600 were less fortunate. The Justice of the Peace of his district (a nobleman, of course) decided what should be regarded as a fair return upon a day's work. The slavey could either accept such compensation or leave it alone. But in the latter case the same Justice of the Peace had the right to have him arrested on a charge of "vagabondage" and could order him to be whipped or condemned to forced labor until such time as he was willing to go back to work at the prescribed rate of wages.

If only there had been a demand for their services, the navvies could have laughed at the prison locks for then they would have been the possessors of a sweet monopoly of sweat and they would have had the merchants and the landed gentry at their mercy. But during the last hundred years all over northern Europe the immense real estate holdings of the Church had been confiscated by the government, and hundreds of thousands of people (monks, nuns, Church officials, and the vast army of happy-go-lucky peasants who thus far had tilled the fields of the monastic establishments) had been deprived of their former livelihood and had been unceremoniously dumped upon the labor market.

Hence the two main conditions necessary for the successful exploitation of a colony were present. A small number of people were possessed of a great deal of surplus wealth which they were eager to invest in almost anything that promised a fair return upon their money. While thousands of others were so poor and hungry and miserable that they were willing to go anywhere, even to the end of the terrible American wilderness, if only they could escape from their present hopeless surroundings.

The American wilderness meanwhile looked quite as bleak as it had done fifty years before. An attempt of Bartholomew Gosnold to found a small settlement in Buzzards Bay in Massachusetts had completely failed. But the first rumors of the recent discoveries of a certain Champlain were at last beginning to spread across the continent. The Frenchman's description of those vast inland seas whose shores he and his Indian friends had visited revived the hope that, after all, there might be something in the theory (then still generally held) that the northern American range of mountains was in reality a narrow strip of land and that the finding of a direct passage from the Atlantic to the Pacific was only a question of time.

In addition, please remember that the average man is incurably optimistic. The terrible fate of the colonists of Roanoke Island had already been forgotten. On the other hand, the stories of the few sailors who had followed Sir Walter to Virginia and who told that the Indians were covered with ornaments which looked for all the world like gold, those wild yarns once more began to be circulated from alehouse to alehouse and lost nothing in the repeating. A few serious-minded people were more impressed with the statement, credited to Sir Walter himself, that Virginian soil was the richest soil on earth and would raise plentiful crops of anything that the hand of man cared to entrust to her mercies. But as such agricultural endeavors implied the diligent use of spades and plows and other implements which are apt to cause calluses on dainty fingers, the prospective immigrants preferred to dream of gold and only laughed knowingly when told that the curse of Genesis III, verse 19, held as good in the year 1600 as it did a couple of weeks after the day of creation.

This refusal to take the matter seriously was almost to cost them their lives, as they were to learn shortly afterward. For the business of founding new trading companies was at last taken in hand by some very reputable merchants. Royal grants were forthcoming with quite unusual speed. It was still highly doubtful whether His Majesty had any right to dispose of lands which, strictly speaking, did not belong to him. But as they did not belong to anyone else, or to be more accurate, as they seemed of such slight value that no one thus far had taken the trouble to claim them for his own, the English charters were deemed to be quite as valid as those signed by their Majesties of Portugal and Spain.

The London Company, which was to have jurisdiction over the southern half of Virginia, was ready first. On the twentieth of December of the year 1606 three ships with forty sailors and more than a hundred colonists set sail for the west. Five months later, when their skippers had not the slightest idea where they were, a convenient eastern storm blew them into the Chesapeake Bay. They dropped anchor and explored the region until they found a convenient place for a fort. It was situated on the banks of a river and they called this stream the James River in honor of their generous sovereign, King James I of England.

Then, at last, they opened the sealed box which contained the secret instructions about the management of the new colony and settled down to enjoy life.

It was the thirteenth of May of the year 1607 and everybody was full of hope.

Six months later, half of them were dead and the others were thinking of means to escape. All their dreams had proved false. The wide bays which looked so well from the seaside were only bogs. The forest stretched a thousand miles beyond the horizon. The "direct passage" to India remained as unfindable as before.

And to cap the climax, the gold of which the sailors of Sir Walter had spoken was only "fool's gold"—the brassy yellow metal known technically as "pyrites," a substance used in the manufacture of sulphuric acid but of no particular value.

No, if ever there was a body of disillusioned and disgruntled men, it was the malaria-infested population of Jamestown.

It is hard to say what foolish things they ultimately would have done if they had been left to their own fate. But fortunately for all concerned they had among them a man who appreciated the value of discipline and knew how to maintain it. That was the glorious playboy of our early historical days, the incomparable John Smith of Lincolnshire. After incredible adventures on land and sea he now became a sort of "one-man colony" and by sheer singlehanded fortitude and good humor he kept the grousing brotherhood together until relief could reach them from England.

Even then it seemed very unlikely that the London shareholders would ever get a single penny of their invested money back. In their despair they took heroic measures to keep the Virginia hearth fires burning. They emptied orphan asylums. They became frequent visitors to the homes for foundlings. They stole boys and girls from the street. But all to no avail.

And then (as the movies have it) the unexpected happened. One of the original promoters of the London Company, John Rolfe, appeared in Jamestown.

This man was interested in tobacco. For several years past Virginia tobacco had been sent to London but no one had bought the stuff. It was too bitter and the connoisseurs stuck to the Spanish variety which was imported from the West Indies.

Rolfe surmised (and he guessed correctly) that the bitterness of the Virginia product was due to the way in which the leaves were cured. Tobacco that was good enough for an American Indian was apparently not quite good enough for an English gentleman. Rolfe made a few experiments and finally devised a method by which Virginia tobacco could be cured so that it tasted quite as sweet as the Cuban variety. The new product was an instantaneous success. Money began to flow to the banks of the James River in a plentiful supply. There was a boom in real estate. So great was the demand for labor that black slaves from the Guinea coast were soon being imported by the shipload (the first of them came in 1619, a date we shall never forget or outlive), and the old neglected grain fields, the disused gardens, yea, even certain parts of the highroads were now used to raise the profitable weed.

The Tudors had had their rose.

The Stuarts now had their tobacco blossoms.

And, believe me, those thrifty Scotchmen knew a profitable posy when they saw one.

The original investors of the London Company had been graciously allowed to bankrupt themselves in an enterprise that had seemed foredoomed to failure. Now, however, the whole world was beginning to smoke Virginia tobacco, to snuff Virginia tobacco, to chew Virginia tobacco.

What more natural than that His Majesty should at once clamor for a share of this unexpected revenue?

Where there was a will there invariably was a way with the members of this ancient and unscrupulous house of Stuart.

In the year 1624 the charter of the London Company was annulled.

Virginia ceased to be the exclusive possession of a small group of private individuals. It became a full-fledged colony with a Royal Governor who drove in a coach and four, who was surrounded by flunkies in livery, and ruled his domains with the assistance of a miniature parliament that was composed exclusively of representatives from among the landed gentry.

History, as I said a few pages back, moves in strange ways her purposes to fulfill.

The "holy herb of the Indians" succeeded in doing what the old dreams of unlimited wealth in the form of gold and silver had not been able to accomplish.

Almost overnight the nefarious weed changed the northern part of the American continent from a howling wilderness into the potential home of millions of respectable English settlers.

*Chapter Nine*

## THE NEW ZION AT TWENTY BELOW ZERO

THE HABIT OF PREACHING is apt to be strong in those who ever answered to the flattering title of professor. And nowhere in the present volume could I hold forth with more eloquence upon certain mistaken methods of historiography than right here. For I have now reached the point at which American history, in the minds of many people, ceases to be just another episode in the endless annals of the human race and becomes something apart; something different; a manifestation of that strange Divine Will which three thousand years before had divided the people of the world into two definite categories; into those who were "chosen" and those who were forever condemned to dwell beyond the pale.

Such an idea may be flattering to the pride of the fortunate "insiders." But it is rather a reflection upon the intelligence and fairness of the Great Spirit, which ruleth all of us. Yea, verily, as I see this world, it is a demonstration of such colossal spiritual arrogance that it would be unbelievable if it were not true.

It greatly annoys me to read the sanctimonious stories told by the survivors of the *Mayflower*. How one particular sailor used to poke fun at the poor landlubbers when they were seasick; how this particular fellow was thereupon stricken down with a terrible disease and was the first to die and to be buried at sea; and how all the other sailors were deeply impressed, because they felt that the just hand of God was upon them.

The poor gob who was obliged to mop up a messy deck ten times a day may have had a perfectly good reason for his uncharitable remarks. And his widow and his children may have regarded the matter in a very different light.

Nor can I agree with Cotton Mather, that it was Providence which had cleared the hillsides of Boston Bay of all pernicious creatures (read "Indians") in order to make room for what the Reverend Doctor was pleased to call "a sounder growth." Undoubtedly Brother Mather regarded himself as a much nobler specimen of the human race than Chief Massasoit, but the poor natives who had all of them died of smallpox or measles a short time before the arrival of the first shipload of Puritans may have failed to understand why they should themselves have to be exterminated in order to provide a group of bungling farmers with a necessary supply of corn. That does not mean that I, who keep a furnace and a couple of open wood fires going that I may with more or less comfort live through a typical Connecticut winter, fail to appreciate the courage which made those people "stick" when every instinct of self-preservation must have told them to go back. They did a good job. But although they were dumped upon a frozen coast during the worst time of the year they were not half as badly off as scores of other early immigrants who died to the last man from hunger and thirst, who were eaten up by the Indians (yes, some tribes did eat human flesh) or disappeared into the wilderness, never again to be seen by the eyes of their white brethren.

These early immigrants knew the risks they were taking.

They had everything to gain and nothing to lose.

They gambled with fate and won beyond their most cherished dreams.

They crossed the ocean to escape starvation, to raise tobacco, to grow rich, and to run their own churches as pleased them. Quite unbeknown to themselves they founded one of the largest empires of modern times and erected a state which, generally speaking, has accepted their ideas as the moral law of the land. Isn't that glory enough for any group of small-town bakers and wheelwrights and tallowmakers?

As for the actual voyage of the Pilgrim fathers, it has been so often told that almost any child is familiar with the details.

The Pilgrims were Puritans. That may mean a great deal and it may mean very little. There never was a Puritan sect as there have been Presbyterian sects and Baptist sects and Methodist sects. Puritanism was a philosophy of life. It was not a product of Protestantism. There have been and there still are many Puritan Catholics. The Crusades were caused by Puritan Mohammedans. There are Puritan Hindus. There are many Puritan Freethinkers. It all depends upon the taste and the inclinations of the individual.

Now there were many people in Europe immediately after the Reformation who felt that the movement toward purging the spirit of man from all worldly desire and temptation had not gone far enough. They knew that something had been gained. The old spiritual prison had been destroyed. But its place had been taken by a hundred new little lockups and the new masters, so it soon appeared, intended to be quite as severe and as exacting as the old ones had been.

But that was not all.

The sixteenth century was a typical post-war period. A number of profiteers had made millions. The princes of northern Europe and England, having "appropriated" (governments and royal families, as is well known, do not "steal"—they merely "confiscate" and "appropriate") the immensely rich possessions of the Church, had bestowed vast riches upon their supporters and had then established a set of religious rules of their own which were just as binding as those of Rome.

Under the circumstances a truly serious man who had hoped that the great reform would give him a chance to develop his own soul after his own convictions was just as badly off as he had been a generation before. He was no longer obliged to be on his guard against the spies of the Inquisition. But Heaven help him if rumor of his heresies reached the ears of the nearest bishop or if he gave offense to the newly enriched classes of ennobled royal henchmen.

Under those circumstances the dissenters did what dissenters have always done. They went underground. They met in deserted stables. They came together in country lanes and when their ministers had their ears cut off or their noses slit, they thought themselves fortunate that they were thought worthy of martyrdom for the sake of something that was much nearer and dearer to them than mere life.

Such conditions, however, could not last forever. The weaker brethren made their peace with the authorities. And the others fled.

In the year 1607 one such group of sorely beset heretics had escaped from England to Holland and had settled down in the good town of Amsterdam. They were dreadfully poor. They lived in the slums and the strong Dutch trade unions (call them guilds, if you think that more romantic) did not look with favor upon this sudden invasion of "foreign labor." As for the invaders, far away from their own villages, deprived of the familiar sights and smells and sounds of rural England, they were miserably unhappy. After a while they could not stand it any longer. And so they moved from Amsterdam to Leyden, which was the chief manufacturing city of the Dutch Republic and there they hoped to have a better chance to make a living and to be a little nearer to those green fields which reminded them of home.

The Dutch authorities, who knew perfectly well what the King of England, with his high conception of a "sovereign by the Grace of God," thought of them ("a pack of dirty little rebels, my friend!"), did not treat these fugitives unkindly. They gave them a place to worship. They allowed them to import their own ministers, to conduct services in their own language. But once outside the meetinghouse, the world in which the poor Puritans found themselves was Dutch, the schools were Dutch, the language was Dutch, and therefore, to the mind of a middle-

62

class Englishman, "foreign" and decidedly inferior.

It would perhaps be unfair to accuse this British colony in Leyden of the dastardly sin of "hyphenation." Let us be charitable and merely say that they were homesick.

Furthermore, they worried about the future of their children. In the year 1621 the twelve years' truce between Spain and her rebellious possessions in the Low Countries would come to an end. It was by no means sure that the Republic would be able to maintain its independence. In case of a reconquest of Holland by the armies of His Most Catholic Majesty, what would become of these English men and women who were known to have left their country because they actually out-heresied their own heretical master?

No, all things considered, it was better for the Puritans to go while the going was still good.

The Puritans on the way to Leyden

Just then the London Company had opened a new drive for prospective settlers in Virginia. The first consignment of Virginia tobacco had just reached the market of London and had brought good prices. The shareholders had taken fresh courage. All that was needed now for complete success was an abundant supply of cheap labor. There was, of course, one serious objection. The Leyden community of separatists (or noncomformists or Brownites or Puritans—whatever they were called) might prove to be a disturbing element in a colony that was predominantly Episcopalian. But America was three thousand miles away and Virginia was very big. Somewhere in the wilderness there probably was a spot where those dissenters could be located without causing too much of a

63

public scandal.

It was not easy to collect the money necessary for such wholesale migration. In the year 1620 it cost as much to get a single steerage passage across the ocean as it costs us today to transport two people in the first class of a fast steamer. Somehow or other the funds were found, but by the terms of the loan the prospective settlers gave up all hope of obtaining individual pieces of land. They were to be part of a communistic enterprise. There were to be no private possessions in their new home save such things as were considered to be part of a man's household goods.

In July of the year 1620 an old vessel of some sixty tons was sent from England to Holland to carry the immigrants to Southampton. Endless delays caused these poor people to spend the greater part of the summer in the harbor of Southampton. At last in September they bade farewell to their native shore. It was really much too late in the year to cross the ocean with any degree of comfort or safety. And furthermore the *Mayflower* (that probably was the name of the ship, although we do not know for certain) was no ocean greyhound. It took her two months to do the distance between Plymouth and the coast of America. Neither can her captain be given a testimonial of unusual fitness as a navigator. Instead of landing his passengers in the Chesapeake Bay (as he had been told to do) he carried them nine hundred miles out of their course, almost shipwrecked them a couple of times on a coast with which he was totally unfamiliar, and finally dropped anchor in an unknown bay entirely surrounded by low snow-covered mountains.

It began to dawn upon the poor travelers that something was wrong. They had started out to work for the London Company and they found themselves within the jurisdiction of the Plymouth Company. Nothing on earth, however, would induce them to go back to the high seas. They sent out a boat to explore the near-by coast and decided upon a site that seemed a little less barren than the rest and there they built themselves a village of their own which they called Plymouth.

So far, so good. But among the passengers of the *May-*

*flower* were some who had a little money and some who had none. The latter (a good many of them of the servant class) had been full of hope of the riches awaiting them in Virginia. Through no fault of their own they saw themselves condemned to a continuation of their humdrum existence. They protested. The charter which they had seen had mentioned Virginia. They believed in law and order. They would go to Virginia if they had to walk.

This looked like mutiny and a very dangerous sort of mutiny. For the number of Pilgrims was dwindling fast through sickness and death and if there were any further desertions, all the settlers would surely perish.

Under such conditions, however, there are always a few energetic men who take charge of the situation and turn defeat into victory. They now came forward and drew up a sort of written constitution for the conduct of the survivors and being saturated with Biblical phraseology, they called this document a "Covenant" and regarded it with a great deal of solemn respect.

All those who signed the piece of parchment (and the disgruntled ones, too, were persuaded to affix their mark) promised to obey such "just and equal laws and ordinances as shall be thought most meet and convenient for the general good of the colony."

This was not meant to be a declaration of independence. It was merely another expression of that practical English spirit which for centuries has been so very characteristic of the English nation and which makes British revolutionists behead their sovereign and their statesmen with every semblance of decency and respect.

What was even more to the point, the thing worked.

The Covenant kept the Pilgrims together during a winter of such severity and during a period of such intense misery that only a strict form of voluntary discipline could prevent the people from committing all sorts of excesses.

If I am not mistaken (but I am quoting from memory) only one man was actually hanged during the first five years of the colony's existence, and that is a very fine record as colonies go.

But undoubtedly the final success of this experiment (and the mere fact that several of the immigrants actually survived that first winter was in itself a great accomplishment), the final and lasting triumph of this settlement in a cold and inhospitable country, was primarily due to the exceptional character of the men who were chosen to be the leaders.

They were strong men of pronounced convictions.

They knew what they wanted.

They were dead serious.

And they had burned their bridges behind them. They had left the old world for good and all. Whatever happened there was to be no return to the Gomorrah of European wickedness.

Thus was founded the New Zion of the West.

And those who lay still under the frozen snow of Cole's Hill knew that all was well with the world and that they had not died in vain.

*Chapter Ten*

## THOSE WHO DESPAIR OF THE MOTHER COUNTRY PREPARE FOR A NEW AND HAPPIER ENGLAND ON THE WESTERN SHORES OF THE ATLANTIC

IT WAS DURING THE EARLY SEVENTIES of the sixteenth century that William the Silent, in despair at the slow progress of the war of Dutch independence, suggested to his followers that they leave their native land and move to America.

"Far better," so he exclaimed, "to experience freedom in the wilderness of a distant continent than to bear slavery amidst the comforts of an uncongenial home."

Since then millions of other men and women have felt that same urge, have put the impulse into practice, and have left their old homes for the uncertain adventure of a new and unknown hemisphere.

Rarely, however, has a plan for a wholesale migration been worked out with more care and more intelligence than that which gave birth to those settlements which soon afterward came to be known as the New England.

A few pages back I said that Puritanism was not a creed or a sect but a point of view. Now let me add that although Puritanism, in the popular mind, is usually associated with the idea of poverty and meekness, there were many members of the ruling classes of England who were staunch Puritans and ready to make every sort of sacrifice for their convictions. This need not surprise us. They were the children and grandchildren of people who had been the contemporaries of good Queen Bess. The austere virtues which were a characteristic of this younger generation were the normal reaction after a period that had drunk too much and had eaten too much and had danced too much and had gambled too much and had exhausted the pleasures of the flesh so thoroughly that people shuddered at the mere mention of the word "pleasure."

Unfortunately for all concerned, just when England was beginning to turn serious, the British crown fell into the hands of a small group of outsiders, men who could not possibly gauge the national temper as Henry VIII and Elizabeth had been able to do. The Tudors, almost without exception, had been tyrants of a very unpleasant sort. But they had known just exactly how far they could go with their subjects without driving them into open rebellion, when it was safe to drop an unwelcome bill into the royal ash can and when it was good policy to bestow a knighthood upon the sponsor of a new law.

The Stuarts, on the other hand, whose ancestors had begun their career "stewarding" (or managing) certain estates in Brittany early in the eleventh century, had done well enough in this world, but they were Scotchmen and not Englishmen, as they were soon to learn to their ever-lasting grief and sorrow.

The autocracy of the Tudors had been tempered by their red-blooded joviality, by a bucolic sense of humor, by the feeling that very often more could be accomplished by a good dinner and a couple of bottles of Malmsey than by a strict appeal to the letter of the law or Scripture.

The autocratic Stuarts were backed by the Presbyterian version of Holy Writ and knew of no compromise. And as a result, from the very beginning of the reign of James I (he succeeded his cousin Elizabeth in the year 1603) there was friction between the crown and the people and that friction continued and grew in importance until it drove the Stuarts into exile and brought England to the verge of ruin.

Poor, slovenly James was indeed a sad case. Think of his childhood and early upbringing! Two months before he was born his mother had watched her husband murder her private secretary, David Rizzio, who was also supposed to be her lover. The little boy with his shriveled legs, his shiftless temper, his secret desire for revenge upon a world that had been cruel to him, was totally unfit to rule a country in which the divine right of kings was being questioned on all sides. His son Charles was able to shed the funny Scottish burr of his father, but for the rest he failed just as completely to understand the true temper of his subjects. James, with all his profound knowledge of Protestant theology, had been at heart a regular pro-Spanisher. To him the King of Spain had always seemed the greatest monarch of the earth and he would have given anything he possessed if he could have gained the good will of this mighty potentate.

That his Protestant subjects held the very name of Catholic Philip in abhorrence and regarded the Spanish court as the anteroom of Hades, made little difference to him. And now, so it appeared, the son was to follow in his father's footsteps. It was very disconcerting to honest Englishmen, whose uncles and brothers and cousins had been burned by the Inquisition as "blasphemous heretics," to hear that their future sovereign, as plain Mr. Brown, had gone to Madrid to woo a granddaughter of one no less than that Philip II who, as the husband of Bloody Mary, had done his best to bring the British Isles back to the True Faith by means of the Armada and the

Jesuits. And when this same Charles finally came to the throne and continued the mistaken policies of his father, when he tried to tax his subjects without their approval, and endeavored to rule the country as if there were no House of Commons, then a great many people began to feel sincerely worried about the near future. That this effort to foist an unlimited monarchy upon the unwilling people of England would end only a few decades later with a final and painful encounter between His Majesty and Jack Ketch was something which no one then could foresee. For the moment it looked as if the Crown would be victorious. Small wonder that many people, despairing of the future of their old fatherland, made plans to save at least part of the wreckage and went forth to establish a New England upon the shores of a distant land while there was still time.

The leader in this movement was one John Winthrop, a Suffolk man. He was the son of well-to-do parents, he studied in Cambridge and then became a lawyer. But he drifted into politics, as almost any honest man was obliged to do in those days when the ancient liberties of England were at stake, and soon he found himself one of the leaders of the opposition to the Stuart tyranny. His fear of Catholic plots was very great. Wherever he looked he saw signs of the Popish menace and one of the reasons why he hoped to establish a British colony on the other side of the Atlantic was his fear that the Jesuits from Canada might in time overrun the entire northern part of the continent. The New England which he hoped to found would stand as a bulwark against Roman aggression when the old England had failed.

Winthrop, however, was primarily a businessman and he proceeded very cautiously. He did not wish to turn his colony into another Virginia. Persons of low morals, people who worshiped the flesh (the "scum" as he called them in his picturesque although somewhat direct English) need not apply. Neither did Winthrop show any tendency to make his new England less intolerant than the old one had been or to turn it into a haven of refuge for all those who elsewhere had suffered for their private opinion.

Within the confines of his Massachusetts domains the Old Testament was to be the law of the land. There was to be a form of popular representation, but the land was to be ruled by the Puritans and for Puritans. The others were either to comply to these ordinations or stay away.

In the month of March of the year 1630 John Winthrop sailed for America. Before he left, he and his associates had quietly passed a measure which soon proved to be a master stroke—the actual government of the colony was to be vested in those shareholders who should migrate to the new world. No more absentee landlordism, no more colonists starving to death while the stockholders, three thousand miles away, were vaguely deliberating about the best methods to relieve their distress.

At first Winthrop had planned to settle down at Salem, where several white people had already built a village. But the Salem colony had not done very well and Winthrop, who feared that it would be bad for the morale of the newcomers if they were regaled with the hard-luck stories of the early arrivals, moved further southward and dropped anchor in a bay which the omnipresent John Smith had visited sixteen years before. In the beginning the village which he built was called Trimontaine, the town of the three mountains. A short time afterward the name was changed to Boston in honor of a city in Lincolnshire which had been the home of several of the immigrants.

If Charles or any of his henchmen had appreciated the true nature of Mr. Winthrop's venture, it is doubtful whether they would have let any other Englishmen proceed to Massachusetts. For the colony actually became what Winthrop had intended it to be—a stronghold of Puritanism. The population increased by leaps and bounds. Less than a dozen years after the founding of Boston there were sixteen thousand people living within the jurisdiction of the Massachusetts Company. More than two hundred ships had visited the harbors of New England, and millions of dollars had been invested in the New England trade.

It is true that Massachusetts could not send a large

number of volunteers to the mother country to help the dissenters in their warfare upon the endless encroachments of the royal masters. But the very existence of a place where their own principles were the dominant factors in the social and religious life of the community gave the home-staying Puritans courage to keep up the good fight. And so well did they acquit themselves of their self-appointed task that Charles lost both his crown and his head.

Once the old country had been purged of its wicked-ness and sin, there was no longer any strict need for a Puritan state outside the national gates. A few people returned. But a new generation of native-born youngsters stood ready to take their place.

They had never known anything else.

The land in which they lived suited them.

They looked around and said, "This is home."

*Chapter Eleven*

## THE DUTCH WEST INDIA COMPANY MAKES THE WRONG INVESTMENT

When Caesar first chased the green-faced savages of the British Isle, the eastern shore of the North Sea consisted of a vast swamp which stretched from the mouth of the Rhine to that of the Elbe and was inhabited by frogs, herons, and by those Germanic tribes whom the Romans (for reasons unknown) called the Batavians. In due process of time the marshes were reclaimed, the rivers were brought to terms by means of a complicated system of dikes, and the descendants of the wild Teutons settled down to make a living as fishermen, pirates, and small-scale traders.

During the twelfth century the herring, for some mysterious cause, moved from the Baltic to the North Sea. A Dutch genius promptly invented a new and superior way of preserving that useful fish. And as all the world observed the Catholic fast days and was obliged to go without meat for half of each week, a pleasant-tasting pickled fish which could be kept for long periods of time without the help of an ice chest was a very welcome addition to the international diet.

Soon the whole of the Continent was eating Dutch herring, and the Dutch merchants were rapidly growing rich. Unfortunately it was not possible to go fishing all the year around. For the herring, at certain stated times, withdrew to the less shallow parts of the ocean that it might there raise its family in comfort and peace and the primitive nets of that period could not follow their prey to such a great depth.

It was necessary to find some other profitable occupation for the ships from Amsterdam and Middelburg while the fisheries stood at a standstill.

Fortunately (fortunately for the Dutch, but not for anyone else) the people of western Europe were so busy fighting each other that they were never able to provide for their own needs. In order to keep alive, Spain and France and Italy were obliged to import large quantities of grain from abroad. The Dutchmen offered to act as middlemen and grain carriers. They went to Dantzic, loaded their vessels with wheat, and sold their cargoes at an enormous profit in Cadiz or Livorno.

Then came the Reformation, and the Hollanders, like all people who live in countries where it rains for the greater part of the year, became enthusiastic partisans of the ideas propounded by Luther and Calvin. This, of course, brought them into difficulties with King Philip of Spain, who by a process of dynastic marriages, murders, and robberies, happened to be their lawful sovereign. Exasperated by His Majesty's ideas upon the subjects of theology and taxation, they threw off the Spanish yoke and began a war of independence which lasted eighty years.

During the first twenty years they were sorely beset. Then their superior ability as navigators began to tell. After the year 1590 the Dutch highjackers were so successful that no Spanish treasure galleon ventured upon the high seas without a convoy of at least half a dozen men-of-war. And then in the year 1595 an adventurous sailor, Jan Huygen van Linschoten, published his famous little book in which he told his compatriots exactly how they could go to the Indies by way of the Cape of Good Hope.

Linschoten, as a boy, had run away from home and had taken service with the Portuguese. That is how he happened to know all about Calicut and Goa and faraway Macao. Even so it took the first Dutch vessels which went to Java more than two years for the round trip. But the profits of such voyages promised to be so enormous that "India Companies" sprang up like mushrooms.

In order to bring some system into the commercial chaos that followed and save the little trading societies from a competitive warfare that would be disastrous to all of them, the leading statesman of Holland, Johan van Oldenbarneveldt, suggested a merger. This was brought about in the year 1602 and within a very short period of time the United East India Company had made herself mistress of those spice islands which more than a century before had lured Columbus on his western voyage.

Like all their contemporaries, the "Gentlemen Seventeen" who managed the affairs of the company and who, during a period of almost two hundred years, administered a gigantic colonial empire without once giving an accounting to their stockholders were thorough believers in the system of monopoly. The Indies were theirs and they meant to keep all foreigners out. But the road to the Indies by way of the Cape was at the disposal of everyone. Evidently it would be to the advantage of the Dutch to have a little Indian route of their own.

During the latter half of the sixteenth and the first quarter of the seventeenth centuries, repeated efforts were made to establish direct communications between Amsterdam and Batavia by way of Siberia. After four or five expeditions had found themselves hopelessly lost in the ice of the Arctic Ocean and one had been forced to spend a most uncomfortable winter on the northern shore of

Novaya Zemlya, the enthusiasm for the northeastern passage died out. But in the year 1608 the learned geographers and map makers of Amsterdam (and just then they were making the charts by which all the world sailed) once more came to the conclusion that the idea was feasible and they persuaded the directors of the Amsterdam branch of the East India Company to give the eastern route one more trial.

Heemskerk, the commander of the ill-fated polar expedition of the year 1596, was dead. He had been killed fighting the Spaniards. But there was a captain in England, Hudson by name, who had gained quite a reputation as an explorer in the services of the British Muscovy Company. The Hollanders sent for Hudson, gave him a contract and a ship and a few dozen sailors, and bade him find a passage to the Indies by way of the North Pole.

On the fifth of April of the year 1609 the *Halve Maen* left the road of Texel. A month later, the ship was in Barents Sea. But it was already "too late in the year" (polar expeditions have a fascinating habit of being either too late or too early) and Hudson was obliged to return. He made directly for the Faroe Islands, where he hoped to get fresh water and fresh supplies and then he called together a meeting of all his sailors and asked what he should do next.

He himself suggested that they sail westward and try to find that large bay of which his friend, the jovial John Smith, had told him a couple of years before and which, according to that honest swashbuckler, might be the long-sought gap in the barrier. The sailors, who thus far had seen nothing more exciting than icebergs and walruses, were all for a plan that would get them back to a warm climate and shouted, "Yes!"

No sooner said than done. The anchor was lifted, and Hudson (as he hoped) was on his way from Thorshavn to Peking, via America and other points west.

On the third of September of the year 1609 he actually found an opening in the land through which the currents raced at such terrific speed that it really seemed like the connecting link between the Atlantic and the Pacific.

Those terrible currents still exist. They play havoc with the inexperienced engineers of small motorboats and they cause many anxious moments to the captains of our transatlantic liners. Technically they are known as the Hudson River. They offer a pleasant mode of communication to those who wish to proceed leisurely from New York to Albany, but they do not run quite as far west as California.

Ere he left, poor Hudson had begun to suspect as much. He made, however, the best of his disappointment and wrote a report which stated that the land he had discovered was rich in fur and fish; that it offered unexcelled opportunities for the settlement of a colony and that the banks of the river which he had explored were very beautiful. A year later he once more sailed for the North, fully convinced that this time he would succeed. He got as far as the Hudson Bay and spent the winter in James Bay. Early the next spring he tried to push further westward (he only had about three thousand more miles to go). But his crew refused to follow him. They mutinied. They put their captain and eight sick men in a small boat and left them to the mercies of the Arctic Seas.

The records of the great voyages of the fifteenth and sixteenth centuries contain much that is not flattering to our human nature. This premeditated murder of a brave captain and eight helpless invalids by a group of disgruntled sailors seems to hold the record for callous bestiality. Our Latin friends can count themselves happy that it was not done by members of their own race. They never would have heard the last of it.

Meanwhile, in Amsterdam, the board of directors of the India Company had taken due notice of what Captain Hudson had told them and then had done nothing. They wanted nutmeg and pepper. They were not interested in scenery. If others wished to profit by the captain's discovery, they were entirely welcome.

Others did so wish to profit. Adriaen Block explored Long Island Sound, sailed up the Connecticut River as far as Hartford, and then by way of Nantucket paid a visit to Massachusetts Bay, seventeen years before the founding of Boston.

Cornelius May went southward, sailed past a cape which he modestly called after himself, and next reached a large bay and river which he called the South Bay and the South River and which in due time came to be known as the Delaware Bay and the ditto river.

As all of these visitors were interested in buying furs and as they paid what the Indians considered good prices in beads, guns, and gin, they were able to establish pleasant relations with the natives who regarded them as a race of Santa Clauses and did not mind if they spent a few weeks on their shores.

These amiable contacts, however, were rudely disturbed when a few occasional Dutchmen remained behind, cleared a bit of land, and commenced to poach upon the preserves of the savages. Then there was trouble and soon the smoldering ashes of a ruined farmhouse told that East and West, after their age-old habit, had met and had failed to appreciate each other. But the number of permanent settlers increased very slowly and although there were many people in the old Netherlands who said that "something ought to be done with these American possessions," very little progress was made. It was difficult to enthuse a Dutch directors' meeting unless there was a chance for large and immediate profit and it was not until the year 1621 that the Dutch West India Company was founded and was given a monopoly of the trade along the coast of Africa and the coast of North and South America, including the banks of the Hudson River.

In due course of time a governor was appointed to administer the territory of the New Netherlands, small groups of political refugees were persuaded to try their luck in a world that was a little less crowded, the island of Manhattan was made the center of the local government and a town was built at the confluence of the Hudson and East Rivers and was called Nieuw Amsterdam.

On paper, all this sounded very beautiful, but those in the know understood that it would not possibly lead to any lasting success. In England and Scotland economic conditions had driven a vast number of working people into such a state of misery that they were more than willing to try their luck elsewhere and even go to America. Furthermore, the system of primogeniture and the strong political position of the landed gentry kept millions of acres from being cultivated and deprived hundreds of thousands of peasants of the chance of ever acquiring a little farm of their own. These, too, were willing to take a risk and joined the army of emigrants.

But in the Dutch Republic, the situation was very different. The old landed aristocracy had been killed off during the long war with Spain, there were no vast estates and the carrying trade, combined with an active industrial development and the tremendous profits derived from the Indian spice trade (not to mention those very considerable extras which were the reward of an occasional highjacking job) had brought about such a high and general degree of prosperity that few people felt the slightest desire to move away.

Under those circumstances the Dutch West India Company, which was never soundly financed (all the surplus money of the Republic had been sunk in the East India Company which was twenty years older) and which kept up an outward semblance of solvency by a disgraceful trade in African slaves—under these circumstances, as I have hoped to make abundantly clear, the company could not possibly hope to make a success of her adventure in American real estate. The mere business of administering her vast foreign possessions proved too much of an undertaking. Young men of ability invariably took service with the East India Company, where they were certain of a career. The West India Company had to content herself with incompetent clerks, broken-down promoters, with all sorts of third-rate crooks who, possessed of a little pull, found themselves suddenly called upon to rule a colony forty times as large as the mother country and surrounded on all sides by enemies, white or copper-colored.

The natural advantages of Nieuw Amsterdam for the purpose of international trade were just about sublime. When the city was visited by a French Jesuit in the middle of the seventeeth century, he found not less than eighteen nationalities represented among the inhabitants of the capital. The same principle of live and let live that had made the Dutch Republic the greatest international countinghouse of the last four centuries seems to have prevailed in the colony. But what could be done without permanent settlers, without farmers, without butchers and bakers and candlestick makers who were willing to stick?

At the eleventh hour an effort was made to populate the colony by reviving that system of feudal land tenure which had gone out of existence in northern Europe hundreds of years before. It led to a great deal of highhanded grafting and it accomplished nothing of any practical value. The time had long since passed when a "patroon" (a common, ordinary landlord) could force his tenants to send their grain to his mill and buy their salt from his store on pain of his displeasure.

To complicate matters still further, the Dutch were forever at loggerheads with their Puritan neighbors of Massachusetts who seemed to live under the apprehension (mentioned before) that the Lord had in some mysterious way created the northern American continent for their own benefit and that the claims of all other races, Swedes, French, Spaniards, Germans, Dutchmen, were almost an insult to Divine Providence. But this hostility on the part of a group of people who only a few years before had sought and found a refuge in the same country which they now accused of every crime under the sun was not the primary reason for the final collapse of the great New Netherland venture.

Neither can we lay all the blame on the shortsighted governors who with very few exceptions were fifty years behind the spirit of their times. In due course of events these incompetent gentlemen would have been decently buried beneath a resplendent escutcheon in some pretty little whitewashed church and their place would have been taken by more energetic and less hidebound youngsters.

No, it was a complete lack of man power and nothing else which made an end to the weird dream of a Dutch empire in America.

In the year 1664, during a war between Holland and England, the New Netherlands were occupied by British troops. Seven years later, a Dutch fleet reconquered the lost colony. But Holland was too much occupied with more profitable adventures in other parts of the world to bother about a stretch of land that had always been a source of trouble, the happy home of corrupt officials, discontented farmers, endless lawsuits, angry dominies, appeals to the States General, appeals to the Stadtholders, appeals for money, appeals for this, appeals for that, and not a penny of revenue.

At the peace of Westminster in the year of 1674 the States General ceded all further rights to the territory of the New Netherlands. The English from their side promised to respect Dutch possessions in Guiana where sugar could be raised in unlimited quantities and where the Dutch planters hoped to recoup themselves for the failure of their northern venture.

Looking back upon the whole procedure, the transaction was not without an aspect of the comical.

The fathers, in their wisdom, swapped New York harbor for a swamp in South America. THEY SWAPPED NEW YORK FOR A PLAGUE-RIDDEN SWAMP IN SOUTH AMERICA!

And they flattered themselves that they had done a pretty clever stroke of business!


*Chapter Twelve*

## THE SWEDES ARRIVE TWO HUNDRED YEARS TOO SOON

THE FRENCH (and I never yet could write a book without some reference to that peculiar wisdom of the French people which seems to humanize whatever it touches), the French long ago gave us a recipe for the writing of history.

"Let us compile, my friends," so they said, "let us compile and out of seven hundred and eighty-four other books, let us make a seven hundred and eighty-fifth."

A history of America in a hundred thousand words can hardly be a compilation. That, at least, is one crime of which I shall not be accused. But it is just as well on general principles to know what the neighbors have written, and so I have read through all the more popular volumes that have been published these last twenty years upon the subject of our national history, and I have discovered a strange mental delusion.

When the authors of most of those learned volumes write about a shipload of English adventurers approaching these shores, there is a hush upon the landscape, the children of Israel are about to cross the river Jordan and take possession of that Promised Land which never really belonged to the poor Canaanites (who have lived there since the beginning of time) and which is now awaiting the hallowed touch of the rightful owners.

But when a Swede or a Dutchman, let alone a German, decides to sink a few florins or crowns or thalers into American real estate and when he fits out a ship of his own and braves a thousand dangers and painfully establishes himself in a mosquito-ridden swamp of the Delaware River or in the heart of Connecticut, there are signs of great agitation among the professors.

Either the "King of Sweden is bitten with the bug of colonization" or "a group of Amsterdam merchants hoped to swell their profits by selling gunpowder and schnapps to the Indians" or "a family of Augsburg bankers was seeking to increase its millions by the exploitation of recently discovered gold mines" or words to that effect.

These statements, as far as they go, are quite correct.

But they are just a little bit one-sided.

Of course those Swedes and Dutchmen and Frenchmen who took the trouble to cross the ocean and grab part of the American wilderness were out to make money. But so were their English competitors. A few British gentlemen actually came to America because they despaired of the mother country and hoped to salvage something of the ancestral virtues by establishing a new and purified England on the shores of Massachusetts Bay. But even a man of the lofty principles of Winthrop was no little angel. He knew perfectly well that with his ideas it would be impossible for him to make any sort of a career in a country ruled by the Stuarts, and being a person of tremendous ambition, he preferred to be Citizen No. 1 in a small village on the Charles rather than to be Citizen No. 47 in a big town on the Thames.

As for those who followed him, by far the greater majority moved from Portsmouth in Hampshire to Portsmouth in Rockingham County because Portsmouth in Rockingham County offered infinitely greater opportunities for material happiness than Portsmouth in Hampshire.

The fact that it was fashionable to go to a Puritan church in Portsmouth in Rockingham County and was regarded with suspicion if one went to a Presbyterian kirk in Portsmouth, Hampshire, may have had something to do with their decision to pull up stakes, but generally speaking, they came for exactly the same reason as Tony the bootblack who makes no bones about it and says, "America a fina country! I maka da mon."

Physics and history have very little in common, but in both sciences one law holds good and that is the law which states that nature abhors a vacuum. Sooner or later (and the sooner the better is nature's slogan) such a vacuum will be filled and whether it be with water, with people, or with air is entirely immaterial.

The American wilderness, ethnologically speaking, was a vacuum which contained a great economic promise. Several people had tried the new world and had found it to their liking. Today when one company makes money out of radio a dozen other companies are formed in just as many minutes. When one man is known to have made a fortune out of Florida real estate, six hundred thousand hopeful idiots pack their wives and children into the family Ford and hasten to Miami.

In the year 1620, when the citizens of Stockholm and Copenhagen and Enkhuizen heard of the enormous prices Virginia tobacco was bringing on the London market,

81

when they saw the pepper quotations of the Amsterdam exchange, they said, "High-ho!" or "High-ha!" (according to the language they spoke) "we, too, would like to have some of that money." And as soon as they had scraped together a few thousand dollars they started a little trading company of their own and joined the rush. The economic histories of that period tell the rest. During the first half of the seventeenth century, West India companies popped up like mushrooms. They grew by night and disappeared with the first rays of the sun. They swept away the savings of thousands of unfortunate people but they brought great riches to a dozen lucky ones. Then the poor victims chanted, "Oh, well, you see it can be done! So let us try again and better luck the next time!" And off they would be on another wild chase for the proverbial pot of money.

There seems to be a strange belief in this world that the people who inhabit northern climes are cool, collected, and phlegmatic. As a matter of fact, most of them would much rather speculate than eat and Heaven knows they are partial to their food.

In Holland the number of chartered, semichartered, and wildcat companies was legion. The Danes could proudly point to five East India Companies, all of them tremendously successful at one moment and hopelessly broke the next. The Russians, deprived of convenient harbors but desirous to obtain their part of the spoils, pushed their colonial enterprises eastward until at last they were able to enter America by the back door and could take Alaska as their share of the great Columbian inheritance.

Before the craze came to an end, even the flags of Austria and Brandenburg, better known to the landlubbers than to the sailors, had made their appearance upon the ocean. But the only serious venture among these minor colonial enterprises was that of the Swedes.

For a long time their good neighbors, the Danes, had tried to keep them cooped up in the Baltic and the castle of Helsingör was better known as a particularly obnoxious stronghold which commanded the Sound than as the home of old lugubrious Hamlet's spook.

But by one of those strange outbursts of energy (which are as sudden as they are mysterious and which occur in nations as they do in ordinary human beings) the Swedes during the first half of the seventeenth century had made themselves the dominant power of northern Europe. Just in the nick of time the iron regiments of Baner, Oxenstjerna, and Torstensson had saved the continent from the horrors of a successful Counter Reformation. The military genius of the Wasa family had put a limit to the ambitions of their half-civilized Slavic neighbors, and the Baltic had been made into a Swedish lake where Poles and Russians gave a wide berth to those vessels that flew the triple-crowned flag.

When soldiers fresh from the battlefields of Lützen and Breitenfeld made their appearance at the mouth of the Delaware River, the English and the Dutch had, therefore, ample reason to feel uncomfortable. But the tremendous territorial acquisitions which had fallen to Sweden as a result of her victories over the Emperor and the Czar had seriously drained her man power. The Swedish-born population of this vast northern empire was only half of what it is today and as long as a Swedish peasant could make himself a new home in Finland (situated just across the Baltic) he was not likely to sail to Fort Cristina (nowadays called Wilmington) which could only be reached after a dangerous voyage of two or three months and which was said to be infested with wild animals and even more deadly natives. And so he stayed where he was, just as his Dutch cousin stayed where he was, and all the fine promises in the world could not induce him to leave his snug farm in Dalecarlia or Norrland.

It was not until much later that the country began to suffer from overpopulation. Then a great westward movement set in and almost a million Swedes pulled up stakes and migrated to America. But they arrived too late to establish an independent colony of their own.

In the year 1655 the Swedish settlements in Pennsylvania and Delaware were annexed by the Dutch. Nine years later all the territory between the Connecticut River and the Schuylkill fell into the hands of the English, and that was the end of Nya Sverige.

Alack and alas! Good intentions, finely emblazoned charters, and beautifully lettered programs never yet made a prosperous colony.

Money is a great help, but it is not everything.

A colony in order to succeed must be a natural outlet for certain classes of people who have strong reasons to leave their old homes.

Those conditions prevailed in England. They did not prevail in France or in Sweden or in Holland.

As a result these pages, although composed in the State of Connecticut, are not written in the tongue of my mother country, but in the Franco-Roman dialect which William the Conqueror forced upon his Saxon subjects during the second half of the eleventh century.

And the people of Philadelphia import their Knäcke-bröd from a baker in St. Paul, Minnesota.

*Chapter Thirteen*

## A FREE COLONY FOR ALL NATIONS

MANY A STRANGE CRAFT has passed from Europe to America these last four hundred and thirty-five years. People have sailed across the ocean and they have flown across and they have traveled in every sort of variety of steamer. In one instance a couple of homesick Scandinavians rowed back to the old country and were none the worse for the experience.

But for sheer discomfort the tub in which George Fox made the voyage, and which leaked to the tune of sixteen inches every two hours (when both passengers and crew were continually kept at the pumps) must have established some sort of record. Not that it made much difference to Friend George. He had been in much dirtier prisons than the hold of this crazy craft. Besides, nothing prevented him from going on deck to talk to the sailors, and if I know anything of the man, he was never unhappy as long as there was a single listener to his pleasant discourse upon the subject of the human soul.

There are two subjects in the field of history which I usually avoid. Not because I dislike them but because I like them rather too well. What is the use of filling long chapters with melancholy details about the growth of the Papacy in the Middle Ages or the development of Puritan New England in the seventeenth century when one might write a merry book about Francis of Assisi or George from Drayton-in-the-clay? These two men stand by themselves. They were artists of life, glorious creatures, extravagant, outrageous, and impossible citizens, they were anything you like. But by the sheer force of their fabulous self-confidence and their indefatigable enthusiasms they did more for the true progress of this world (and did it in less time) than ninety per cent of all the respectable saints and divines whose effigies frown down upon us from those edifices which Friend George designated most disrespectfully as "steeple houses" and which not infrequently had closed their doors to the little brother of the daisies and the woodchucks.

Now as far as the first of those two is concerned, I don't run any risk of devoting too much space to him. The Catholic colony, now known as the Maryland Free State, was in every respect superior to the Calvinistic settlements along the coast of New England. But the spirit of tolerance which made itself manifest along the banks of the Patapsco seems to have been entirely due to the superior personal qualities of George Calvert, the founder, and it is impossible to decide in how far His Lordship had been inspired by the kindly philosopher of the Umbrian mountains and how much of it was practical politics.

But with George Fox the story is different.

The great difficulty with all movements that remain strictly spiritual and do not degenerate into a hard and fast system of religious dogma is this: that one can never hope to trace the influence which they exert on the development of contemporary events with any degree of accuracy.

One can state definitely that organized opposition to the institution of slavery first made itself felt in Pennsylvania. But does that mean that the Civil War was brought about by the followers of William Penn? I don't know.

The whole world now recognizes that the first people to insist upon prison reform were those same Friends who had spent so much of their own time in the pestilential dungeons of Old and New England. But was it George Fox directly who taught us to regard the criminal as a sick man rather than as a wicked scoundrel or is it the general spirit of the times? Again, I do not know.

Any man who has ever studied the "concessions" which Penn drew up for his colony in America is struck by the similarity of that document and the scrap of parchment upon which a few years later Thomas Jefferson wrote down his conceptions of individual and national liberty. Are we, therefore, right in suggesting that the famous skeptic from Albemarle County was at heart a Quaker?

Historical parallels, when they arise (which is very rare), make such a plausible appeal to our innate sense of order that we are easily tempted into conclusions which are by no means borne out by subsequent developments.

Of this much, however, I feel convinced, that if William Penn had been allowed to continue his experiments for a few years longer than he actually did, if his successors had been as capable as he himself, in short, if Quakerism had been able to make itself the dominant factor on the American continent instead of Puritanism, the history of our country would have been infinitely less violent and as a nation we would have been a great deal more lovable and happier than we are now.

The Penn régime in America did not last very long. Fifty years at the most. But in that short space of time the Quakers lighted a beacon of spiritual righteousness which has never quite ceased to illuminate the dark and hidden corners of the local landscape. Most important of all, they did this without making any undue fuss about their personal holiness, without laying claim to being better than their neighbors; without even trying to force upon their neighbors those ideas and principles which happened to suit their own tastes and predilections.

That is a pretty fine record for a group of people who for more than half a century were at the mercy of every piffling little magistrate, who were hanged and quartered and whipped to death for no other crime than that they seemed to hold certain opinions, considered dangerous to the greed of Anglican bishops and the dignity of Puritan clerics, a small band of faithful men and women who were under constant temptation to revaluate their suffering into a sense of superiority and who had every reason to regard themselves as the chosen children of God.

Those strange but interesting heretics, who insisted upon taking the words of Jesus seriously, had been quietly going from the whipping-post to the hanging-pillars for almost two generations when they stumbled across an unexpected and powerful protector.

The Quakers, who did not believe in the established Church of England, who did not believe in any established church anywhere at any time, were in the habit of holding separate meetings of their own. Those gatherings were of a very peaceful nature. The Quakers did not believe in physical violence and kept away from all political life. The magistrates, of course, knew this. But in those good old times justice was a form of revenue. When business was slack, it was good sport to drag a Quaker to court and fine him a couple of pounds for refusing to take off his hat in the presence of the judge. Furthermore, as these strange people did not believe in lawyers, there was no danger of their ever suing anyone for false arrest.

It is a very curious thing, but many of the world's most ardent reformers have been rich young men who lived in comfort and ease until by a mere chance they were brought into contact with the brutalities of everyday existence and were so shocked and horrified by their experience that they remained rebels until the end of their days.

This had been true of Buddha and St. Francis and George Fox and now it was the turn of a young sport-about-town by the name of William Penn.

One fine day the local gendarmerie of the town of Cork decided to organize a little raid and gather in as many

Quakers as could be found at the nearest meetinghouse. Following the usual procedure they took their charges to the police station to hold them there until they could be tried by a convenient judge. Imagine the horror of His Honor when a real gentleman was discovered among the prisoners. The magistrate was abject in his apologies. Of course it was all a mistake and would the young man overlook this most regrettable event and consider himself free to go home whenever he pleased?

No, the young man would not, and that, as far as we know, seems to have been the way in which William Penn drifted into the Quaker movement, and took his stand with the oppressed and bedraggled followers of the new faith.

Young William had always been more or less interested in religion. Even in his college days he had believed so strictly in man's right to find salvation after his own fashion that he had succeeded in getting himself fired for nonattendance at chapel. But as the son of Admiral the Hon. Sir William Penn of Wanstead House, Essex, he had spent his first twenty years in a sphere of society in which it was not considered good form to make a public showing of one's emotions and he had never had the courage to break away entirely.

Once, however, the decisive step had been taken, he stopped at no halfway measures. He discarded his uniform, renounced his ambition to become a soldier, wrote pamphlets explaining his strange creed for the benefit of all scoffers, and managed to make himself the center of a celebrated lawsuit in which the jurymen, by their refusal to find the prisoner guilty as directed by the presiding judge, established a legal precedent which has been respected ever since, both in England and in America.

That, however, was not his only encounter with the authorities. Penn was forever preaching and was forever being sent to jail and was forever being pardoned and then was sent to jail again for some new crime of a highly Christian character. All the time, however, he was making converts and the situation threatened to become slightly ludicrous when to the great satisfaction of his exasperated relatives he got interested in the idea of establishing a Quaker colony in the American wilderness.

The Quakers knew a great deal about America. Like the early Franciscans they were always going upon all sorts of queer expeditions. They were likely to drop in on the Sultan of Turkey, or the Tsar of Moscovy, or the Dey of Algeria at the most unexpected hours. And because they were simple and unaffected folks and had none of the annoying characteristics of the average professional prophet, they were almost invariably well received and (as long as they dealt strictly with non-Christian potentates) they seemed to have suffered practically no harm.

The Grand Padishah may have been slightly astonished when good Mary Fiske, fresh from a long sentence in a Yorkshire jail, walked in on him at his camp before Adrianople. But he behaved like a gentleman, he listened with serious mien to her message, and he gave her the freedom of his empire with the offer of a private body-guard.

As for the Moscovite and the Moor, they, too, had behaved with unexpected decorum and when the irrepressible Friends visited them and told them how much nicer this world would be if all the people really liked each other and stopped quarreling and stealing their neighbors' possessions, they had said yes with great solemnity and invited their strange visitors to stop for supper.

Far different was the reception that awaited these modern apostles in America. Quite a number of them were hanged. Others were whipped from village to village. And as for the women, they were forever at the mercy of those New England divines who liked to turn every case that concerned a pleasant-looking young woman into a witch-hunting affair and then made the best of their opportunities.

Under those circumstances, the members of almost any other sect would have given America a wide berth. The Quakers, it must be admitted, rather enjoyed such violent tussles with fate, and besides, they took an almost child-like interest in the welfare of wild people and wanted a chance to prove to all the world (and to the New Englanders in particular) that there were other and more profitable ways of settling the native problem than the usual ones, suggested by the shotgun and the whisky bottle.

And then in the year 1670 they had their chance.

Sir William Penn was dead and had left his son a claim on the Stuarts for eighty thousand dollars. The Stuarts were right royal borrowers, but when the day of payment came around, they suddenly felt the stir of the ancestors and could be as penurious as the meanest Glasgow moneylender. But they were not without a certain artistry in the realm of finance. They were always willing to repay a debt with something that did not belong to them. And so after several years of negotiation they bestowed upon William an immense tract of land which was called Pennsylvania (after the young man's father) and which was supposed to lie somewhere between Maryland and Delaware and to run west and north as far as you please.

On the first of December of the year 1682 Penn left England for his new possessions in the good ship *Welcome*.

That was the beginning of one of the most interesting colonial experiments of the days before our national independence.

This new settlement was not just going to be another enterprise owned, managed, and exploited by a board of absent directors. Far from it! And Penn, who was a good deal of a sloganeer, expressed himself quite clearly when he called his domains "a free colony for the benefit of all mankind."

But in his naïve enthusiasm he went much too far. He even insisted that the original inhabitants of the country were human beings and when he delivered himself of such an outrageous statement, the other colonists knew him for what he really was—a foolish visionary with unpractical and dangerous ideas. To them the Indian had been one of two things, either a sad joke, which must be humored with gin and colored beads, or an invention of Satan, planted on these shores to defraud God's chosen people out of their righteous inheritance and therefore at the mercy of every good Christian with a reliable musket.

When the Quakers, in obedience to their Master's "Great Law," actually put the theory of "friendly White, friendly Indian" into practice, did not cheat the Indian, did not go to church carrying half a dozen arquebuses and bludgeons, but instead left the children to the care of the nearest squaw while they walked solemnly to the nearest meetinghouse, the other colonists knew that there must be a secret treaty between the Devil and this man Penn and they took steps to protect their own possessions against the consequences of such a wicked and foolish policy of kindness and conciliation, and hastily laid in an extra supply of gunpowder.

When in addition to all these enormities the yearly meeting of the Quakers of 1696 declared the institution of slavery contrary to the teachings of the New Testament, it became clear to all decent citizens of Virginia and Massachusetts that this absurd experiment in colonial statecraft must soon come to a bad ending. Unfortunately they were right.

There seems to be a singular fatality about all efforts to turn the dead words of Jesus Christ into a living rule of conduct. During a few years men like George Fox or Francis of Assisi or William Penn are so successful that we are apt to say, "Now the thing has been done! The world has heard the simple words that will set it free from most of its troubles. It is still a long cry from Paradise. Children will continue to catch the measles and old folks will die of this and that, but the foolish jealousies and hatreds and envies of everyday life will be thrown overboard as silly superfluities."

And then, just as soon as the first enthusiasm has worn off, when it begins to dawn upon the world in general that these men are not really Gods in disguise, that they possess no secret formula that will suddenly set the world free from poverty and pestilence, then the cry is raised that they are miserable impostors and hypocrites and deserve to be hanged on the highest gallows.

Poor Penn, who had wasted his patrimony on his colony, who had devoted all his time in and out of jail to the happiness of his fellow men, fell upon evil days. His children died or turned drunkards. One of them even became a notorious character in the city called Philadelphia. His trusted friends cheated him and his private secretary tried to defraud him of more than sixty thousand dollars and when Penn refused to be blackmailed managed to have him imprisoned for debt. And meanwhile the other colonies, by their treatment of the natives, caused outbreaks of border warfare which at times made the position of the Quakers very difficult.

In the year 1712 a merciful stroke (nature ofttimes shows herself kinder than the human race) made Penn oblivious of the little worries of everyday life. During a few more years he was able to wander through the pleasant lanes of his country house. Then he died and with him the wonderful dream of George Fox came to an end.

But not entirely.

Great men are like the floods of Egypt that come and go and leave the country happier and richer and more fertile in noble ideals for their temporary presence.

The Quakers as a sect obeyed the laws which rule all organized forms of society. They soon lost that spiritual pliancy which had been the greatest asset of their founders. Even so they retained a degree of charity and kindliness and tolerance which made them superior to those Calvinists and Episcopalians who were their neighbors and within the boundaries of their own colony they maintained a measure of personal freedom which for a long time made Pennsylvania unique among the colonies.

Of course I know all the arguments against them. They were penurious and close-fisted and terribly solemn. They never went to the theater. They did not care for music and they lived dreary and drab lives. Granted! But they had one enormous merit. As a rule they minded their own business.

*Chapter Fourteen*

# COLONIZING BY GOD AND BY GUESS

IN EVERY ONE of the handbooks of navigation of the sixteenth and seventeenth centuries there is a chapter devoted to the useful art of dead reckoning.

In those days, as soon as a ship had left port, it was "at sea" in the true sense of the word. No wireless information, no submarine telephones, no tide charts, radio compasses, forecasts of weather and icebergs, or any of the other appurtenances which have changed the modern ocean liner into a sublimated ferryboat. The average skipper, of course, had a much greater personal familiarity with the stars than is possessed by the seafaring men of today. With the help of these useful orbs and a few simple instruments he often performed the most extraordinary feats of seamanship. But when storms and fogs and bad weather continued for a long time prevented him from making the necessary observations, then he depended for information as to his true position upon his log line, his compass, and his own good luck.

Or, in the parlance of that pious day, he sailed "by God and by guess."

If he were lucky, he would reach port.

If fate were against him, he would not.

It was all in the day's work. Amen.

Our ancestors, who were still sufficiently near the days of the medieval Church to understand the use of symbols, loved to speak of the Ship of State.

We people of a more sophisticated age, who know how easily a ship can be destroyed by a sudden internal explosion and how quickly it can be wrecked by bad management on the part of the officers, are less fond of this pleasant simile. But during the seventeenth century, a great many Ships of State still proudly sailed the waters of the

Colonizing by God and by guess

international ocean and few of them had been entrusted
to a more incompetent skipper than the magnificent galleon which flew the British ensign and was supposed to
obey the commands of a certain Captain Stuart.

It never foundered because most of the crew knew their
business so well that, in a pinch, almost any boatswain
could take hold of the wheel and bring the vessel about
before it was too late and it had been broken to pieces
on the Rocks of Popular Discontent.

I might continue this pleasant allegory for a little longer,
but I am afraid that my supply of nautical terms is somewhat limited and I had better come to the point I wished
to make at the beginning of this chapter—that the colonial
policy of England during the seventeenth and eighteenth
centuries was a policy entirely by God and by guess.

The Puritans were the only exception. They at least
knew what they wanted. But the other settlements just
"happened."

A few of them had been started as speculative investments in real estate, financed entirely by private corporations. Others were founded by honest men and women who only recently had escaped from the religious and economic despotism of the people in the Massachusetts Bay region.

Still others were meant to be experiments in philanthropy and endeavored to provide a home for the social misfits of the mother country.

Two of them had originally belonged to other nations and were afterward incorporated into the British Empire by force of arms.

One was the private property of a benevolent Catholic gentleman who curiously enough lived up to his promise of "religious tolerance" with such honesty of purpose that he incurred the bitter enmity of all his Protestant neighbors.

Another large slice of territory had been handed over to a rich young Quaker in lieu of a royal debt that could not be paid in cash.

Several more owed their existence to this same cause and were the result of the well-known Stuart habit of rewarding faithful servants with promissory notes upon something that belonged to someone else.

The last of the Stuarts, known to his followers as Henry IX and by profession a cardinal, died in France in the year 1807.

He was a good and kindly man but it is said that he was not very bright. If he had been possessed of the good-natured philosophy of his amiable but entirely worthless great-great-grandfather, King Charles, he might well have contemplated the new map of America with sardonic astonishment. For rarely, during that period of history upon which we possess some concrete information, has an undertaking, conceived in such utter spirit of haphazard indifference, borne such astonishing fruit.

## Chapter Fifteen

# EMPIRE BUILDING BY ROYAL RESCRIPT

THE ENGLISH CHANNEL is not very wide.

A fast steamer will carry a Continental tourist from Calais to Dover in little more than an hour. But once he has passed through the British customs, he is in a different world which will continue to puzzle him for the rest of his days.

Take one little example.

In Europe baggage is always more or less of a nuisance. It has to be dragged to one corner of the station and has to be weighed. Then a receipt has to be obtained. Then the receipt has to be paid for, and everything is very formal and according to a definite paragraph of a definite law, passed on a definite day of a definite year by a duly appointed royal commissioner of railroads.

In England, a fellow in a red tie leisurely carts one's bags to the luggage van; deposits them there as seems to suit his fancy, and disappears with a tip and a cheerful "good morning." Arrived at the spot of destination, another citizen in a red tie collects such parts of the van's contents as one may claim as his own, packs them on his little truck, and without further ado takes them to a taxi.

"But," asks the foreigner, who feels that such absence of official supervision is almost criminal, "don't you people lose an awful lot of trunks that way?"

"No," the Englishman replies, "nothing much ever seems to be lost. Perhaps once in a while a bag goes astray. But we are accustomed to the system. I suppose we got the habit of doing the thing this way in the days of the stagecoach and it works. So why change it?"

In short, the English system (if it can properly be called by that high-sounding name) seems to be to let things take their course, to give the individual the greatest possible freedom and to restrict interference on the part of the government to a few necessary if unpleasant details such as policemen and magistrates and courteous though quick-fingered executioners. Whereas on the Continent the public is regarded as a helpless imbecile who could not possibly get along in life without constant supervision on the part of the government.

This philosophical treatise upon the "customs of nations" may seem slightly out of place in a chapter that deals with the history of the seventeenth century, but it was just that eternal meddling on the part of the authorities that made the French lose their empire in America and that has since then accounted for so many of the colonial failures of other European nations.

If Mr. Nobel had invented his dynamite a couple of centuries earlier and had offered an annual prize for the man who had achieved the greatest possible distinction in the field of discovery, the majority of his rewards would undoubtedly have gone to several of the subjects of good King Louis.

Those Frenchmen walked and rode and sailed and canoed and snowshoed across the hinterland of Canada with such a sublime disregard for their personal convenience (not to mention a dozen forms of slow and painful death) that a chronicle of their adventures reads like a sublime but forgotten chapter of *The Three Musketeers*.

And then, in the end, they accomplished nothing.

Whereas their English neighbors stuck as closely as possible to convenient rivers and bays and founded the greatest of modern nations.

It was all very sad from the French point of view, but it was absolutely inevitable.

For France in the seventeenth century was rapidly degenerating into an overcentralized monarchy. The power of the feudal aristocracy had been broken, while the power of His Divine Majesty the King had been made absolute.

Now it is a well-established fact that the nobility of a country ceases to be an important factor in the development of the state as soon as it ceases to exercise "leadership" and prattles sweetly of "service."

During the seventeenth century the English nobles continued to be the recognized potentates of the communities in which they happened to live and never went to London if they could possibly help themselves. Their French colleagues, meanwhile, felt highly flattered if they were allowed to take care of the royal canaries and were permitted to dwell permanently within the presence of their illustrious master.

Thus, while in England the crown was obliged to be very circumspect and dare not press any laws unless they enjoyed the cordial support of the county squires, the French sovereigns ruled their realm as they pleased or as seemed best to their mistresses and an occasional minister.

The French as a nation do not like to travel outside of their own country and furthermore they are proverbially ignorant of the habits, customs, and morals of other nations which they think slightly ridiculous and wholly barbarous. And as for the French kings, they might know every stone and tree along the road from Paris to Versailles, but of geography in general they had not the faintest notion.

I do not mean to imply that the Stuarts spent the midnight oil poring over the maps in Mr. Blauw's well-known atlas. But in their case that was not necessary. They exasperated their subjects so thoroughly that whole droves of them fled across the ocean and in this way the interests of England were well taken care of. But even this the French monarchs failed to do.

It used to be customary to speak of the great French Revolution of the year 1789 as if it had been caused solely by the misery of the masses. "Let them eat grass if they cannot have cake," etc., etc. Now at last a less sentimental but more truthful conception of history is beginning to shatter this idea. The peasants in many other countries of Europe were not only invited to eat grass, but they were actually forced to consume that tough herb to keep alive. As a result they were so weak that they lacked the energy necessary for a successful rebellion. Whereas the sans-culottes and the other butchers from the provinces who waged that bloodthirsty upheaval seem to have been fairly well fed. Otherwise it seems impossible that they could have been quite as energetic and as successful as they proved themselves to be.

True enough, the French peasants lived in squalor. But the mighty palace of Versailles was nothing to boast of when it came to cleanliness and comfort, and judging by the unwillingness of the average French provincial to leave his village, his condition cannot have been quite as hopeless as some of the historians of the Revolution would have us believe.

It was the old, old story of the lack of man power which accounted for the slow development of the French possessions in North America.

When the explorers returned to Paris and told of their discoveries, of the unlimited miles of the territories which they had added to the French kingdom, His Majesty and his immediate advisers felt that something ought to be done, but where in the name of their seven hundred pastry cooks were they to find the necessary number of settlers?

Very gradually a few thousand hardy individuals moved more or less voluntarily to the neighborhood of Quebec and Montreal. As soon, however, as that much had been accomplished, the logical and orderly French mind got busy and committed the usual error of "centralizing" the new townships as thoroughly as if they had been villages in Burgundy or Gascony. Thereafter everything that people wanted to do in distant Canada must first of all be referred to the officials in Paris. If a man wanted a hunting-permit, he must send his application to Paris. If a governor desired to rid himself of a stupid subordinate, he must first consult his superiors in Paris. Under such circumstances, all private initiative was soon destroyed, and a colony (especially in those days) depended for its rapid development upon the sort of people who are at their best when left to their own devices and who never under any circumstances ask the help of the central government.

But there was another reason why the people of the New

France lagged so terribly behind their Dutch and English neighbors. In the territory that had been settled by the Protestants there was little or no friction between the civil authorities and the clergy. Occasionally there was a quarrel between different sects of Calvinists or Lutherans, but in such a case the minority wandered forth to build a Zion of its own in another part of the forest and the community at large benefited by the extension of the English sphere of influence.

In Canada, on the other hand, the government and the Church were forever at loggerheads with each other. At a very early date the Jesuits had descended upon the country and had taken charge of the poor savages who were undoubtedly in great need of everything that the good fathers could teach them. But that extraordinary society of saintly and learned men (the shock troops of the Catholic Church) never quite accepted the theory according to which the State is supposed to be superior to the Church.

In one part of America, in Paraguay, the Jesuits had even succeeded in establishing a state of their own which was recognized as an independent nation, and maintained an army and behaved like a sovereign state for almost a century. In Canada they never got as far as that, but they and the other missionaries greatly resented what they called the undue interference with their work on the part of the royal governors and they were the sworn enemies of those dignitaries as long as Canada remained a French dependency.

The French government, of course, hoped to make some money out of those American possessions and it was the duty of the colonial officials to show a profitable balance at the end of each year. How and in what way the necessary number of furs was collected did not interest them. As far as they were concerned, the whole of the native population could die from an overdose of rum if only the storehouses of Montreal were kept well supplied with bearskins and beaver pelts.

The Church, on the other hand, only saw the slow degradation which overtook the natives as the result of such a policy and the honest fathers did their best to prevent it. During a great many years the French possessions were practically ruled by the Bishop of Quebec and trade came to a complete standstill. But that was not all. The pernickety savages, far from appreciating such kindness, mistook it for an expression of weakness and under the leadership of the Iroquois they almost pushed the entire French population into the ocean. Thereupon there was a great hue and cry on the banks of the Seine. A strong man, a certain Louis de Frontenac, was hastily dispatched to the St. Lawrence River that the heathen might be brought to terms. But as soon as he had slaughtered a sufficient number of Indians to discourage the others from further warlike activities, the old game of wire-pulling began afresh. The lady friends of His Majesty, as beautiful as they were pious, shed copious tears upon the royal table whenever the fate of their clerical protégés was mentioned. One after another the bishops returned. Soon afterward the energetic governor was called back to Paris "to render an account of his recent activities" and then everything was as it had been before.

At one moment during the seventeenth century, during the reign of Charles II, it would have been the easiest thing in the world for the French to annex the whole of the Atlantic seaboard. For just when war had broken out between France and England, the French had one of their best regiments in Montreal and the English were practically without troops.

But at this very moment and in the midst of the most serious crisis in the history of New France, some silly fool in the mother country managed to have the governor general of Canada recalled at the request of a dissatisfied cleric and when the error had been repaired the chance for a successful invasion of New England was gone.

Meanwhile on paper the empire of New France looked magnificent.

It stretched with a grandiloquent gesture from the Arctic Circle to the Gulf of Mexico and its frontiers were carefully defined by a series of heavy leaden plates upon which the servants of His Majesty had engraved the legend that the land in which these lay buried belonged to Ludovicus—whatever his number.

But in practice it was a poverty-stricken, priest-ridden wilderness, neglected part of the time, suffering from an oversupply of laws and regulations at other times, never allowed to develop its own resources according to the wishes of its own inhabitants and at the mercy of every petticoat intrigue and royal whim.

Even as late as the latter half of the seventeenth century there was a chance to save this valuable possession for France. In the year 1685 Louis XIV revoked the Edict of Nantes by which Henri IV had guaranteed unto his Protestant subjects equal political rights with their Catholic neighbors. During the next twenty years the Huguenots were the victims of a very cruel and stupid form of persecution. Their life at home was made almost unbearable and they asked permission to go elsewhere. Those industrious men and women would have given anything if they had been allowed to found a loyal French state on the other side of the ocean. But their requests were curtly refused. And when they insisted, the frontiers were closed to them.

Of course whenever people really want to get out of a country (or get in) they do get out (or in). Within the next five years more than fifty thousand Huguenot families managed to escape from France. They wandered to England and to Holland. They carried nothing with them but their thrift, their ability, and their credit. That baggage, however, proved sufficient for all their needs. In less than no time they had firmly re-established themselves in business and trade. And those same people, who might have been most useful bulwarks of French culture in distant parts of the world, now strengthened the forces of those who only waited for an opportunity to despoil France of the last of her colonial possessions.

*Chapter Sixteen*

## HORIZONS OF HOPE

PEOPLE NEVER CEASE TO MARVEL at the so-called "suddenness" of fate. In the next street a house "suddenly" falls down, an old neighbor "suddenly" dies, a famous European dynasty is "suddenly" wiped out.

As a matter of fact, as all scientists, most newspapermen, and even a few historians know, nothing ever happens "suddenly." The collapse of the house, the demise of the dynasty or the neighbor may seem to be accomplished within a very short period of time. But the forces that brought about the state of decay which made the matter of collapsing and demising a question of minutes and seconds had been at work upon their secret task for years and years in advance.

Reverse the process and you will find that the "sudden rise" of a republic, the "sudden" acquisition of wealth on the part of a family, the "sudden" manifestation of genius in a hitherto obscure fiddle player are all of them the result of certain mysterious plans which were worked out with infinite care in the patient laboratories of time.

Only a few pages separate us from that great political upheaval which "suddenly" will turn thirteen quarreling little colonies into a strongly united political power. But how was this "sudden" change brought about? Was it caused by the hardships of a long military campaign or by the necessity of greater economic co-operation? Or was it the result of one man's ability as a statesman?

Of course not.

The Revolution was a mere incident, although noisy enough to attract a great deal of attention. The real groundwork, however, for the new enterprise had been laid centuries before. But it had been done so quietly and so unobtrusively and most of it had been accomplished by such very simple people that few of the contemporaries were then conscious of the fact that something unusual was going on in this world.

Our statistics upon the subject of seventeenth- and eighteenth-century immigration are not entirely reliable. About a few of the groups of newcomers we know a lot, about most of the others we know practically nothing.

But enough information has been gathered to give us a fairly accurate idea of the sort of people who then took the trouble to cross the ocean.

They came from all classes of society and for every conceivable reason.

In the first place there were the Negroes who were dumped upon the American shores by the bitterly competing companies of English and Dutch slave raiders. Those unfortunate creatures, however, do not properly belong in our tabulation. They came here because they could not help themselves and they were doomed to suffer for a sin which they had never committed.

Then there were the "bonded servants." The bonded servants of the seventeenth century were really day laborers and small artisans and bankrupt shopkeepers who could not afford to pay for their own passage. In exchange for a certain number of pounds and pennies they agreed to let themselves be "bound out" to some colonial master for periods varying between five and seven years. Generally speaking, it seems to me that these poor creatures did not get a square deal. The cost of transportation in those early times was a great deal higher than it is today. Four hundred dollars for a single fare was quite a normal price. Even so, seven years of chores and drudgery in return for a steerage ticket seems a bit stiff. But the prospective immigrant probably reasoned that this was the only chance he had of ever getting away from his miserable home. Once those seven years were over he would be free to do as he pleased and would have a chance to begin work upon a career of his own.

Next there were the small capitalists, the fortunate folk who had saved or made or inherited a few hundred pounds, who had read the full-page advertisement in which Brother Penn described the glories of his sylvan Paradise and who decided to get their share of those treasures and free homesteads before it was too late.

Then there were those who belonged to some sect or other that was being persecuted by some particularly persevering group of magistrates and who hoped to find some nook in the wilderness where they would be allowed to pray and preach as they liked.

Then there were those who had been born with that cheerful affliction known as the "Wanderlust" who went to America solely because they were bored at home and felt the need of a change.

Then there were those who felt an equally urgent need of a change because the bailiffs were after them.

In short, it was as motley a crowd as ever pulled up stakes and moved from one part of the world to another.

But as soon as they landed, all these people, these religious fanatics, bonded servants, sporting younger sons, insolvent tradesmen, dissatisfied noblemen, escaped felons, runaway sailors, dispossessed farmers, agreed upon one thing: that this was a better world than the one they had just left behind. Not an easier world, for only the hardiest among the colonists could hope to survive. But a world of unlimited opportunities, a world of vast spaces, a world where a man still could stretch out his arms and could say, "Behold, I am free!" and could pick up his bags and start forth to walk and could walk for ten years and still find himself in the midst of the forests and the plains.

And long before anyone along the Atlantic seaboard had ever dreamed of combining the rival colonies into a single state, the people who inhabited the territory between the Charles River and the Chesapeake Bay were possessed of one characteristic that was to provide them with a useful common ideal during the many trying years that were to follow so soon. I refer to the conviction that the future happiness of every man in the new world depended exclusively upon his own efforts and that those who had chosen to live on the outskirts of the wilderness were masters of their own fate in the strictest sense of the word.

●　　●　　●　　●　　●　　　　●

A few hours before an inward-bound vessel is boarded by the pilot the dim outline of a rocky coast begins to make its appearance. To the early discoverers, bound for the gold of Zipangu, it spelled delay and disaster. To the millions that came afterward, it meant their first glimpse of the horizon of hope.

Learned treatises have been writ upon the psychological changes that take place in the prospective immigrant, of the how and the why and the wherefore of the American character.

. . . . . . .

But in this instance I can do without the guidance of these erudite tomes.

I, too, have seen that slender dark line.

## Chapter Seventeen

## THE ROYAL AND IMPERIAL GAME OF LAND GRABBING

THERE IS AN OLD STORY (I don't remember where I first heard it) about a certain professor of ichthyology, who one day was lecturing upon the stirring subject of that noble fish which is called the sturgeon. In his left hand the learned doctor carried a sheaf of notes painfully culled from all the books that had ever been written upon the subject of Acipenser Rubicundus. His right hand held a short cane with which he pointed at a fine large picture of the subject under discussion. As the slow minutes ticked away, he waxed quite eloquent.

"Gentlemen," he said, "the sturgeon—"

At that moment the door opened. A shiny old sturgeon, hoary with the weeds and the wisdom of ages, came quietly swimming into the room and made for the speaker's platform.

For a moment the man of science was puzzled. He hardly

knew what to make of this interruption. Then he got hold of himself and with great dignity he asked, "Will one of you gentlemen kindly remove this creature, that I may go on with my observations?"

When I read the learned works of some of my European brethren, I am often reminded of this yarn. They work so terribly hard. They are so tremendously conscientious. They will spend a lifetime in the search of a single missing document and they wade through bales and bales of printed and written material, that they may explain just a few years of such important movements as the great migrations or a few of the less obvious aspects of the feudal system and the development of dynastic states. Meanwhile they seem to overlook the quite obvious fact that the Middle Ages are still in full swing on the other side of the ocean and that modern America is the ideal laboratory for the study of a large number of social and spiritual and economic phenomena which had run their course in the old world centuries before the birth of Columbus.

A few examples will tell you what I mean.

In Europe people ceased to wander from place to place twelve hundred years ago. In America the migrations are still in full swing and in Washington the problem of new hordes of barbarians clamoring for admission is quite as much of a problem in the year 1927 as it was in Rome in the year 227.

The Great War has swept aside the last remnants of feudal Europe. In our American cities the feudal system is still as active as ever before and those who doubt my word had better make a study of Tammany Hall or any of our great political organizations.

And as for that rivalry between the different dynasties which caused so much suffering in Europe during the seventeenth and eighteenth centuries, that rivalry in a modified form continues in America with such uninterrupted violence that fully one third of our newspaper space is devoted to the subject. Of course, the methods which are employed in the year 1927 are different from those that were current in 1727, but the Habsburgs and the Bourbons and the Romanovs and the Hohenzollerns and the Wasas fighting for large parcels of European land could have given many a useful hint to the groups of financiers who this very morning are making war upon each other for the possession of certain monopolies in oil or grain or coal or electricity.

The past is always picturesque. Distance lends enchantment, for it covers the greasy spots on His Majesty's plumed hat with a charitable layer of dust. But the great interdynastic struggle of two hundred years ago was every whit as stupid and as wasteful as the conflict between the groups of financial interests who are now fighting for the possession of our water power and our rubber.

There was just one difference.

The campaigns of the eighteenth century were conducted from the saddle of a horse.

Those of today are directed from the seventeenth floor of a skyscraper.

As for the main outline of the history of the dynastic period of the Louises and the Georges, it is fairly well known and not very interesting.

The theological frenzy of the era which followed immediately upon the Reformation had spent itself. People were beginning to feel slightly foolish when they thought of the oceans of blood spilled in the name of brotherly love. They were no longer willing to go to war for the greater glory of an unintelligible paragraph in some equally obscure chapter of a holy book. But now they were just as eager to fight for the sake of certain dim but greatly revered principles of "legitimate succession." And the hours which had formerly been wasted upon a perusal of the official catechism were now devoted to the study of genealogical timetables and directories.

The taste in popular slogans had changed, but the human race had remained the same and now the average citizen went forth just as seriously to "vindicate the good right of George or Louis" as his grandfather had done a hundred years previously "to uphold the glory of the true God."

As the European dynasties were really a close corporation of professional sovereigns who for hundreds of years had been marrying their first, second, and third cousins, it was often exceedingly difficult to discover exactly who, among a dozen candidates for a particular throne, was the "legitimate" one. And the "near legitimate" ones could always get hold of a convenient body of so-called "judicial advisers" who (in return for a certain consideration) were willing to bolster up any and all claims of their temporary employers.

They were curious wars, these eighteenth century conflicts, and not unlike a great international game of cards. All the nations who took part (and as a rule the whole Continent was dragged in before the fight was over) tried to get hold of as many tricks as possible and then, when it was time to talk of a settlement, they said to each other, "Now I have got four of your provinces and nine of your big cities and twelve thousand square miles of your colonies in India and fourteen thousand square miles of your provinces in America and a couple of thousand of square miles in Africa and three hundred and eighty-two of your merchantmen, and let us see—you have got five of my provinces, but only six of my big towns and ten thousand miles in India and twenty-five thousand miles in America (that is pretty bad, I must grant you!) and nothing in Africa (that is better!) and two hundred and seventy-nine of my merchantmen. Now that makes four plus nine plus twelve thousand—" and so on and so forth, until by that process of wrangling known in unofficial circles as "horse-dealing" they had reached an agreement that seemed fairly honest to all concerned.

That the natives of Africa and Asia and the colonists of America who were invariably forced to take part in these quarrels, although they were not in the least interested in them, should also have been asked for an expression of opinion, never seemed to have dawned upon the powers that ruled in Paris and London and Vienna and Amsterdam.

But once more I must warn you not to be too severe with our benighted ancestors.

Only a few years ago we ourselves turned the heart

of Africa into a battlefield where Kaffir murdered Kaffir for the greater glory of the Germans or the Allies. We made shambles of Chinese cities which did not belong to the people who were fighting for their possession. We drove countless Indian and African natives into a conflict that did not touch their lives in any way, form, or fashion. And when it was all over, a small number of old gentlemen played dice for scraps of territory and barrels of oil and had the brazen effrontery to say that they were stealing each other's colonies to "assure the peace of the world."

The dynasties for whose benefits these ancient wars were fought no longer exist while the odds and ends of American real estate for which our great-grandfathers gambled and which they threw away or swapped as useless investments now bear such high-sounding names as "The Dominion of Canada" or "The United States of America."

As for the series of Franco-English wars which finally made the northern part of the American continent English and destroyed the power of the French, these have been described so often and so eloquently that I shall go into no details. For the sake of convenience and historical accuracy our schoolbooks talk of King William's war and Queen Anne's war and King George's war and the French and Indian war and they tell us that these conflicts lasted from 1689 to 1697, from 1701 to 1713, from 1744 to 1748, and from 1755 to 1763, and they duly recount those famous battles in which our side gained only "a moral victory" and they give a slightly more glorious description of those encounters in which the British actually forced the French to evacuate some isolated blockhouse and to surrender a garrison consisting of thirty-seven soldiers and thirty-eight squaws.

But those occasional outbreaks of violence between small groups of red-coated and blue-coated members of the military profession were really of very small importance if we compare them to the silent tragedy enacted during those fateful years along the frontier of the great American wilderness.

The statesmen of the eighteenth century who thought

exclusively in terms of protocols and compacts and official memoranda never even suspected what was happening. But while they were drawing their pretty little dotted lines across the map of the New World and were telling each other who should have what, other forces were at work which soon afterward were to undo the painstaking labors of these hide-bound Excellencies with an almost sublime disregard for official precedent. I refer, of course, to the rapidly increasing number of European immigrants.

Generally speaking the men and the women who had left the overcrowded cities and villages of the old world and who had settled down on a little clearing in a Pennsylvania forest or who were trying to raise a few stalks of grain on a stony Massachusetts farm were very simple folk. They read few books except the Old Testament. Their interest in politics did not extend beyond the limits of their own county. They lived a monotonous existence (from our point of view), ate what they had raised themselves, drank what they had distilled in their own kitchens and wore what their wives had woven for them. But like all primitive organisms they knew what they wanted and what they wanted was expressed in just one word "LAND."

"Oh, dear me!" exclaimed a much perturbed official in faraway London when he heard that a hundred Rhode Islanders had gone west. "But those people simply can't go there. That part of America belongs to France."

"Can't we!" answered the men who were putting the harness on their ox-teams.

And they went.

It is true that sometimes they came to grief. Detachments of French soldiers would drive them back or for greater convenience would kill them on the spot.

Alas, those French blockhouses, which looked so formidable on paper, were supposed to protect a frontier that stretched all the way from the Gulf of St. Lawrence to the Bay of Mobile. There were very wide gaps between these fortifications, and through these gaps a steady but irrepressible stream of immigrants now began to flow with uninterrupted monotony into the rich forests and fields of the West.

On a small scale the same thing had already happened along the Atlantic seaboard. When the Dutch had claimed far more territory than they were able to handle, the surplus population of New England had quickly taken possession of the pleasant valleys of Connecticut and the English farmers had raised their crops on the ramparts of Dutch fortresses and nothing had happened because these people needed each other and could not be bothered by the artificial allegiances of their European homes.

In the eighteenth century it was the turn of the French to learn that it is useless to fight against the laws of nature. The government in Paris had at last begun to understand the importance of their American possessions. They had sent a large number of troops to Quebec and Montreal and New Orleans and Fort Vincennes and Fort Detroit and those soldiers had more than held their own against the British. But all their bravery and their skill were of no avail when the disinherited masses of the East made their bid for the free farms of the West. When finally in the year 1759, by a stroke of good luck, the English conquered the town of Quebec, the chain of French fortresses which was supposed to protect the territory of the Great Lakes and the Mississippi valley was broken for good and all.

Here and there an old French name reminds us of the tragedy that took place in those distant regions in the days of our great-great-great-grandfathers. And that is all.

*Chapter Eighteen*

## JANUARY 5, 1769
## THE BEGINNING OF OUR MODERN ERA

THIS CHAPTER is merely a suggestion. But it may help us to understand the history of the last two hundred years a little better than we do now.

For the sake of convenience and in his pride of achievement, a certain historian of the Renaissance divided the past of the human race into three periods: Antiquity, the Middle Ages and Modern Times. Modern Times, of course, represented his own era. Prehistoric man he left out because he had never heard of him. And he let the Classical Period end with the fall of Rome and decided that the conquest of Constantinople by the Turks had brought about the end of the Middle Ages and the beginning of Modern Times.

This division has for a long time been in urgent need of a thorough revision. Rome never fell and the statement that it did is apt to create an erroneous impression. The Middle Ages may or may not have come to an end when the Turks took Constantinople, but other events caused a much greater disturbance among the medieval conceptions of life than the successful European invasion by Suleiman the Great.

In the present book, however, my main concern is with the history of America.

I wish to state that on our continent the Middle Ages came to an end on the fifth of January of the year 1769.

On that day a certain James Watt obtained a patent for his newly perfected "fire-machine."

*Chapter Nineteen*

## GEORGE GRENVILLE TURNS "EFFICIENCY EXPERT"

THE ROAD OF RUINED EMPIRES is thickly strewn with the remnants of discarded systems. Indeed, nothing in public or private life seems to conduce so inevitably to failure as strict adherence to some rigid form of law or behavior and as a rule the more efficient the system, the greater the final collapse.

As long as the British Empire had been "on the make," so to speak, everything had gone well enough. The men who were sent to the corners of the earth to fight the spiritual monopoly of the Church and the economic monopoly of Spain had not been hampered by too many restrictions from the home government. They had been allowed to act as independent agents and they had done whatever seemed practicable and expedient at the moment. Sometimes, if it afterward appeared that they had gone a little too far in their eagerness, they ran, of course, the risk of being made His Majesty's scapegoat and of being hanged or decapitated for their trouble. But such incidents were all in the day's work and they did not interfere with the enthusiasm of the survivors.

But by the middle of the eighteenth century the rough work of empire-making had been done. The time had come for centralization and organization and classification and (as the inevitable result) taxation. The Raleighs took their bow and when the curtain went up again, behold the noble figure of George Grenville in the rôle of the "Boy Patriot," and wearing the uniform of a Lord of the Admiralty.

It may seem unfair to drag the name of Grenville into the present discussion as if poor George alone had been responsible for the loss of the American colonies. But Grenville was such a perfect representative of that type of official mind which can do more harm in less time than any other known agency of human ingenuity that he must play his little part and cannot hope to escape for at least four or five pages. Don't think, however, that this is going to be straight comedy. A decided tragic strain runs through the whole performance—the tragedy implied in the words "wasted effort."

For George was really a very conscientious and intelligent servant of the crown. There was not a man in the whole of the British Isles who got up so early, who went to bed so late, who spent quite so many hours in fussing about the details of his job, as this much abused Chancellor of the Exchequer.

In the days of Queen Bess he would have been very useful as the bookkeeper of a company of gentlemen adventurers.

The frontier fortress

In the days of George III he was downright dangerous as the man who was asked to tell the American colonists when, where and in what manner they were expected to pay their share in the upkeep of the empire.

With Charles Townsend he probably believed that the colonists were "children of England's planting, nourished by the indulgence of the mother country until they were grown to a good degree of strength and opulence." But what sort of a pose was he to strike when old Colonel Barre answered, "Children planted by our care? No, indeed! It was our oppression that planted them in America and it was our neglect that made them grow up," and when the Americans, as one man, rose to applaud these seditious utterances?

For although the New Englanders and the Virginians and the Carolinians were too well grounded in the ancient laws of obedience to the King to dream of forming a nation of their own, they felt that they had a serious cause for grievance. They had left the old country to rid themselves of certain impositions which were irksome to their sense of personal freedom and to gain a more abundant supply of bread and butter for their children. But as soon as they were free the home government had reached across the ocean and once more the pioneers found themselves caught in the meshes of an official net that was disgusting to them and from which they had hoped to escape for good when they sailed from Bristol, England, to Boston,

Massachusetts.

Whether they liked it or not they must sell everything they produced in English markets and through English intermediaries although Dutch or Spanish merchants in Dutch or Spanish markets might offer them much better prices than their own countrymen. With the exception of such tools and agricultural implements as they could fabricate on their own farm, they must buy English-made goods or go without.

And whatever they imported or exported must come to the harbors in English vessels, manned with English sailors and commanded by English captains.

During the last half-century of border warfare between the English and the French it had been comparatively easy to circumvent all such regulations. But now peace had returned and George Grenville was told to find sufficient revenue to pay the interest on the hundreds of millions of pounds which England had borrowed to pay her armies and navies.

Grenville, like most members of his class, was not devoid of a certain rough and ready instinct for practical politics. He preferred a quarrel three thousand miles away to a quarrel right at home and he decided that it would be a good deal easier to increase the taxes of the American colonists (who were simple-minded farmers and lived at the other end of the world) than to incur the displeasure of his own neighbors who would promptly hoot him down in Parliament and who would cut his wife and keep his sons out of all lucrative jobs. The tremendous sacrifices which the mother country had made to protect her dearly beloved children in New England and Virginia against the cruel encroachments on the part of the French and the Indians gave him an excuse for a number of measures that were meant to increase the revenue of the fiscal agents in Charleston and Philadelphia and incidentally help England to retrieve her fallen fortunes.

In the first place the old Navigation Law which had become practically a dead letter since the days of Cromwell was to be strictly enforced and smugglers were to be tried by an admiralty court and no longer by those complacent juries of their fellow smugglers who regarded the crime of which the defendant was accused as an act of supreme patriotism.

In the second place, those vast tracts of western land which had just been taken from the French were closed to immigration until the home government should have been able to make an inventory of its new possessions and should have decided what measures must be taken to protect the interests of their newly acquired Indian subjects.

In the third place, a large number of the necessities of life, such as molasses and sugar (and afterward tea) were to be taxed for the purpose of indirect revenue, and finally all official documents, newspapers, playing cards, deeds, contracts, mortgages, were to be adorned with a pretty stamp which His Majesty's fiscal agents were ready to sell at prices ranging all the way from a penny to a couple of pounds.

Compared to the vast sum which even the humblest of our citizens are nowadays obliged to surrender to the Federal Government in Washington, these odd nickels and dimes exacted from the pocketbooks of the early settlers seem highly insignificant. But it was not the money, it was the principle. The professional orators of the colonies referred to these outrageous measures in flaming sentences, talked about liberty and death and the hideous principle of taxation without representation. They forgot that, had they remained at home, they would have enjoyed just as little "representation" in Parliament as they did after they had moved to Georgia or New Jersey. For in those blessed days less than ten per cent of the English people ever came near a voting-booth. The other ninety per cent were silent partners. They paid the deficit and kept their mouths shut. The leaders of the American opposition knew this perfectly well. What they meant, of course, was that they hated like thunder to pay any taxes at all and that they used the slogan "no representation, no taxation," because it was picturesque and implied that the tax-dodgers were really fighting for a noble and unselfish principle of political righteousness.

For a long time, however, nothing happened.

The home government continued to pass new laws and regulations.

The colonists continued to break those new laws and regulations as soon as they were passed.

And George Grenville sat up nights to "study the question" and then rendered verbal reports that were so profound, so solemn and so dull that George III at last fired him for no other cause than that he was so insufferably long-winded.

## Chapter Twenty

## DUTCH TEA AND FRENCH MOLASSES

THE INHABITANTS of the English colonies in America needed many articles which they could only obtain from abroad.

In order to pay for those articles, they must have money.

In order to get money, they must be able to export certain goods and sell them abroad.

All this sounds very simple and, as a matter of fact, it is very simple. Provided, of course, that you can get the raw material for the manufacture of the articles which you hope to export at such a price that you can sell your final product for a little more than it has cost you. If, on the other hand, you are forced to buy your raw material in one single market and must pay whatever price that market insists upon, then you run a grave risk of being assigned to the bankruptcy court.

The Americans of the eighteenth century, as indeed all other people of the eighteenth century, consumed large quantities of what our fathers used to call "likker." In New England they drank rum; in New York they preferred gin; in Canada they remained faithful to their trusted old cognac; but everywhere they drank. Yea, they drank so much that in certain of the states rum was the most important article of export. But in order to make rum the Puritan distilleries had to have large quantities of sugar and molasses. These necessary ingredients could be imported quite cheaply from the neighboring islands of the West Indies. The majority of those islands, however, belonged either to the French or to the Dutch. According to the current English law, they were therefore "out of bounds" and the New Englanders were obliged to buy their sugar and molasses in the mother country where the merchants made the best of the monopoly which their government had so kindly placed at their disposal.

Question: Did the New Englanders, as obedient subjects of His Majesty, King George, therefore sail across the ocean to buy their sugar at one hundred dollars a ton in London or Bristol?

Answer: They did not. As obedient but none the less intelligent subjects of His Majesty, King George, they sailed to Guadalupe or St. Eustatius and bought their sugar at thirty dollars a ton.

Question: Did the government of His Majesty King George like this?

Answer: It did not.

Question: Did this prevent the New England skippers from continuing the evil practice of rum or sugar running?

Answer: It most certainly did not.

And there, indeed, was a fine subject for a prolonged debate.

It is a curious fact that one can go back as far as the Babylonians and find that people will stand almost any form of abuse as long as the government does not interfere with the things they eat and drink. Sometimes I even doubt whether beer has not provided more bloodshed than theology and that is saying a great deal. When the British government had quarreled with some particular group of dissenters, there had always been certain other dissenters to take the side of the Crown and to gloat over the misfortunes of their enemies. But the moment Parliament put a tax on rum or tea or coffee, it was on dangerous ground, for then it touched something which was as dear to the Quaker spinster as to the Baptist deacon or the most hardened of agnostics. True enough, the tax was very light, only three pennies on the pound, but it was a nuisance, for every time a peaceful citizen made himself a cup of the delectable brew he knew that he was aiding and abetting a law which he felt to be unjust.

In the end, the humble teacups (the proverbial scenes of so many storms) provoked a hurricane that was to rock more than one ocean and all that for an expected annual revenue of only $200,000.

But who could have foreseen such an outcome?

Let us be honest—no one.

At first the American colonists bravely set forth to do without tea. But they had always drunk tea. The poison was in their system. They must have tea.

"Very well," said the skippers from Nantucket and Plymouth, "we can smuggle tea just as easily as sugar," and they sailed forth to Curaçao and returned with nice fat cargoes of tea, very cheap as to price, imported directly from the Dutch East Indies. This made it possible for people to have their usual cup without feeling that they were unfaithful to their principles and within a few months the storehouses along the New England waterfront were filled to bursting with Dutch tea. This meant a serious loss to the English tea-dealers and they became very angry. English merchants with a grievance are a dangerous folk. Parliament decided that something must be done. Accordingly, large quantities of tea, grown by the British East India Company, were dumped upon the American shore and with the help of a government subsidy were offered to the public at a much lower price than the Dutch article.

The honest smugglers (and they belonged to the most influential classes of society) felt that the government by underselling them was guilty of a gross breach of commercial etiquette. Their publicity department got busy. Newspaper articles and broadsides denounced as "traitors" all those who drank British tea.

It has always been easy to stir up the feelings of people

120

who are inclined toward Puritanism. They are so much in the habit of stifling their true emotions that they will welcome almost any occasion for a little "legitimate excitement." Here and there ships carrying English tea were burned by mobs of delighted citizens. In Boston a group of young men (quite nice young men, too) disguised as wild Injuns, boarded three vessels that had just arrived from British India and notwithstanding the fact that there was smallpox on board they bravely dived into the hold and for the benefit of a large and enthusiastic gallery they threw every bale of tea into the harbor. In Massachusetts they became popular heroes. But in England they were denounced as low-down brigands who ought to be delivered to the sheriff and hanged.

But nothing was done. And when it became clear that violence would go unpunished if committed in the name of patriotism, there suddenly were a great many professional patriots.

At regular intervals the

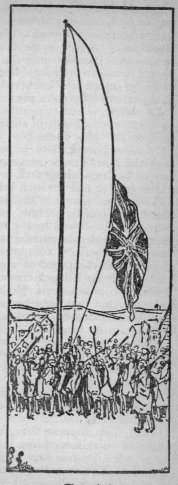

The rebels

121

luckless officers whose duty it was to sell stamps were attacked by bands of rowdies, their houses were looted and their stamps were burned. Those bashful citizens who believed in obedience to the law of the land, whether they approved of it or not, and who actually bought stamps and pasted them on their legal documents ran forever the risk of being tarred and feathered. And it was impossible for the courts to offer them protection.

Of course, it was impossible for the home government to tolerate such a state of affairs. A government that ceases to "govern," that issues laws and then allows the mob to defy those laws, cannot hope to survive. It must either take the most drastic measures to enforce its will or go out of business altogether.

But how to enforce such laws and at such a distance?

There were courts in the American colonies. Of course, there were courts, a whole lot of them. But those courts were like the courts in the mother country. A jury was supposed to decide whether the defendant was guilty or innocent. The jury, composed of the intimate friends of the accused, composed of men who were in hearty sympathy with the alleged crime of the prisoner, invariably declared him innocent. No matter how convincing the evidence that had been gathered by His Majesty's attorney the culprit went scot-free.

What to do next?

Pass an emergency bill which declared that in the future certain cases, to be hereafter enumerated, should be taken to England for trial? That could be done. But it would cause a great deal of resentment. For an ancient and hoary principle of English law stated (in the most positive terms) that no man could be tried outside of his own bailiwick.

Well, then, suppose the government pass another emergency measure suspending the right of a free-born citizen to be tried by his own neighbors. That, too, could be done but it was treading upon highly dangerous ground. It really meant answering one injustice with another; it was a question of fighting the devil with the devil's own fire, a very dangerous precedent and not to be thought of except in case of an actual outbreak of revolution.

Meanwhile some sort of action had to be taken. For the colonists took the question so seriously that they forgot their own little quarrels and sent delegates to a Congress

What price loyalty?

in New York City to protest against the illegal policies of the home government. Evidently matters were rapidly drifting to a crisis and under such circumstances the best thing to do is to clean the slate and begin all over again. Parliament still could have retired with some dignity and while insisting that it always had had and meant to continue to have the right to legislate for England and her colonies, it could make it clear that it intended to do nothing illegal and was willing to listen to reason.

But Parliament was no longer in a mood to listen to reason and began to mutter vague threats about re-establishing order with all the power at its disposal. Now, "power," in the terms of a government, means just two things, policemen and soldiers. And that brings us to the second state of development of the war for independence.

A large number of troops were sent to the seat of disturbance and were told to patrol the cities and villages where the outrages against the tax officials had taken place. Patrolling, however, is dull work. Even the best disciplined of soldiers are apt to lose their temper when turned loose among a hostile population. Besides, they carry guns. They can shoot. When a crowd of naughty little Boston boys begins to pelt them with snowballs, they can get rid of their pent-up anger with a volley that kills perfectly peaceful citizens and throws an entire city into a state of panic.

It is all such an old, old story.

And it bears out what many an historian has begun to suspect, that the past never teaches anyone anything, that every generation has to learn its own lesson anew by making its own mistakes.

"Pessimism," you will say.

My friends, I am sorry, but I did not make this world.


*Chapter Twenty-One*

## THE HOMESPUN WISDOM OF THE FRONTIER

AND NOW WE SHALL HEAR a good deal of musketry and we shall see small groups of deadly tired farmers wading through the sleet of impassable country roads and we shall see armies of grumbling redcoats shuffling through the dust of dangerous country lanes and endlessly we shall hear the question, whose fault was it? Why this fury of Englishmen against Englishmen? Why this spilling of the blood of one's nearest and dearest relatives?

And again I must answer that we don't know. There are certain events in the history of mankind that seem inevitable and the American Revolution was one of those.

If it had not come in the year 1776 it would have come in the year 1777. If some political genius had been able to avert the outbreak of hostilities in 1777 it would have taken place in 1778.

For this was not merely a conflict of interests.

It was a clash of ideals.

And in such a case there is only one answer—war!

It is always a little embarrassing to sit in the seat of mighty Zeus and dispense justice upon the ancestors with the grandiloquent remark, "So and so was to blame, and all others go out scot-free."

Be it therefore said in a spirit of great humility that in my opinion the British government committed one grave error of judgment. The King and his Parliament and his ministers continued to think of the colonists as Englishmen. In a legal and political sense they undoubtedly still were Englishmen, but they were Englishmen with a memory. They had a clear vision of the almshouse in which they were born, of the pauper's grave into which the body of their mother had been dumped. They never forgot the pangs of hunger, the beatings which they had received while their father was in a debtor's prison. They remembered these things and they remembered them with the dull resentment of those who have suffered a misery that was not of their own making. And then the escape—the voyage in a foul immigrant ship—the putrid food—the corpses that were thrown overboard—and finally the arrival on the shores of the New World to become the bondsman of some penurious Pennsylvania farmer, the drudge of some terrible Puritan housewife, and work —work—work for five or six or seven or eight years that they might gain their freedom, two suits of clothes and a barrel of flour.

And then, the painful journey into the wilderness—the dirt of the lonely log cabins—the aching back from those interminable rows of trees that had to be felled—the aching arms from those endless boulders that had to be put into neat rows before a little corn could be planted—the wife who had died from lack of medical attendance—the neglected children that somehow had to be fed and

washed—the insects that destroyed the crops—the rats
that killed the chickens and the mosquitoes that made
life into a worse hell than ever devised by the insatiable
Jonathan Edwards.

And then—at last—a little prosperity—a new wife—a
third one or a fourth—children big enough to handle a
plow and tend a pig—a house with more than one room
—a short stretch of road that was passable—a few neighbors who could be depended upon in case of sickness or
childbirth—the joy of being the sovereign lord of a small
clearing in the woods and not being obliged to say "Yes,
sir!" to any man alive.

And then—one fine morning a letter—a large envelope
bearing an official seal—a hard-to-decipher document
which stated that the King's Divine Majesty, duly supported by a decree of Parliament of such and such a date,
*doth hereby command and instruct His Majesty's most
loyal subject . . . or otherwise to suffer . . .*

All of it perfectly right and just and legal, but remi-
niscent of the one thing the colonist had hoped to forget—
the past.

Men who live by the grace of their own prudence and
the labor of their own hands are apt enough to be impa-
tient of all authority. People to whom the word "authority" has always been synonymous with "oppression" have
only one mode of redress that will satisfy their pent-up
feelings, and that is open defiance.

In the cities near the seaboard it was easy enough to
keep the populace under control. The merchant who held
the notes of ninety per cent of his neighbors could bring
a pressure to bear that was unanswerable. The minister
of the Gospel who discoursed upon the inviolability of
public officers and the sacredness of private property was
able to take care of the other ten per cent.

But in those endless tracts of land between the Ohio
and the Mississippi bills of exchange were apt to be lost
and clergymen who preached an unpopular doctrine could
be asked to return to "civilization." For there the individual farmer was merchant and preacher and soldier
and king and he ruled his realm as pleased him and all

others take warning.

Those Englishmen who did not understand that spirit (about ninety-seven per cent of the total population) could always get a hand when they rose in Parliament and held forth about the poverty-stricken yokels of some obscure Tennessee county who meant to inform His Majesty King George III that the people of Watauga no longer meant to recognize his supreme authority.

But it was not quite so simple to get hold of those obstinate rebels and hang them as an example to the others. Indeed, it soon became clear that such a course was impossible and the rebels who knew this made the best of their opportunity.

.    .    .    .    .    .    .

The men who handled a spade all day or wielded an ax from sunup to sundown were as a rule too tired to commit their thoughts to paper. They read few books and wrote none.

But they sometimes spoke their minds and we know fairly well what was in their minds.

They were not particularly interested in the theory of government. They knew what suited them, what was fit for those small communities which they had built along the outskirts of the empire.

They lived in too close a companionship with guns and pistols to be fond of fighting.

But the wilderness had given them their chance—the only chance that would ever come to them in all their life. And that chance they refused to surrender.

They did not regard themselves in the light of a chosen people as the Puritans had done a hundred years before.

They had few ideals about themselves.

They fully recognized their many failings, their habit of blasphemy, their drunken sprees after years of soul-destroying drudgery, their sentimental tears, their occasional outbreaks of cruelty, their ungovernable tempers, their disrespect for all forms of written law.

But they did not insist that the world love them and point to them as exemplary citizens. All they asked was to be let alone.

And when the outside world would not or could not do this, they said, "Well—" put some powder upon the pan of their guns, and waited.

Their endless struggle with nature had taught them patience.

And in questions like these it was so much better to let the other fellow make the first mistake.

*Chapter Twenty-Two*

# LAWYER ADAMS OF QUINCY, MASS., AND HIS COUSIN SAM TURN TO PRACTICAL POLITICS

IF THE ENGLISH GOVERNMENT of the year of Grace 1775 had been a little more familiar with conditions in the American colonies they would have been able to save themselves a lot of trouble. They would have made use of the bad feeling that existed between the money-lending towns and the money-borrowing rural districts, they would have played one party out against the other and by gaining the good will of either the merchant class or the farmers, they would have assured themselves of a very useful body of allies.

Fortunately for the cause of free America the British officials blundered magnificently and by a series of colossal errors forced the seaboard and the mountains to make common cause and to forget (temporarily at least) those economic differences which made a Yankee banker almost as unpopular in an agricultural community as one of His Majesty's duly appointed and ordained "gougers" and "stamp collectors."

Now, revolutions (I believe that I have said this before in another book) are usually made up according to the following pattern:

Ten per cent of the people are willing to hang for their

128

principles.

Ten per cent are willing to hang but are not particularly happy at the prospect and therefore wish to know if. the purpose for which they are fighting cannot be achieved in some less violent fashion.

Forty per cent (who call themselves "practical" men) sit on the fence until they know which side is going to win, when they join the army of the victors.

That makes a total of sixty per cent. The other forty per cent believe in "law and order" at all costs and either execute their former neighbors if those happen to be unsuccessful or themselves get hanged if it is proved that they have guessed wrong.

It may be claimed that I am a little too bloodthirsty in these pages. I am sorry but anyone who has read through the literature of that period (as printed on both sides of the ocean) will know that the gallows were ever present in the minds of those who joined the rebellion and those who remained loyal to the British crown.

This may come as a shock to those who shy at the word revolution, who prattle sweet nonsense about a wicked German sovereign on an unblemished British throne, who shudder when they are told that in the eyes of the average Englishman of the year 1778 George Washington was a veritable Lenin (only much worse because he had so much less cause for discontent). For their special consolation, however, I can truthfully add that this was a most genteel and respectable revolution, as revolutions go. No Bastilles were stormed. No Winter Palaces were plundered. There were no wholesale executions of civil prisoners. No secret tribunals made it their business to establish a reign of terror.

On the contrary, the very best people took part in the uprising and whenever the fortunes of war forced one general to surrender to another, the event was made the occasion for an exchange of the most urbane civilities, and a mutual expression of good will that would have brought tears to the eyes of Hindenburg and Foch.

This may have been due to the fact that in the eighteenth century war was a gentleman's profession and was conducted according to a definite set of rules. One could never foretell who would win the next battle. Wherefore it behooved the victor to step carefully and treat his opponent as he himself hoped to be treated should he happen to come out second-best.

And furthermore, there was very little of that feeling of personal animosity which had made so many European wars a struggle for extermination. Several of the British governors and their subordinates had been exceedingly annoying administrators, slow-witted, pettifogging dignitaries who regarded all colonials as an inferior species of the human race and who had treated their American subjects either with a display of that haw-hawing geniality which will arouse even the meekest of us to murder or had forced them to stand for hours in cold and dark anterooms until their Excellencies had finished their third bottle of port.

But that type of persons, although they may be guilty of great cruelty during a moment of panic, are rarely very cruel. Such atrocities as thus far had been committed on the American continent had been caused by the religious hysteria of the settlers themselves and there was no blame attached to the British officials.

It was, therefore, not so much a question of what England had actually done in the past that made the Americans rise in wrath against the mother country as fear of what England might do in the future unless the rights and prerogatives of the colonists were duly protected against further royal and ministerial encroachments.

All this the leaders of the rebellion knew. They were, therefore, willing to give occasional free rein to the mob (one cannot hope to make an omelet without breaking a few eggs!) but the rabble (and the merchants and plantation owners who were the leaders of the rebellion were aristocrats and had very little use for anybody outside of their own class), the small fry, the common multitude, must be kept well within bounds that all things might be done in order and with decency and according to the ancient and honorable laws of a community of free and independent yeomen.

. . . . . . .

This chapter bears the name of one John Adams and his cousin Samuel, but please do not get the impression that these two men alone were responsible for the agitation that led to a declaration of independence. Both John and Sam, although in many ways miles apart, were so typical of the sort of patriots who stepped forward to assume command that they will serve our purpose as well as any other couple of whom I can think at this moment.

The Adamses were of old English stock and had moved from Devonshire to Massachusetts during the late thirties of the seventeenth century. They had become farmers and had worked hard to get ahead. As soon as Harvard College had been founded they had sent their children there to learn all there was to be learned and join one of the professions. John (Harvard 1755) had studied to be a lawyer. He was not exactly a cheerful neighbor. "A man of convictions," we would call him, but withal a person of tremendous usefulness during a period of unrest, a rock-ribbed, humorless and aloof personage, as indifferent to royal displeasure or popular approval as a chunk of Vermont marble.

Quite different was his cousin Samuel, who had graduated fifteen years earlier, who knew every Tom, Dick, and Harry in the town, who would cheerfully lock the door of his brewery as soon as he heard that there was a chance of a little excitement, a clever ward leader who was just as much at home at the tea party in Boston harbor as at a formal convention of Massachusetts townships.

As for the opposition which these two men joined, it was still a very harmless affair. The people of the colonies, although they did a lot of reading, were Englishmen and they intended to remain Englishmen. They believed in the power of human reason. Let their fellow countrymen across the ocean only know what was happening in America and all would be well.

Meanwhile in order to enlighten their British cousins and nephews they intended to write pamphlets, draw up

131

resolutions, call together a "Continental Congress" of representatives from all the different colonies (duly convened in Philadelphia on the fifth of September of the year 1774), institute Vigilance Committees (so-called Committees of Correspondence which were to keep all good patriots informed of every new act of official tyranny) and build up a perfectly sound and legal case which in the course of time would not fail to convince the most obstinate of British Tories of the justice of the American claim.

It was the month of April of the year 1775.

The stage had been set for the second act and the curtain was ready to rise.

*Chapter Twenty-Three*

## THE COMMANDER OF HIS MAJESTY'S COLONIAL FORCES IS OBLIGED TO REPORT SOME VERY BAD NEWS

ABOUT FORTY YEARS AGO a certain Captain Charles Boycott got into trouble with the peasants of the estate he was managing in County Mayo, Ireland. In consequence whereof he was declared "out of bounds." No one would speak to him. No one would buy anything from him. No one would sell him anything. No one would feed him, deliver his mail, milk his cows. In short, as far as his Irish neighbors were concerned, he ceased to exist.

This particular method of bringing pressure to bear upon one particular person or group of persons has since been known as "boycotting" and wherever it is applied there is bound to be a great deal of trouble.

In the first place it is exceedingly humiliating to the people concerned. After a short while it is apt to get on their nerves. And in the second place it drives the victims to exasperation because they have no plausible way of redress.

ample, the Chinese of Canton refuse to eat
eans or to wear English cotton, in short, if
to boycott American and English products,
thing in all the world the English and Amer-
nts can do about it. They are helpless, for no
n be Chinese or Eskimo, can be made to eat
o wear cotton if he prefers to do without. And
hey are helpless and know it, the sufferers are
se their temper, to do foolish things, to clamor
hips and write letters to the newspapers urging
immediate war.

The leaders of the group of malcontents in America
knew this. That the Continental Congress in Philadelphia had adopted a so-called Declaration of Rights in
which the different grievances of the colonies were re-
spectfully enumerated was a first step in the right direction. But official documents are rarely read by the masses
of the people. At the best they cause a slight disturbance
among a few officials who say, "Pooh-pooh! This is sedition. We must do something about it!" At the worst they
are simply forgotten.

But this same Congress, ere it dispersed, had adopted
a resolution which promised to be more far-reaching. Not
a single true friend of liberty, the delegates declared,
would henceforth try to import or export British-made
goods or would consume such articles if they were offered
to him for sale.

This measure, I am sorry to say, caused a great deal of
suffering in the colonies. There still were a good many
merchants who intended to remain loyal to the mother
country and who thought it their good right to deal how
and where and with whom it best pleased them. These
were now delivered to the mercies of lynch law. Their
stores were broken into. Their goods were destroyed.
Quite frequently they themselves were tarred and feathered and driven away from the place of their birth by
mixed mobs of patriots and hoodlums.

But in England, too, the blow was felt. And loud were
the howls of the British traders and manufacturers that
something must be done right away and at once to bring

these renegade colonies to reason.

When the English newspapers reached A... showed the wide extent of the anti-colonial fee... the people of the mother country, the leader... position in Boston and Philadelphia and Norfo... to understand the seriousness of the situation. At... any moment they might now expect that the home g... ernment would begin a policy of retaliation, would send troops to Massachusetts and would declare a blockade of the entire American coast. Under those circumstances it was well to be prepared. Here and there active Committees of Correspondence (the unofficial bodies which had taken charge of the conduct of the revolution) began to buy kegs of gunpowder, to make a census of the number of available flintlocks, to look for suitable cellars where arms might be hidden from the gaze of those English officers who were said to be traveling around in disguise and whose supposed presence was a continual source of irritation.

This accusation, although based entirely upon hearsay, was true enough. The intelligence department of Lieutenant General Thomas Gage, who commanded Boston, was on the job and His Excellency not only knew that the colonists had hidden a considerable store of arms in the village of Concord but also that Samuel Adams and John Hancock, the two most adroit leaders of the opposition, were at that moment conducting a campaign of agitation in Middlesex County. It was decided to despatch a number of troops to destroy the hostile ammunition and incidentally capture the proscribed patriots and send them to London to be tried before an English Court.

But during such periods of great popular excitement there are wheels within wheels and spies that spy upon spies and still other spies that spy upon the spies that spy upon the spies and it was quite impossible to maintain a secret.

More than twelve hours before the expedition of Colonel Smith started northward, William Dawes and Paul Revere and Samuel Prescott, three young Americans sent out by the Committee of Safety in Boston to warn the people of Middlesex, were racing toward Lexington that Hancock and Adams might be given a chance to escape.

Therefore when early the next morning a detachment of the Tenth Infantry marched across the Common of Lexington, they found themselves faced by a group of determined and excited farmers.

Who then fired the first shot will always remain a secret.

But a shot was fired.

Next a volley crashed across the peaceful green, and eight Americans lay dead.

It was as if the whole countryside had awaited the sound of those fatal muskets.

The English succeeded in reaching Concord, but on the way back to Boston they were exposed to a constant fusillade and it did

The signal

not cease until Gage had sent Lord Percy with a couple of field pieces to protect the rear guard of his defeated army and bring the stragglers and the wounded home.

If the colonists had possessed more deadly weapons than the uncertain fowling-pieces of their grandfathers, hardly an English soldier would have returned alive. As it was, the British lost 273 dead, wounded and missing, or one third of their total force, before they finally reached the Charlestown ferry and withdrew behind the fortifications of Boston.

The news of the fight spread like wildfire. Far and wide the messengers of the Committee of Correspondence galloped to bring the good tidings to those who might still

---

vords. t three dred and rseman. He ilies went in k in Westmore- Vernon, an estate Edward Vernon, the belonged to his half- in the year 1752. They two brothers. When Law- he whole family had weak had taken him to the West ed just the same and George had You could still see it in his face. the reason why he smiled so rarely.

hesitate in their devotion to the cause of the colonies. And from all over the west, from the furthermost corners of the south, lean and hungry pioneers were marching in the general direction of Massachusetts that they might be present at the next encounter and avenge the martyrs of Concord.

Suddenly Gage found himself cut off from the rest of the world. An attempt to dislocate the insurgents from the height of Bunker Hill cost him more than 1500 of his men. Efforts to reach a settlement by an amicable parley failed.

But that was not the worst.

On the tenth of May of the year 1775 ~~~~ ond Continental Congress came together at Phil~~~~

This time delegates from all of the ~~~~ ~~nies were present. That meant that for the ~~~~ ~~r history the grievances of all the America~~~~ chance to be aired in one and the same roo~~~~ gravity of the situation made these jealous little independent nations forget their mutual suspicions and rivalries.

The die had been cast.

The colonists, much to their own surprise, had suddenly been caught in an act of open rebellion. They might not be particularly fond of their Presbyterian or ~~~~ or Dutch Reformed neighbors, but as the wit of ~~~~ bellion remarked, it was a question of "hanging to~~~~ or being hanged separately and the prospect ~~~~ lows is apt to make strange companions-at-ar~~~~

And so for once there was an eager will~~~~ operate, and the bankers and the pawn~~~~ moneylenders from the seaboard, who ~~~~ known and disliked as "the aristocr~~~~ work together with the unshaven ~~~~ grubby frontier, who were usual~~~~ democrats" and who w~~~~ held ~~~~ polished citizens of t~~~~ bellion had started ~~~~ land, it could not p~~~~ hearty support of th~~~~ banks of the Potom~~~~

Otherwise not a man who could not see a joke, and not a heavy churchgoer, either. For the rest, as long as you did what you were supposed to do you could be sure that he appreciated your efforts and would take your side if you got into trouble with some busybody selectman whose chickenyard had been plundered by a couple of hungry soldiers. But God help you when you fell asleep at your post, when you discovered that you had urgent business in the rear as soon as a British man-of-war had got your range. He would bawl you out right then and there and once going he could curse like the marines. But that was all right. Sure it was all right. This was war. It wasn't a pink tea. Anybody ever hear of a war that was fought without swearing? And he would see to it that you got well fed if he had to pay for your grub out of his own pocket. Yes, that was right, too. He would not take a cent for his services. Said that he was rich enough and meant to make no money out of something he merely considered his duty. He had not wanted the job much anyway. He had a nice place down there in Virginia and all the land and the slaves he needed. The people in Georgetown said they knew for a fact that he was a millionaire. Well, perhaps not quite that. But rich he certainly was. And he had married another hundred thousand dollars. A widow lady, a mighty handsome woman, Martha Dandridge by name. And there were two kids. Or rather they were hers. But the colonel had adopted them and was now educating them as if they were his own. All in all, a fine gentleman. Not the sort you'd slap on the back. No, not exactly. But if he decided to go somewhere, you somehow or other decided that you would go there too. Leadership they called it. Well, he had it. And he had needed it in the olden days. He had been all through the Indian wars. He had been captured by the French. He had saved whatever could be saved of Braddock's old battalions. But a few years later he had got even. For it was he who had taken Fort Duquesne from old Louis and had called it Fort Pitt. And so they had made him commander of all Virginian troops and that while he was only twenty-three years old. No, he was not a Presbyterian. He went to the

Episcopal church. But he was no fanatic. Live and let live was his motto. And so as long as you did your duty, he would not bother you, and if you had something of importance to say, you could say it provided you did not use any more words than you could help, for he was busy and he was not very fond of speech-making.

So much for the man.

What about the "situation"?

It was so terrible that it was almost funny.

In the first place, there weren't any cannon.

The retreat from Lexington had shown that no militiamen, however brave, could stand up against gunfire. And as long as Gage had his field pieces, Gage was going to be master of Boston.

At this critical moment the rebels met with a stroke of great good luck.

There were two forts in Northern New York. They were called Ticonderoga and Crown Point. In the olden days they had prevented the French and their Indian allies from breaking into the English possessions by way of Canada. Now that Canada was no longer a French colony they were quite useless from a strategic point of view and were used as arsenals. A couple of old veterans were all the garrison they had.

On the tenth of May a Vermonter by the name of Ethan Allen and a troop of his Green Mountain boys had taken these forts and one Benedict Arnold, turning an old schooner into an emergency warship, had sailed down Lake Champlain and had captured Fort St. John. Suddenly the rebels found themselves the proud possessors of forty cannon. And in the fall, when thick layers of snow covered the Berkshire Mountains, an ingenious Boston bookseller managed to haul all this valuable plunder from the heart of New York state to Dorchester Heights in Massachusetts. They were loaded with the shot taken from the British supply ship, the *Nancy,* and then at last the great Atlantic seaport was at the mercy of the Americans.

On March the seventeenth of the year 1776 the British and those Americans who wished to remain loyal to King

George sailed away for Halifax in Nova Scotia.

It was a very different army that marched into the conquered city from the unruly and ill-disciplined mob that General Artemus Ward had presented to the commander-in-chief almost a year before on the green of the Cambridge common. And it was a very different crowd that watched these well-drilled regiments cook their soup on the green meadows of the old common.

As long as the red-coated soldiers of His Majesty had patrolled their streets, these good people had been obliged to call themselves Englishmen.

Now they were free to make their choice.

For the moment the American forces seemed to be victorious, but before they made a decision they wanted to know something else.

"What was happening in Philadelphia?"

## Chapter Twenty-Five

## MR. THOMAS JEFFERSON OF ALBEMARLE COUNTY, VIRGINIA, SHOWS THE SUPERIOR ADVANTAGES OF A CLASSICAL EDUCATION

UNTIL SOME FIFTY OR SIXTY YEARS AGO it was the custom to look back upon the Middle Ages as a highly colorful period of pageants and princesses-in-distress and saints and torture racks, a sort of glorified melodrama that had lasted almost ten centuries.

The modern historian has done some very useful blasting among the picturesque but dangerous ruins of a none too charming past. We now know that the men and women of the eighth and the twelfth and the fourteenth centuries were really very much like ourselves, that the differences which strike us as so very important were merely artificial differences, and that underneath their mailed shirts and their velvet coats our ancestors were animated by the same ambition that keeps us going—the all-overpowering desire to survive.

And one of the fields in which we were obliged to modify our opinions was that of architecture.

Our grandfathers looked at a medieval town and said, "Those huge walls and towers are very interesting. They were of course constructed to protect the inhabitants of the cities from attack on the part of their enemies, the robber barons and the kings."

Today we know that that was only part of the truth. The medieval system of defense had a twofold purpose; it was expected to keep the enemy outside and the citizens inside.

For those noble fights and sieges of which we read with so much pleasure in the novels of Sir Walter Scott were rather dismal affairs from the point of view of the average man.

The people of the Middle Ages were not familiar with the idea of nationalism. They were loyal to their own home but rarely thought in terms of nations or states. They accepted emperors and kings just as we accept many institutions which we do not exactly like but which happen to exist and which are so well entrenched that we feel powerless before them.

When the King of France went to war with the King of Spain, it was of course to be expected that the troops of the King of France would besiege the fortified towns of the King of Spain and that the troops of the King of Spain would besiege the fortified towns of the King of France and that the garrisons of the towns which belonged to the King of France would do their best to keep the fortress entrusted to their care safe for their master in Paris and that the garrisons of the towns which belonged to the King of Spain would fight like demons to protect their redoubts and bastions from the sullying touch of the Valois mercenaries.

Meanwhile the poor distracted burghers were expected to suffer and starve in silence until the fight was decided, when they were plundered by the victorious enemy or were asked to bestow such a large share of their worldly goods upon the brave fellows who were supposed to have protected them that they were ruined in either case.

I need not tell you that they did not like this. And as soon as they had eaten a sufficient number of rats and mice to have shown a decent sense of loyalty, they were apt to open the gates of their town and say to both contending parties, "Do whatever you please, but for Heaven's sake make an end to this foolish hacking and shooting and let us go back to business."

It was of course the duty of the garrison to prevent such treason. Hence, as I said before, the fortifications of the Middle Ages served a twofold purpose and they were built in such a way that the garrison could turn its bullets and arrows upon friend and enemy alike.

The men who took charge of the American Revolution resembled a medieval garrison. For not only must they keep the Britishers out but at the same time they must prevent the loyalists from making common cause with the English.

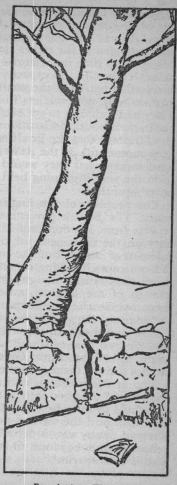

Revolution. The victim

143

Now that it is all over we are apt to forget that the number of people who remained loyal to the King was very large. Almost without exception these troublesome citizens belonged to the richer classes and that was their undoing. Since time immemorial they had been professional moneylenders. In this capacity they had incurred the deep and lasting hatred of the small farmers. These same small farmers were now soldiers in the army of independence. They had a chance to get even. And they were so vociferous in their public declarations about the fate that awaited any "traitor" that the loyalists, willy nilly, were forced to keep m.... ...mericans had lost the war, it is hard to say wha.... ...But the rebels from the very beginning held .... ...yalists never squeaked.

The problem of the English was not settled quite so easily. The British government, according to the latest reports from London, was hiring every available mercenary on the Continent for the purpose of bringing the colonists to terms. But the prospect of such an invasion did not cause Washington and his advisers to spend too many candles in midnight deliberations. They had seen enough of the English professional officers not to fear them overmuch. Furthermore they were familiar with the country, they knew the sort of tactics that were best suited for fighting in the wilderness, and they were close to their own base of supplies. No, the prospect of a campaign against the clumsy German peasants of His Majesty did not disturb them overmuch.

The problem that caused them profound anxiety was this: would the good feeling that now seemed to animate the whole country hold out to the end? Could they keep their men and the civilian population together until the common enemy should have been defeated?

Sooner or later it was to be decided, not only whether Englishmen or Americans should rule over these fertile regions along the Atlantic seaboard, but also which of two contending factions should be the dominant party in the new American nation, the aristocrats, the merchants and moneylenders of the cities, or the democrats, the farmers and small storekeepers of the frontier?

Now that the enemy stood before the gate, co-operation was the first essential of success. And in order to bring about such co-operation, it was necessary to devise a platform upon which the two parties could unite, if only for a short time, if only for a couple of months or years.

Washington was too busy drilling his recruits to occupy himself with that task. John Adams was lacking in that personal magnetism, in that power of intimate persuasion without which nothing could be accomplished in a gathering of such diversified elements as had now met for the second time in William Penn's ancient capital. Once more a Virginian came to the rescue.

Thomas Jefferson, like Washington, was a southerner. He also belonged to the best families of the land, for his father had married a Randolph. But there the comparison between the two men ceased. For Washington was by birth and environment an aristocrat—a member of that small group of plantation owners which at an early date had taken possession of the fertile soil of the lowlands. Whereas Jefferson was a true child of the frontier, had spent his early youth among the farmers of the distant Blue Ridge Mountains and had seen very little of the more artificial civilization of the East until he went to the college which Dutch William and his English wife had founded in Williamsburg in the year 1693.

Early in the sixteenth century it was said of Erasmus, the great humanist, that he liked the Popish way of living but the Lutheran way of thinking. With an equal degree of truthfulness it can be stated of Jefferson that he liked the aristocratic way of thinking and the democratic way of living.

Washington, while fighting the armies of the King of England, was quite willing to be called His Excellency and allowed himself to be surrounded with a pomp that in the eyes of his many enemies smacked suspiciously of that royal etiquette which was supposed to fill the hearts of all good patriots with unfeigned disgust.

Far different, Jefferson. Since early childhood he had been plain Tom to all his neighbors of Albemarle County.

He thoroughly despised those graces of life which the hardy men of the frontier regarded as unnecessary affectation on the part of a race of weaklings. But when it came to that independence of mind which is most often found among those who have never been obliged to worry about their daily bread and butter, then Jefferson was an aristocrat of the aristocrats.

There seems to be a common belief that revolutions are made by the down-trodden and poverty-stricken multitudes of the slums. Alas! Those poor, dumb masses of underfed humanity play only a secondary role. When they are needed, they are called upon to serve as cannon fodder. The actual work of tearing down and building up is done by men with a different sort of background. And foremost among the ranks of those who have risked their lives and their personal comfort for the sake of an ideal stands the type of radical aristocrat of whom Jefferson was so true and noble a representative.

Like Washington, Jefferson also suffered bitterly at the hands of those who failed to understand him. Like Washington, he was envied, slandered, maligned, and vilified with a bitterness that seems incredible to these later generations. And like Washington (and all truly great men) he accepted the ingratitude of those whom he had benefited as part of the day's work. He fully understood and appreciated the true nature of the service which he had rendered to his country. And he knew (as we ourselves know today) that it was his shrewd brain which had bestowed upon the thirteen quarreling little colonies that common declaration of faith which in the eyes of the rest of the world lifted the Americans out of the class of mere "rebels" and put them foremost into the ranks of those who since time immemorial had fought for the right of man to decide his own political allegiance.

The members of the first Continental Congress had still talked a great deal about "loyalty." The few radicals who had foreseen that a breach with the mother country was inevitable had not been able to convince their more conservative neighbors. Since then a great deal of water had flowed through the Schuylkill. The English had been defeated in the first encounter with the patriots. But the breach between "city" and "country" was wider than ever before and in several of the provinces there was the prospect of a civic rebellion or even worse, an outbreak of anarchy.

Under those circumstances it was felt that only a very drastic measure such as the overthrow of the old form of government and the proclamation of an independent republic could really bring all the contending factions together. Such a bold step would make the breach with the mother country definite and irreparable and it would give new courage to the halfhearted and the lukewarm by offering them their choice between a noble death on the field of battle or an ignominious demise on the gallows of His Majesty.

On the seventh of June of the year 1776 Richard Henry Lee (born in the same Virginia county as Washington), after prolonged consultations with the political leaders in his own colony, offered the following resolution:

*in the first place, that "these United Colonies are, and of right ought to be, free and independent states, that they are absolved from all allegiance to the British Crown, and that all political connection between them and the state of Great Britain is, and ought to be, totally dissolved":*

*in the second place, that "it is expedient to take the most effectual measures for forming political alliances":*

*and in the third place, that "a plan of confederation be prepared and transmitted to the respective colonies for their consideration and approbation."*

John Adams of Massachusetts seconded the motion, and a committee was appointed to draft a formal document which should explain to the people at home and to the world at large exactly in what manner and by what exasperating means the King of England had forced his erstwhile loyal subjects to take such a drastic step and sever all connections with the mother country.

This famous committee consisted of Benjamin Franklin, Roger Sherman, Robert R. Livingston, John Adams, and Thomas Jefferson.

Sherman and Livingston had been elected to gain the good will of New York (a colony rightly suspected of strong loyalist tendencies) and they did not take a very important part in the preliminary discussions. Franklin and Adams made a few suggestions which slightly modified the inner structure of half a dozen sentences. The Declaration of Independence, therefore, as it stands to this day, was the work of Thomas Jefferson and embodied not only his political convictions but his general philosophy of life as well.

Independence

Jefferson, in contrast with Washington, had read widely. Few authors had made such a deep impression upon him as John Locke, the contemporary of Spinoza and one of the earliest champions in England of the new and startling principle that man was entitled to his own convictions. Where Locke first got this notion we do not know. But during the latter half of the seventeenth century he had been an exile in Holland, just a century after the people of that country had declared their independence from Spain in a document which had stated that "all sovereigns have been appointed by God that they may rule their subjects as shepherds who watch over their flocks," and furthermore, that "the subjects have not been created for the benefit of the king, but the king has been created for the benefit of the subjects."

Jefferson, in his Declaration of Independence, followed the method used by his Dutch predecessors. First of all he explained his general ideas concerning the theory of life and of government. Next he enumerated the grievous injuries which His Majesty King George III (*vice* Philip II) had inflicted upon his longsuffering subjects, the people of the United States of America (*vice* the people of the United Netherlands). Then he summed up with the verdict that the aforementioned subjects had been left with no other mode of redress than to declare themselves independent.

The Declaration was duly read and discussed in the Continental Congress, a few slight changes were proposed and all this took so much time that the committee did not get ready with the final draft of the document until the evening of the fourth of July. On the fifth of July a few copies were printed and were sent to the commanding officers of the revolutionary forces. Finally on the eighth the Declaration was in such shape that it could be read to the people of Philadelphia who for that purpose had come together in City Hall Square.

On the nineteenth of July (due to slow work on the part of the New York delegation) it was decided to have the Declaration written down on a large sheet of parchment.

On the second of August, the official scribe got through with his task and then at last the work of affixing the signatures could begin. Of those whose names appeared at the end of this extraordinary document, eight had been born outside of the colonies and eighteen were of foreign origin. The other half could claim descent from English ancestors.

So did our nation on the day of its birth truly represent that ideal of a common brotherhood of man which the hardships of life in the wilderness had forced upon the disinherited masses of the older world.

## Chapter Twenty-Six

## KING GEORGE III BECOMES A POPULAR HERO IN HIS OWN COUNTRY

MEANWHILE what did the people in the mother country say of these scandalous proceedings?

At first they said nothing. They were busy trying to recover from a long period of war. They had little time and less inclination to listen to the supposed grievances of a "few colonists."

But gradually it began to dawn upon them that this was something more serious than a quarrel among people who lived in trees.

And as soon as they understood the underlying principles of the conflict, they grew angry.

After all, who had benefited most from the defeat of the French in Canada?

The Americans.

And who had been obliged to pay for the upkeep of those armies that had won the victory?

The English.

Was that fair?

Most certainly not, as far as the honest Britishers could see. And they made it quite clear that in their opinion the New Englanders and Virginians ought to offer to contribute at least a few pennies and pounds toward the millions which the war had cost.

They were familiar with the colonial slogan, "No taxation without representation," but they themselves were rarely represented in Parliament and they paid taxes just the same. What was good enough for the people in London must be good enough for the people in Boston.

But there was something else.

Whether they were represented in that body or not, they felt that Parliament was the bulwark of all British liberties and ought to be regarded as the fountainhead of all authorities in the British Empire.

Their fathers and grandfathers had fought a long and bloody war to establish the superiority of Parliament over the Crown. And here came a certain Mr. Jefferson, an obscure farmer from somewhere in Virginia, and boldly claimed that the jurisdiction of Parliament was restricted to the British Isles, that, on a somewhat larger scale, Parliament was nothing more important than his own foolish House of Burgesses, and that the colonies would govern themselves after their own sweet pleasure or know the reason why.

This was nothing short of high treason. Once such opinions were tolerated, what was to become of those hallowed ideals for which Cromwell and his Ironsides had fought at Naseby and Marston Moor?

Therefore the sooner the colonists learned that they, together with all Englishmen, were subject to the will of Parliament, the better.

Now His Majesty King George III was a very dull man, but he was not a fool, and he shared the political ability of his famous cousin, King Frederick of Prussia. His wishes in regard to his American possessions coincided entirely with the prejudices of his subjects. Here was his chance to make the Crown the champion of the rights of Parliament and at the same time gain the good will and the support of the National Assembly in his private quarrel with the obnoxious Whigs. It was such an opportunity as comes only once in the lives of most sovereigns and George made the best of it. During the next seven years the most touching harmony existed between the King and his subjects and in all matters pertaining in the American rebellion, the people and their sovereign thought and felt as one.

It is true that a few of the ministers, notably William Pitt, had questioned the practical aspects of some of the laws that had been forced upon the colonists. Furthermore one member of Parliament, by the name of Edmund Burke, had delivered himself of some flowery bits of oratory upon the problematic rights of the American radicals.

But Pitt, when it came down to a question of principles, agreed heartily with all those who held that Parliament by right was and ought to be the court of last appeal in all matters pertaining to the government of the Empire. And as for Burke, he was born in Dublin, and so of course he was "agin the governmint.".

Small wonder, under these circumstances, that the English people were not particularly squeamish in the methods they employed to bring the rebels to terms. Life, or rather existence, in the British army at that time was so harsh that very few Englishmen were found willing to enlist. Convicted yeggmen and highway robbers, when placed before the choice of jail or service in His Majesty's army, chose the latter. But their number was relatively small and it was necessary to send abroad for the necessary number of recruits.

At first Catherine of Russia was approached and was asked for the loan (for a decent remuneration, of course) of twenty thousand Cossacks. Her Majesty, after some preliminary correspondence, declined this request and several years afterward, as we ought to remember with gratitude, she went so far as to grant the new republic a small but very welcome loan of golden rubles.

There remained the small potentates of northern Germany. These worthies, notably the reigning granddukes of Hesse-Cassel, of Brunswick, and of Anhalt-Zerbst, were then engaged upon the hopeless task of changing their rustic residences into so many imitations of the Court of Versailles and were in dreadful need of ready money. They were delighted to avail themselves of this unexpected opportunity to refill their empty treasure chests and during the next seven years they sold not less than thirty thousand of their subjects into the slavery of foreign service. As their Serene Highnesses were paid an extra sum for every man killed or wounded, they had every reason to wish for a long and bloody conflict.

So much for the white allies of England.

As for their Indian friends, they did not prove of great value. Already the French had discovered that these poor savages were of very little use in actual battle. As long as everything went well, they murdered and plundered like lions, but as soon as there was the slightest sign of a panic, they disappeared and were swallowed up by the woods. The English made use of them during the Revolution but rarely as part of the regular army. However, by liberal offers of cash and whisky in return for bona fide colonial scalps it was possible to enlist the enthusiasm of a great many of the redskins and several of their massacres, notably that of the Wyoming Valley in New York State in the year 1778, where three hundred settlers were murdered by the Senecas, were remembered by the colonists with a bitterness which in some regions has not died out to this day.

Fortunately for the rebels after the year 1778 when France, Spain and Holland had joined in the war, the English could no longer devote all their attention to the problems of America. Generally speaking, however, the majority of the people in the mother country clearly realized the importance of the struggle and long before news of the first series of defeats reached London they were eager for the government to strain every nerve to bring the Revolutionists to terms.

That England failed nevertheless was due to a multitude of causes. In the first place, the British were fighting a war three thousand miles away from their base of supply. In the second place, their soldiers never became thoroughly familiar with the methods of skirmishing best suited to the country. And finally they used mercenaries while the American army was composed of volunteers.

It has been said (with more or less truth) that the Gods are always on the side of the largest cannon. In the case, however, that both parties are fairly well provided with artillery, the victory is bound to go to those who have a personal stake in the quarrel. The Vermonters and Rhode Islanders who followed Washington through the slush and sleet of Delaware knew that if they failed to fight their damnedest, their farms would be burned down by the enemy, their cattle would be stolen, their wives and children, very likely, would be sent to Canada or Nova Scotia. The poor Hessians, on the other hand, engaged in this war at seven pounds, four shillings, four pence halfpenny (which went into the pocketbook of their illustrious master), had absolutely nothing to gain but an occasional pot of ale and enough food to keep them alive.

And so they said to themselves, *"Warum sollen wir uns da anstrengen?"* And they went into action with one eye upon the enemy and the other upon the nearest exit.

Let those who ever spent a couple of uncomfortable years under the shell fire of a quarrel that did not interest them throw the first hand grenade.

As far as I am concerned, those Hessians were very wise men.

## *Chapter Twenty-Seven*

## LORD NORTH IS FORCED TO KEEP AWAKE

LORD FREDERICK NORTH belonged to a family that gave England a great number of distinguished politicians and Epsom salts. He was the most amiable statesman who ever gambled for the fate of an empire and lost. He was never ruffled or cross. He could say something funny in the midst of the most acrimonious debate. And when he was bawled out by the members of His Majesty's most loyal opposition, he pulled his wig over his eyes and quietly went to sleep.

Alas! During the period between the years 1775 and 1783 the noble lord had little chance to practice his wit and quite frequently he was obliged to keep awake long after bedtime. For things went none too well in the distant colonies and he, poor man, had to bear the blame.

First of all there had been the failure of the attempt to reconquer America from the north. The city of Boston, which was supposed to have served as the main base of supply for the army of occupation, had been forced to surrender and the whole of New England had fallen into the hands of the rebels.

After due deliberation (a period of rest which had given Washington that for which he prayed most of all—time in which to organize his raw troops) a second plan of campaign was drawn up. This was more or less Napoleonic in its bold aggressiveness but the execution was so far from Napoleonic that it failed completely. It intended nothing less than a division of the northern American territory into two halves by a military cordon that should stretch in an almost straight line from Montreal to New York. Two armies were to be employed simultaneously. One was to march from Canada to the mouth of the Hudson River. The other was to proceed from the mouth of the Hudson River to Canada.

So far so good.

The city of New York, that hotbed of loyalism, was taken without great difficulty but Washington and the greater portion of his army were allowed to escape. This exposed the western flank of the British forces forever to an attack on the part of the rebels, as they were to learn to their disadvantage at Trenton and Princeton.

Meanwhile another strong division had followed the old frontier road along the banks of Lake Champlain and had recaptured Fort Ticonderoga. Then, however, that delightful and popular playwright, John Burgoyne, who happened to be in command, succeeding in losing himself in the wilderness of northern New York and together with all his troops and train (the latter more welcome to the Americans than the former) he had been captured near Saratoga, the well-known and fashionable watering-place of the early years of the Republic.

That practically ended the second campaign. For although the English had gained several victories in other parts of America and had even occupied Philadelphia, the capital of the Revolution, their success had not broken the resistance of the colonists. On the contrary, it had given the courage of desperation to many a hitherto lukewarm member of the Continental Congress and it had emboldened that body (which on the approach of the redcoats had fled in the general direction of Lancaster, Pa.), to agree upon a series of articles of confederation and perpetual union which has made the name of "The United States of America" something more than a hollow title. And by the end of the second year of war, the prospects of a speedy British victory were as remote as ever. It is true that Washington and his men passed through a miser-

Winter quarters

able winter in the village of Valley Forge, twenty-four miles away from Philadelphia. But somehow or other they survived even this terrible experience. By this time they had suffered so much through the inefficiency and indifference of Congress, that the callousness of a few Pennsylvania farmers, who sold all their produce directly to the British (whose pockets were filled with golden sovereigns) and let their own countrymen starve (because they could not pay in cash) was merely an unpleasant experience to be forgotten as soon as the actual fighting was resumed.

As for the commander-in-chief of this desperate cause, the behavior of Washington during these trying times was sublime. Ninety-nine men out of a hundred would have retired before the constant campaign of calumny—before the innuendoes of the New England democrats—who detested and distrusted the Virginia aristocrat—the contemptible little plots and cabals which tried to gain the commandership-in-chief for such renegades as Charles Lee (a survivor of Braddock's ill-fated army who ostentatiously had taken the side of the rebels and who secretly tried to sell the revolution to his former countrymen) or for any other adventurer who could brag of his campaigns in the old world.

But Washington never allowed himself to be disturbed by such little incidents. He knew that he was personally held to blame for the loss of Philadelphia. He knew that the New Englanders regarded their own General Gates, the hero of Saratoga, as an infinitely more capable strategist. He knew all this and he kept his peace, made his rounds, drilled his men when they had shoes and could go out into the open, taught them the theory of war when they had no shoes and were forced to remain indoors. Some day or other, of this he was convinced, there would be a break.

The break came early in the next year. It came in the form of a letter and it told the lonely man in Valley Forge that on the twenty-second of December ultimo his good friend, Dr. Benjamin Franklin of Philadelphia, Pennsylvania, had reached Paris and had taken a room in the pleasant and not too expensive suburb of Passy.

*Chapter Twenty-Eight*

## DR. BENJAMIN FRANKLIN, THE WELL-KNOWN PRINTER OF PHILADELPHIA, PA., CALLS UPON THE DESCENDANT OF SAINT LOUIS

THERE IS A TENDENCY among certain classes of our society to regret the good old days of the Republic when God was in His Heaven—when the laboring man touched his cap and worked ten hours a day in return for a large silver dollar—when all the simple virtues of life were practiced everywhere—when Arcady had been recovered along the banks of the Charles River and the Potomac.

The people, however, who talk that way seem to overlook one little item that really made that era the golden age of American civilization (and that would have enraged them greatly)—the sublime independence of the average individual.

Where, oh where, in our blessed civilization of monotony and standardization, are those magnificent creatures who crowded the stage at the time of the great revolution, only a hundred and fifty years ago?

What marvelous men and what a delightful originality!

They were not the sanctimonious heroes of which our story books love to tell. They patronized the alehouses for warmth, comfort, and a congenial social atmosphere. They loved widely, if not always wisely. They got the uttermost farthing out of every commercial deal. They often backed their faith in a particular horse with an appreciable sum of money. They handled the King's English with a fine flourish of the pen, read the Emperor's Latin without the help of a dictionary, and were not ashamed to confess to a certain predilection for quotations from the classical authors of Greece.

They could hate with a persistent relentlessness, but they would give their last penny to keep a friend out of the poorhouse or the bankruptcy court.

Not infrequently they were mean and spiteful and harsh, but whatever they did, they were themselves, and if you did not happen to like them the way they were, you knew what you could do about it.

It must be confessed that they were not exactly good citizens in the modern sense of the word. They would wear anything that suited their taste without paying attention to the prevailing fashion. They would eat and drink whatever they liked without asking whether the neighbors ate and drank the same things. Even in such important matters as religion and politics they would take their conscience as their guide and would be serenely indifferent to the accusations of heresy which were soon being whispered among the less enlightened members of the community.

A dangerous policy, we say, and one which in modern times would lead the average citizen to business failure and would make him socially impossible.

But the men who made our country never seem to have

bothered overmuch about that "practical success" of which we have heard so much during the last seventy years.

"Jewels and houses and stocks and bonds and horses and carriages," so they would argue, "are all very well as far as they go, but they don't go far enough. This world is a vale of tears and all material goods are perishable. Today we are rich. Tomorrow we may be poor. But there is something of which neither God nor man can deprive us. That is our own integrity and that strange mixture of inherited and acquired characteristics which goes by the name of 'personality.' Let us cultivate that rare virtue beyond everything else and all will be well with the world."

Some day we shall wake up (indeed, it seems that we have already begun to wake up) to the marvelous and entertaining heritage bestowed upon us by these solemn Founding Fathers (and how they would have roared could they have heard that title!). At present they lie buried underneath tons and tons of sentimental nonsense and we can only reconstruct them from a few fortunate fragments that have escaped the ardor of the patriotic professors. And if we happen to know Benjamin Franklin better than most of his contemporaries, it is due to the fact that this jovial genius gave away the secrets of his soul with such liberality that three-score official "lives" have not been able to undo the first impression left behind by his straightforward and plain-spoken autobiography.

Franklin was not an aristocrat. Most decidedly not. Although he met more kings and dined with more dukes and told funny stories to more countesses than any other man born on the western coast of the Atlantic Ocean, he was of very simple birth.

He was the tenth child of a poor English immigrant who during the latter half of the seventeenth century had moved from Northamptonshire in England to Middlesex County in Massachusetts.

He had been taught reading and writing almost as soon as he had learned to speak and before he was eleven he had set to work in his father's soap factory in Boston.

Three years later he had been given a more congenial job in the printshop of one of his half-brothers who was the editor and publisher of the famous *New England Courant*.

From that day until the end of his long and active life (he died when he was eighty-four) he was never far removed from the composer's stick. You know how it is—once the love of the composing-room gets into your blood, you are never quite happy unless you live in the atmosphere where a dirty urchin hollers occasionally for "Copy-y-y-y!"

Boston, however, did not hold this young man very long. He was considered too much of a radical, too outspoken a "freethinker" to please the parsons who still dominated that part of the world. And so at the age of seventeen he packed his little bundle and moved to New York and began the career of a wandering apprentice which by way of New York and London carried him to Philadelphia which was to be his home town. From that moment on it is almost easier to say what he did not do than to enumerate the endless variety of careers in which he engaged before the Revolution claimed all his attention and turned him into a statesman.

He invented a new sort of type. He experimented with the ink used on the press of his *Pennsylvania Gazette*. He taught himself Latin, Spanish, French, and Italian. He helped found the American Philosophical Society. He was postmaster general for the colonies and speeded up the mail service until New York had three Philadelphia deliveries each week. He was the first successful rebel against the Puritan Sabbath and spent his Sundays perusing his own studies instead of listening to the secondhand wisdom of someone else. He studied the cause of earthquakes, perfected the well-known Franklin stove, and gave his native city an adequate system of street-lighting. He received the Copley medal of the Royal Society in London for his new-fangled invention known as the Franklin rod and since introduced into all parts of the world as the lightning rod. Under the pseudonym of Richard Saunders he printed an annual little booklet which became known as *Poor Richard's Almanac* and which was on every Christmas table in America during the latter half of the eighteenth century. He opened and operated the first public lending library. He was a member of the General Assembly of Pennsylvania for thirteen years. He was colonial agent in London for his own state, for Georgia, for New Jersey, and for Massachusetts. And when at home he used to cart the paper necessary for his many publications by his own hand from the warehouse to the printshop so that his neighbors might see that he did not consider himself too good for his job and intended to remain plain old Ben Franklin, the printer.

When the mother country and the colonies got into a quarrel about taxation, he tried at first by all means at his disposal to bring about some sort of a compromise. When he saw that the English government was unable or unwilling to appreciate the standpoint of the settlers in America, he became an outspoken advocate of force to the limit and he backed his opinions with every cent he owned or could borrow. The leaders of the rebellion tacitly accepted him as an unofficial Grand Old Man of the Revolution and when it became clear (as it did very soon) that the thirteen United States could not hope to win their war without the support of some other country, they asked Franklin to go abroad and see what could be done.

The new republic was in desperate financial straits. But it produced certain raw materials which were badly needed in Europe. Benjamin Franklin, trained in the school of the Puritans and the Quakers, could drive a bargain with the best of them. He was past his seventieth year. But he seemed possessed of life everlasting and besides he was the only champion of liberty whose name was widely known abroad and who, by sheer weight of his personal prestige, would not run the risk of being refused admission to the anterooms of French and Spanish and Dutch ministers and bankers.

Accompanied by two of his grandsons, the old man crossed the ocean and after a dreadful and seasick voyage in the little *Reprisal,* he reached the coast of France in December of the year 1776.

His instructions were of the vaguest. Congress had not even taken the trouble to provide him with a letter of credit. But by a stroke of good luck, the *Reprisal* had been able to capture two English merchantmen on the way over and the sale of their cargo of lumber and brandy provided the American delegate with enough pocket money to see him through for one or two months.

The kingdom of France at that moment was not unlike the Roman Empire of fifteen centuries before. The French people (that is to say, the upper classes, for the lower classes did not count) had reached that point of civilization which is apt to be so disastrous to the national character. For centuries they had lived in the handsomest houses the ingenuity of their architects had been able to devise and which stood planted in the heart of the most beautiful gardens ever designed by the most brilliant of landscape architects. Their cooks were the most famous of the world. Their literature was copied by all the writers of the Continent. Their court was the school of manners for all the best young men of western, northern, and central Europe. The standard of conversation, even in the most remote of their hamlets, was such as to make foreign visitors gape. Their tunes were fiddled by all the virtuosi of all the concert halls. In short, they had for so long enjoyed the best of everything that life had lost its zest, that every old emotion tasted as flat as boardinghouse mashed potatoes and that they were willing to give almost anything for a new sensation—for a new thrill.

At that precise moment, Dr. Franklin appeared in their midst. The old printer had never studied psychology but he did know men and women. If he were to gain the good will of this rich and powerful nation, he must appeal to their sense of the dramatic. Wherefore he turned actor and played his role so brilliantly that two years later, France concluded an alliance with the rebellious colonies and declared war upon Great Britain.

How did he manage to do this?

By the simplest of expedients, by absolutely remaining himself.

The immensely bored courtiers of King Louis, accustomed to the dull formality and the affectations of their own little Versailles, suddenly found themselves face to

face with a pleasant old man in a beaver cap and a coat of the vintage of the year 1730, who talked to them as if they had been his own grandchildren and who, if they were very good, might give them a hickory nut or an apple, "grown in his own garden."

Thank heaven here at last was something new.

France went wild about this philosopher from the backwoods.

In less than a month, everyone in the whole country knew the old man at least by sight. Peddlers carried his engraved portraits and plaster-cast busts from the Pyrenees to the Meuse. Every snuffbox and shaving-mug, in order to be up-to-date, must show the benign countenance of the "Apostle of Liberty." Lovely ladies wore Franklin bracelets and rings. The populace at large went Franklin-mad and only a man with the iron constitution of the old printer could hope to eat his way through the endless official banquets, luncheons, and suppers that were arranged in honor of this most distinguished guest and live.

Meanwhile the poor old ambassador had a few troubles of his own which would have destroyed all but the most hardened of political skeptics.

When he arrived in France, he discovered that he had been preceded by two other American delegates. One of these, Silas Deane by name, an honest Connecticut Yankee, had already established several highly profitable commercial relations between the colonies and the Continent. He had discovered that Pierre de Beaumarchais, the musical watchmaker of the court of Louis XVI, the composer of the enormously popular "Marriage of Figaro" and the "Barber of Seville," was a regular America fan, willing to help the colonists in every way he possibly could. Of course whatever was to be done must be kept a secret from the French authorities and so Deane and de Beaumarchais had worked out the following ingenious plan.

In Paris the business house of Rodriguez Hortalez & Cie. made its appearance. It was closely associated with the firm of Diego Gardoqui in Madrid. Soon large quantities of gunpowder and rifles and uniforms began to arrive in the French ports of the West Indies. As luck would have it, the vessels bearing this precious cargo often lay side by side with clipper ships from Nahant and Providence. And two weeks later, no one knew exactly how, these same barrels of gunpowder, consigned to some honest trader in Guadelupe or Haiti, would be unloaded by members of General Washington's quartermaster department and those rifles with which the natives of Basse Terre were supposed to have been shooting ducks would be discovered in the hands of Pennsylvania militiamen.

And no matter how strenuously His British Majesty's ambassador in Paris complained of this outrageous breach of neutrality, the French Minister of Foreign Affairs—*parole d'honneur!*—could not possibly tell him how it had happened.

Of course an absolutely illegitimate transaction like that depended for its success upon absolute secrecy. It was impossible to keep any accounts or books. No notes must ever be exchanged to show that the venture enjoyed the active support of the French and Spanish governments. The smugglers just had to take each other's word, trust each other's integrity.

As long as Deane handled this account, everything went well. But as soon as he was forced to co-operate with Arthur Lee, the second delegate sent abroad by the Committee of Secret Correspondence of Congress, his troubles began. This Arthur Lee was a brother of Richard Henry Lee who as a delegate from Virginia had offered the famous resolution that led to the Declaration of Independence. By professions he was a doctor and a lawyer, but he utterly lacked that equanimity of soul which alone could have brought him a lasting success as a medical man or as an attorney. He was forever seeing plots. All the men with whom he came in contact were crooks and thieves. Beaumarchais was not trying to assist the colonies because he had gone almost silly on the subject of popular liberty! No, he was in the business for the money there was in it. Deane was not a distinterested patriot who had spent the last penny of his private income to further the cause of the Revolution. Don't you believe it! Deane was a grafter who lived in splendor in Paris while his patriotic countrymen starved in their miserable dugouts in Valley Forge. And so on and so forth and only Lee was honest.

Congress, always eager for a little scandal, for an official "investigation" that should give some of its members a chance to appear in the limelight, took Lee's charges very seriously and asked Deane for an accounting. How could Deane, who for years had been doing forty different things at the same time, possibly tell what had become of the sums that were supposed to have passed through his hands ten or fourteen months before?

But this answer did not satisfy his judges. He was recalled and although his innocence (of which Franklin never doubted) was soon established, he died as a voluntary exile in England, while Lee lived to become one of the most bitter enemies of the Constitution of the United States and a general nuisance to all those who meant well by the country.

This unpleasant incident, together with a number of minor quarrels, provoked by Lee's bumptiousness and general lack of tact, awaited the attention of Franklin when he arrived in Paris. He did not allow himself to be ruffled. He had been engaged in other fights ere this. Quixotic and generous Beaumarchais, who for all his troubles had heard himself called a rascal and a robber by the very people for whom he had made so many sacrifices, was no longer in a mood to volunteer his help. But others came to his assistance. The mass of the French people, delighted by the personality of the American envoy, were solidly behind him. And the court, still smarting under the defeat of a generation before, was willing to listen to reason. That reason came in the form of a young Bostonian who had hastened across the ocean with the information that the entire army of Burgoyne had been captured by the Americans and that practically all of the northern territory was now in the hands of the revolutionists.

Four days after this cheerful bit of news reached the French capital, the French Minister of Foreign Affairs sent word to Doctor Franklin that he would be glad to see him any time at his convenience. And two months later, France recognized the independence of the United States of America, a move which England answered with a declaration of war.

That, however, did not end Franklin's usefulness in Europe. During seven long and anxious years he remained on the Continent, buying supplies, arranging for loans, equipping privateers, settling quarrels between his subordinates, cajoling other nations into commercial or political alliance, and bestowing by his mere presence a certain luster upon a cause that was badly in need of all the glory it could get.

As for himself, he was old and he asked for very little. The great Voltaire had embraced him before all the famous men of France.

That surely was reward enough for a true philosopher.

*Chapter Twenty-Nine*

## M. JEAN JACQUES ROUSSEAU WRITES A BOOK AND M. LE MARQUIS DE LA FAYETTE GOES TO STUDY THE DELIGHTFUL CHILDREN OF NATURE IN THE AMERICAN WILDERNESS

AT THE AGE OF THIRTEEN, Marie Joseph Paul Yves Roch Gilbert du Motier de La Fayette was an orphan, the possessor of one of the longest and noblest names in France and so rich that he did not know what to do with all his money.

The background of the second hero of this chapter, Jean Jacques Rousseau, had been rather different. He, too, had been left without the care of a father and mother before he had grown out of boyhood. But he had obtained his first glimpses of life as an engraver's apprentice, a footman, and a tramp, and until he was well past fifty he was never quite certain about his next meal.

And yet, in some mysterious way, the careers of these

two men, so curiously separated by every possible barrier of birth, breeding, and previous condition of servitude, were to cross each other for the benefit of a country which neither of them had ever seen.

For Rousseau turned author and prophet and philosopher and became the champion of the highly novel and interesting doctrine that all modern forms of civilization were evil; that true worth was only to be found among those savages who had never been exposed to the devastating influence of the white races; and that the only hope for the ultimate salvation of humanity lay in a return to nature.

Such a gospel was bound to appeal to a nation which (as I have stated a few pages before) had become so thoroughly saturated with pleasure that life had lost its zest and which, not being under the immediate necessity of working for a living, was willing to give three quarters of its net income in exchange for a new emotional experience.

A mere cursory perusal of the works of Jean Jacques was as thrilling as a flight in one of the new-fangled balloons.

And so behold the whole of French society returning to the simple manners of the earliest ancestors!—the queen milking her dear little cows—the king working at his forge—duchesses running dairy farms—famous painters depicting the blessed innocence of small girls holding little baa-baa lambs with pink ribbons around their necks!

What more natural than that the heir to one of the largest estates in France should fall a willing victim to this craze for Goodness and Virtue—for sweetness and light?

And then Paris was thrown into a general state of excitement by the first stories of the American war for liberty. To the average Frenchman of that day (and of today) anything that happened outside of his own frontiers was illimitably remote. Stockholm was situated somewhere on the outskirts of the inhabited world. A realm of darkness and Eskimos. As for Philadelphia, it was the last station before the planet Mars.

And now the unexpected, the unbelievable, yea, the impossible had happened. The humble farmers who dwelled in the farthest recesses of a somewhat doubtful continent had brazenly done battle upon the forces of the all-powerful monarch of the British Isles and had actually defeated those beautifully garbed warriors.

Such a thing would never have been possible unless those noble heroes had from earliest childhood denied themselves all those luxuries and pleasures which lay at the root of European corruption and decadence.

With a sudden shock the French people realized that the paradise of which the new philosopher had been preaching with such great eloquence actually existed. It was situated along the banks of the Susquehanna and the James rivers and it was called America. After that, there was only one thing to do, to dress *à l'Américain,* to eat dishes *à l'Américain,* to assume the air of a humble *paysan du forêt de la Pennsylvanie.*

Young La Fayette, hopelessly bored with the routine of his regiment of dragoons, got a more severe attack of the disease than most of his fellow officers. Finally the urge became too strong for him. He defied the very explicit orders of his king (who wanted him to stay at home a few years longer), escaped to Spain, and from there made his way to South Carolina.

His English at that time was not quite perfect and most of the people whom he met on the road to Philadelphia wondered by what strange turn of fate such a nice and bright French boy should ever have been carried to their particular neck of the woods. Congress, too, was slightly bewildered. A letter from Silas Deane explained in great detail that M. de La Fayette belonged to a family that went back to the days of Julius Caesar, that he was an amiable and engaging young gentleman, and that his name on the staff of General Washington would be of tremendous publicity value not only in France but all over the Continent.

That sounded very well but almost every ship that touched at an American port was carrying a full cargo of hungry European officers who told wondrous stories about their prowess in battle, sported orders received from a dozen sovereigns and who, on the strength of their past reputation, demanded to be made brigadier generals or admirals with salaries in proportion to their rank.

In the beginning, Congress had actually hired a few of these bibulous swashbucklers. But they had been rather a failure. And any man who now arrived in the national capital with a sword presented to him by the Emir of Podolia and a golden snuffbox forced upon him in return for his invaluable services by the Emperor of Kathay was apt to be an object of suspicion.

Young La Fayette, however, convinced his hosts that his intentions were of the purest. He came strictly as a volunteer and he would not accept a penny for his services. Congress pricked up its ears, and on the thirty-first of July of the year 1777 the Marquis de La Fayette "in consideration of his zeal, illustrious family and connections" was made a major general in the army of the United States.

A day later he was presented to Washington.

At first the commander-in-chief was somewhat puzzled what to do with a major-general of nineteen. He could not very well ask his roughneck mountaineers to take this child seriously. But he soon came to appreciate the very fine qualities of this young French nobleman and began to understand that a man who leaves his wife and his child and his country and a couple of million a year for the sake of an ideal is not a common everyday character.

It would have been absurd to expect that a second lieutenant of dragoons, trained in a small garrison in Europe, should overnight be changed into a great strategist, capable of conducting a campaign in the wilderness. But that was not necessary. The great value of La Fayette lay in the field of the morale. His presence made the cause of America fashionable. In the eyes of the European aristocracy (still the most valuable element in every state of the old Continent) the Revolution had "arrived."

From then on other distinguished foreigners, bona fide military men with long experience in the art of war, began to pay serious attention to this strange and uneven fight at the other end of the world. A former general of Frederick the Great, the Prussian Baron von Steuben, became the drill master of the American troops and put them through their paces until they ceased to be a mob and became an army.

Another German, Johann Kalb (better known as Baron Jean de Kalb), who had crossed with La Fayette and had been made a major general, also, rendered highly valuable service as an organizer and paid for his enthusiasm with his life when his raw troops stampeded and left him to the mercy of the regulars of Cornwallis while they themselves ran away.

While Kosciuszko and Count Pulaski added a dash of reckless Polish bravery to the operations around New York and before Savannah.

But other valuable allies now hastened to the support of the good cause. The strange new ideas of Rousseau, reinforced by the doctrines of liberty and equality which had been gathered in the famous Encyclopedia of Diderot and his friends, had found their way to every corner of Europe. In Holland they had led to the foundation of a political party which hoped to change the government of the country from an oligarchy into a democracy. When King George asked the Republic for the loan of two Scottish regiments which had been in Dutch service ever since the days of the revolution against Spain, the opposition fought the project so bitterly that the States General were obliged to refuse His Majesty's request.

A little later a translation of a pamphlet entitled *Common Sense*, written originally by an obscure Englishman, Tom Paine, and intended as a defense of the principles of the American Revolution, forced the English minister in the Hague to register his painful surprise at such an open expression of pro-Americanism.

It was at that very moment that the Congressional agents approached the merchants of Amsterdam and discreetly sounded them out about a loan and a commercial alliance. The merchants were willing to discuss the possibilities of such a plan but since their country was neutral, they requested that all negotiations take place abroad and that they be kept a strict secret. The Americans agreed, and after a short while a preliminary agreement was drawn up and was sent to Philadelphia for approval. Unfortunately this highly compromising document fell into the hands of the English when they captured Henry Laurens, who was bound for Amsterdam (and a loan of ten million dollars) and who had taken no precautions whatsoever to prevent his trunkload of diplomatic correspondence from being captured by the enemy.

London was greatly annoyed by these unfortunate incidents. To make matters worse, a short time before, the American Revolution had boldly sailed into a Dutch port, when John Paul Jones, a former English skipper but now a very successful American captain, had taken his prize, the *Serapis,* into the harbor of Texel. Instead of arresting this "buccaneer" as the English minister at The Hague had suggested, the Dutch people had made Jones into a national hero and wherever he and his strange crew had shown themselves (out of the two hundred and twenty-seven sailors under his command only seventy-nine were Americans) they had been received with loud expressions of popular approval.

The discovery of a plot to place a loan in Holland, coming so shortly upon the refusal of the Dutch government (under the pressure of the American sympathizers) to return the *Serapis* to her rightful owners, made England declare war upon Holland.

No Dutch troops, during this struggle, crossed the ocean to join the Americans and the French, but the Dutch fleet kept several English squadrons engaged in the North Sea and most important of all for the success of the Revolution, the vast wealth of the old republic was placed at the disposal of her younger sister at a moment when the finances of the United States were in a hopeless muddle. The lack of a strong central government had made it impossible to devise a system by which the Revolution could pay its way. Most of the thirteen states were bankrupt. The dollar was not worth its weight in paper. And the troops were constantly on the verge of mutiny for lack of the commonest necessities of life. France had promised golden mountains, but her treasury was empty and the ministers of King Louis, try as they might, could not make both ends meet. Wherefore such loans as Franklin, and after-

171

ward Adams, managed to obtain were usually in the form of drafts to be used for the purchase of supplies within the French dominions but not under any circumstances to be converted into cash. The seven million dollars in real money which were raised in the Dutch Republic therefore came as a veritable godsend.

The bankers who arranged for this transaction were not actuated by any unselfish love for the cause of America. They were businessmen and as such they believed in sentimentality but not in sentiment. They expected that upon the return of peace their own country would derive some benefit from its past generosity and that the American government would show its appreciation and its gratitude by granting the Dutch Republic a favorable commercial treaty. In this they were to be bitterly disappointed, but that was something no one then could foresee. And meanwhile the gold transports from Holland, addressed directly to General George Washington, Esq. (and not to Congress), found their way across the ocean and upon several occasions prevented a recurrence of those outbreaks of near-mutiny which had become only too common during those last four years of Congressional neglect and indifference and which sometimes made Washington fear that he would have to fight the war for independence single-handed.

## Chapter Thirty

### THE MOTHER COUNTRY MAKES THE BEST OF A BAD BARGAIN AND THE MEN FROM THE FRONTIER MAKE THE BEST OF A GOOD ONE

IT LOOKED like a stalemate. Indeed it did. England at war with France, Holland, and Spain (for Spain had joined the allies in the hope of getting back Gibraltar and her island possessions in the Mediterranean) had her hands full in Europe. Her ruthless indifference toward the right of neutral nations on the high seas had forced several of her more powerful competitors to form a protective alliance, the so-called "armed neutrality," and to make themselves the champions of that vague code of ethics known as International Law.

But after three years of war it began to dawn upon the world that the Americans were receiving the help of an ally who invariably spread disaster when he took part in a military conflict. That was Brigadier General Distance.

The Romans, so it seems, had been the only people able to hold their own against this indefatigable opponent.

The military leaders of the Middle Ages had always suffered defeat when this terrible warrior, followed by his merciless associates, the famous Captains Miles and Kilometers, appeared upon the scene. And now old man Distance had joined the staff of George Washington. After that, no matter how hard the English tried, no matter how bravely they fought, they found themselves outmarched and outdistanced on every field of battle. Thus far, in all their wars, they had been able to depend upon their navy. But ships were of little use in the Allegheny Mountains and no men of war could safely hope to sail across the "drowned lands" of Illinois. Footwork was to be the decisive factor in this encounter and footwork, after two or three years, has a tendency to become somewhat monotonous and to undermine the discipline of the best regulated troops.

Even gay Lord North began to talk of compromise, suggested that the mother country and her erring children might let bygones be bygones and start again on a new and sounder basis.

Let us confess—since we are trying to tell the truth—that this message did not fall upon deaf ears. The American people in general were beginning to feel the results of three years of commercial stagnation. Their finances were in hopeless disorder, and Congress was too weak and too inefficient to bring about that union of all the country's manifold forces without which a definite victory would always be out of the question.

173

The loyalists (and they still formed a large if discreet portion of the population) were as willing as ever to listen to the sweet sounds of peace and good will that reached them from England. In short, a decided wave of "defeatism" swept across the country.

One American general even went so far as to try a "coup de main" by which the rebellion should be brought to its logical conclusion and America should be saved for King George. He himself (at a price) was to be the hero of the occasion. Fortunately, the English officer who had charge of the negotiations fell into the hands of a small band of camp followers who dimly felt that something was wrong with the mysterious papers which this young gentleman carried in his boots and who surrendered their prisoner to an officer of the regular army.

In this way the plot, which had many ramifications, was discovered. And as so often happens in such cases, the poor intermediary, a certain Major André, was hanged while Major General Arnold, the commander of the highly important fortification of West Point, who had tried to sell his country to the enemy, made good his escape and died peacefully (if not happily) as a brigadier general in the English army.

That dreadful and shocking affair proved to be a turning-point in the history of the United States. It was shortly afterward that General Distance began to make his presence felt in all seriousness and all along the line the footsore British troops were beginning to move slowly in the general direction of the Atlantic seaboard.

Their progress, however, was greatly impeded by the endless train of fugitives that followed in their wake. The loyalists began to understand that the game was up. They had put their money on the wrong horse, or rather in a contest between an eagle and a lion, they had chosen to back the quadruped, and the poor beast was slinking home. Such of their goods as they could carry away they loaded upon trucks and forwarded them to Nova Scotia or New Brunswick. But their houses and their gardens and their farms and their ancestral heirlooms they left behind and these now fell into the hands of the victorious boys from the western hinterland. In several states it seems that not less than half of all available real estate changed hands during the period between 1775 and 1787. And the new owners (or whatever you call people who acquire property in that way) belonged for the greater part to the class of disinherited farmers from the frontier and their sudden wealth greatly strengthened the prestige of the democrats, while the forced departure of the loyalists weakened the cause of the aristocrats.

But in other ways did the democrats increase their hold upon the country. They were now given a chance to settle the question as to who should own the great wilderness of the western frontier. The French were gone but their fortifications had fallen into the hands of the English and that was just as bad. For the New Englanders and the New Yorkers and Virginians and Pennsylvanians who had taken charge of the Revolution seemed quite indifferent about the future of the farmers who lived along the frontier and who were called upon to deal directly with the British garrisons. They felt about these distant compatriots as we feel about people in Idaho and Wyoming. When we read in the papers that they have suffered from a flood or an earthquake, we are very sorry and we say, "Something must be done about this!" Sometimes we go as far as sending them a check. But they live so far away from our own little back yard that their suffering rarely provokes anything more serious than a polite and wholly academic interest and a letter of condolence.

The pioneers knew this.

Thus far they had always been held in check by royal French commissioners or Jesuit padres or the officers of His Majesty's forces. The royal commissioners and the Jesuits were gone. Remained the troops of King George. As the war approached its end the outlying posts were gradually recalled and then at last the people of the frontier were given a free hand.

It was a sad day for the native inhabitants of these wild regions. Driven by some obscure instinct of self-preservation, they had taken the side of the English, and full of British rum they had been guilty of abominable atrocities against defenseless American farmers.

Now they were to pay the price.

One after another the different tribes of Indians attacked were killed off, or were forced to move further westward. The more highly civilized groups of Indians who lived in the woods of northern New York and who had developed a federal form of government which Franklin had praised to his fellow members of Congress as an example that might be followed by the United States, tried to put up some semblance of resistance. But they were badly defeated by a large American force under one John Sullivan from New Hampshire, and to make his victory complete, Sullivan went so far as to destroy all their fruit trees and their corn patches, so that the survivors were doomed to die of hunger. A good many people protested against the barbarous severity of this sentence, but Congress welcomed Sullivan back as a hero and favored him with a vote of thanks.

That was the end of the Indian menace as far as the United States were concerned and from that moment on there was no longer any danger of an attack from the rear. But in the East, also, the Americans were successful. French soldiers and German drill masters and Polish volunteers and Dutch money, aided and abetted by our old friend General Distance, were gradually wearing out the veteran regiments of His Majesty, King George.

In the year 1781 the English tried their last bit of strategy. Their campaign in the north had ended in failure with the evacuation of Boston. Their effort to separate the east from the west by occupying the Hudson River valley had ended with the defeat of Burgoyne at Saratoga.

Now they meant to mass their troops in the south and then work their way up northward.

This expedition ended disastrously with the surrender of Lord Cornwallis together with his entire army at Yorktown on the nineteenth of October of the year 1781.

When news of the disaster reached London, King George remarked that "It was nothing," and added that no one in England should think that even the greatest of disasters would make the smallest alteration in those principles of conduct which had directed him in the past. But Lord North stayed serious long enough to whisper in deep gloom that it was the end. Whereupon he resigned from office and left the business of negotiating for a cessation of hostilities to his successor, the Marquis of Rockingham, and to those same Whigs whom half a dozen years before he had driven from office.

The peace conference which opened in Paris in the spring of 1782 lasted almost two years and it became a sort of geographic and economic debate in which Benjamin Franklin and John Adams showed themselves far superior to their opponents.

Finally on the third of September of the year 1783 the treaty of peace between Great Britain and the United States of America was signed with all due formality.

Two years later Adams was appointed minister to the court of St. James.

The representative of the new Republic upon the occasion of his being presented to the King deported himself with that ungracious rectitude of mind and behavior which in his part of the world was known (and respected) as a manifestation of honesty.

But His Majesty delivered a pretty little speech which deserves to be remembered.

"Sir," he said, "I wish you to believe (and I want what I say to be repeated to your compatriots in America) that I have done nothing during the late contest but what I thought myself indispensably bound to do by the duty which I owed to my people. I will be very frank with you. I was the last to consent to the separation. But the separation having been made and having become unavoidable, I have always said, as I say now, that I would be the first to meet the friendship of the United States as an independent power."

At last the mother country had accepted the inevitable.

## Chapter Thirty-One

## THE COMPROMISE THAT SAVED A NATION AND FOUNDED AN EMPIRE

AMERICA WAS FREE, but in the words of that profound philosopher of the fifteen-dollar-a-week clerk, the excellent Rube Goldberg, "Now that the people of the United States of America had got their liberty, what were they going to do with it?"

I am afraid that the question was not the least bit funny to such men as Adams, who expected an immediate outbreak of anarchy, or to Washington, who found himself called upon to do policeman's work and whose great personal following alone saved the country from a very dangerous outbreak of mutiny.

For revolution, as you will know without my telling you, is something negative. It may be necessary. It may be even desirable. But also, by the very nature of its ultimate purpose, it must be something negative, like a surgical operation or the destruction of an old building that has outlived its usefulness.

Thus far the American rebels had been held together by a common ideal which consisted mostly of things they did not want to do. For example, they did not want to pay taxes to the British government. They did not want to have bishops of the official British church appointed for America. They did not want the King to tell them that they must keep out of certain western lands which were supposed to be reserved for the Indians. They did not want Parliament to put a duty on their tea and on their glass and on their paint. They did not want to do this and they did not want to do that.

But now the period of the "don'ts" had come to an end. The much less exciting era of the "do's" had begun. And that, as the successful rebels were to discover almost immediately, was something different again.

In the first place they had ceased to be subjects of a foreign crown. They had become citizens of a republic of their own.

But how was that republic to be ruled—what sort of a republic was it going to be anyway—how was it going to get the necessary money for the support of an independent army and navy and diplomatic service and postal department and health office and a few thousand other questions?

Until recently the Americans had not known what the word "deficit" meant. His Majesty's government had most kindly looked after all such little details as defeating the French, keeping the savages away from the white man's farms, maintaining law and order and paying for the upkeep of the armed forces. That day was gone forever. And so the Americans began (but without any great show of ardor) to ask themselves and each other, "What sort of government ought we to have?"

At once the old difference of opinion between the city and the farm, between the seaboard and the frontier, made itself felt.

On the part of the democrats, Mr. Thomas Paine pleaded for a Res Publica—a true "Common Weal"—an "asylum for all mankind"—a confederation of sovereign and independent little states.

The aristocrats did not like this idea. A loose confederation of sovereign and independent little states sounded very well on paper. But what could a nation hope to accomplish in this wickedest of all worlds without Force with a capital F? And what did Force mean but a strong national government? Even now did not the different colonies suffer greatly from their inability to maintain their own good rights against the rest of the world?

There was the question of the English tariff. Since the treaty of Paris the mother country had begun to treat her former children just as she treated the rest of the world and she now insisted that all American goods brought into her harbors pay duty. The Americans would like to retaliate. But how could they? By passing thirteen bills regulating the tariff of thirteen little states? The very idea was absurd.

There was the question of those millions of paper dollars with which the different state legislatures had flooded the country and which in many neighborhoods had caused a complete standstill of credit and business. Did anyone expect these same state legislatures to withdraw that worthless paper and go back to the colonial standard of gold and silver? Of course not. There was too much profit in it for too many petty politicians.

There were the I.O.U.'s of the army for supplies and for food and for clothing signed under the stress of immediate necessity by some hungry officer or soldier. What were the poor farmers and merchants to do with these scraps of paper? Offer them for presentation to the treasurer of Pennsylvania or Delaware? A lot of good that would do them. Those communities had been bankrupt for years and their promissory notes were being used for wallpaper and as writing-pads.

There were the endless difficulties connected with interstate commerce. Could New York levy a tax on all goods brought in from New Jersey and vice versa?

The Articles of Confederation of the year 1777 still bound the different states together in some sort of a league and European powers, whose interest it was to do so, could (and occasionally would) recognize this League of Independent States as a regular nation. But popular enthusiasm for America had run its natural course. The war was over and the foreign creditors were beginning to clamor for cash or at least for some interest upon their money. A certain amount of revenue was coming in from the sale of that vast western territory which the treaty of Paris had placed at the disposal of the Americans and which (so it was hoped) might eventually be converted into a few new states.

But who was to handle that money?

And so on and so forth until all but the most eager enthusiasts for a pure democracy had begun to understand that something definite must be done and must be done quickly.

A first convention called together in Annapolis to settle a tariff quarrel between Maryland and Virginia accomplished nothing. Only five states took the trouble to send delegates. After a few feeble discussions of the desirability of a strong central government they all went home again. But Hamilton, Washington's former aide and a firm believer in the aristocratic idea of government, had been among those present and this very intelligent person knew that the time had come for a radical change or everything would be lost.

And so certain discreet gentlemen met in the back rooms of certain discreet hostelries and letters went back and forth and as a result it was announced that a formal convention would be called together in Philadelphia in the month of May of the next year.

At first only seven states were represented, but gradually the others followed suit (with the exception of Rhode Island). On the first of June the meeting at last got under way.

In this hour of crisis (the country had now been without a central government for almost a dozen years) the different states momentarily forgot their ancient quarrels and rivalries and sent the very best among their citizens and did not hamper them with too many instructions.

The convention sat behind closed doors. But from the report of the debates printed in 1827 and from the many private memoirs published afterward, we now know what happened during those four months when the fate of our country hung in the balance. The extreme democrats were not present and the out-and-out aristocrats were absent, too. The majority of the fifty-five delegates were people of fairly moderate views, lawyers and merchants and soldiers who had done their share during the difficult years of the rebellion, who wanted a sensible republic with a sensible form of government, but who were not at all inclined to try strange new experiments of statecraft.

Like all good businessmen they knew that nothing is ever accomplished by a committee unless it consists of three members, one of whom happens to be sick and another absent. Most of the actual work of drawing up the necessary documents was therefore left to a certain James Madison of King George County, Virginia, who was the author of an enlightening little pamphlet, entitled *The Vices of the Political System of the United States*. This Mr. Madison had taken a prominent part in the calling together of the Annapolis convention and he had come to Philadelphia with such a sensible and workable plan for a constitution (the so-called "Virginia plan") that he was immediately assailed as an enemy of democracy by all the representatives of the smaller states who regarded every suggestion of centralization as an attack upon the rights of the small nations.

They therefore submitted a plan of their own, the so-called "New Jersey plan," which the big-state people denounced as an effort to enslave the more important provinces to the advantage of the weaker ones.

There was a crisis. It looked as if the small-state delegates would bolt the convention.

But His Excellency General Washington was in the chair and one did not bolt conventions while His Excellency General Washington was in the chair. No! One did not!

And then there was Doctor Franklin, now a very old man but a very wise one, who smiled pleasantly when things went well, told funny stories when the debate grew too hot, and occasionally invited disgruntled delegates into a little anteroom of his own until they were ready to smile again and the business of constitution-making could go on.

Anyway—and this is the most important point—the convention did not break up. A compromise proposed by the delegation from Connecticut was adopted and in September of the year 1787 the Constitution of the United States of America was ready for public inspection.

The ratification by the different states was very slow and it was accompanied by all that bitterness which the convention itself had so narrowly avoided.

The "lowborn" felt that the "highborn" had put something over on them; that the president of the Republic was to be merely another monarch; and that the Congress provided by the Constitution was to be another British Parliament which would undertake to rule the union without any regard for the sovereign rights of the smaller states. The "highborn" on the other hand maintained that all these arguments were nothing but cheap expressions of the spirit of mob rule and that the new government of the country was so beautifully balanced that the executive branch, the legislative branch, and the courts would never be able to usurp those powers that did not actually belong to them. And they published a series of articles which were afterward done into a single volume called the *Federalist* and which proved to be a veritable handbook for all those who wished to study the Constitution without more personal prejudice than necessary.

In those states where the conflict between democrats and aristocrats had always been most bitter, the ratification gave cause for a renewal of the old fight and in some of them the number of yeas was only slightly larger than that of the nays (187 to 168 in Massachusetts). But gradually one state after another expressed its approval and even Rhode Island, which had refused to take part in the convention, repented of its ways and agreed to continue as part of the United States and not set up as a nation of its own.

Since that memorable day so much has been written and spoken upon this subject by such very learned people that I feel like a little boy who is going to tell Fritz Kreisler how to play the violin. And yet one cannot undertake to print a book about America without devoting a few words to the subject.

The Constitution, as I see it, is one of those documents (like Goethe's *Faust* or Dante's *Divine Comedy* or Milton's *Paradise Lost*) which are praised in proportion to the amount that they are not read.

Everybody will at times say, "Oh, the Constitution!" but very few people among those enthusiasts have taken the trouble to study it seriously. Children at school are, of course, the exception. They are forced to read it and as a result most of them come to hate it and regard the whole document as a dreadfully dull piece of writing, a fit counterpart of all that vast literature that has become anathema because it is part of the "prescribed reading" of our colleges and high schools.

But it is really one of the most interesting documents of the last two hundred years. As it was the result of a compromise, it shows few signs of having been divinely inspired. But a paper set of rules of government which managed to survive the great scientific and economic and political upheavals of the last hundred and forty years, which is as vital in 1927 as it was in 1787, a political decalogue of such tenacity of life is surely no ordinary, everyday document of state.

Today constitutions are neither very rare nor very important. With the exception of England every country now has a constitution or a couple of constitutions. But we seem to be the only land blessed with a constitution that will work.

And that result is due in the first instance to the sound common sense of the men who had come together in Philadelphia in 1787.

Just when it seemed that this recently launched Ship of State was bound to be thrown upon the rocks of partisanship and was going to perish miserably amidst the turbulent waves of anarchy, Madison and his colleagues came to the rescue, corrected the compass, and presented the crew with such an excellent set of charts and sailing-instructions that the little vessel was saved from destruction and was able to continue its voyage toward the limitless sea of the future with every assurance of a successful voyage.

On March the fourth of the year 1789 the first Congress elected under the new rules came together in New York. Three weeks later from the steps of the Federal Hall and amidst the jubilation of the entire country, His Excellency General George Washington was proclaimed President of the United States of America.

And still a few weeks later good King Louis of France stood awkwardly in the banqueting hall of his palace of Versailles and amidst the dead silence of his faithful subjects told the representatives of the French nation how he wanted them to save their common fatherland from ruin.

. . . . . . .

This is a strange world and it takes all sorts and manner of men to make the wheels go round.

The Adamses and the La Fayettes and the Franklins and the Washingtons and the Rousseaus and the Hamiltons and the Jeffersons and the Joneses and the hook-nosed descendants of Adhémar of Bourbon, they make their bow, they rush upon the scene, they speak their little part, and *phut*—Clio puts them away in her old and trusted box.

Then this patient goddess quietly sets the stage for the next act and gives us a comedy or perchance a tragedy and we look at it and we are moved to tears or to laughter and we are quite sure that no one but ourselves ever witnessed so wonderful a performance.

## Chapter Thirty-Two

## MR. ALEXANDER HAMILTON OF THE ISLAND OF NEVIS (B.W.I.) PUTS THE COUNTRY ON A SOUND COMMERCIAL BASIS, AND GEORGE WASHINGTON, ESQ., RETURNS TO MOUNT VERNON, AN OLDER AND SADDER MAN

THE GREEK WORD "aristos" means "the best" and the Greek word "kratia" means "government." An aristocracy therefore was supposed to be a "rule of the best," or as Alexander Hamilton expressed it in terms that sounded agreeable to his political friends, "Aristocracy means a government by the wise, the wealthy, and the good."

Aristocracy has always been a noble ideal. Indeed it would be difficult to suggest anything superior to a "rule of the best." There is only one difficulty. It is often quite hard to discover who exactly are the wisest and the goodest (the wealthiest are found easily enough) of any given community. But in periods of great stress, when the emotions are running wild and oratory has temporarily darkened the reason of even the most sensible of men, such slogans (or their opposite) are apt to be taken seriously and to become part of the temporary code of morals and ethics.

We, however, who have accepted democracy as the best of all political compromises can look back upon that period of our history without getting excited and we are able to study the events of that day without taking sides. And then it becomes clear that the men who made our Constitution had striven with all their might to devise a system that should resemble as closely as possible an elective monarchy, and that they had taken every precaution lest the office of temporary sovereign fall into the hands of anyone not fully qualified for this exalted position.

Furthermore they had been very careful lest the people whom they loved in theory but whom they distrusted and hated in practice should be able to exercise any direct influence upon the choice of the executive. They had made no bold declaration of any such intention, but they had left this matter to the discretion of the different state legislatures who were asked to devise ways and means by which their citizens could select a small number of electors without granting too much power to the poorer classes. These electors, highly respectable citizens, were thereupon to come together and, untrammeled by any instructions from their constituents, they were to say, "In our opinion the Hon. So-and-So of there-and-there is the man best fitted for the presidency. And we shall therefore ask him to be the head of our nation during the next four years."

In the year 1789 the choice had, of course, been unanimous. The very trees and shrubs had shrieked the name of "George Washington!"

But no man alone can attend to all the details of the

186

administration of almost four million people. He needs assistants.

Washington chose his ministers with great care and considerable intelligence and did not allow himself to be influenced by his personal preferences. John Adams had been elected vice-president and was therefore not available. But Thomas Jefferson, who disagreed with his neighbor of Fairfax County upon almost every subject except his devotion to the common fatherland, was now back from his mission to France and he was made Secretary of State, while Alexander Hamilton was put in charge of the most embarrassing relic left behind by a succession of incompetent Continental Congresses, a totally depleted national treasury.

The bank

Hamilton was eminently fit for the job. When little more than a child on the island of St. Croix, where he lived with his relatives, young Alexander had been left to take care of a thriving business enterprise during the temporary absence of his employer and he had done so well that he had attracted the attention of some kind-hearted people (not relatives) who had given him money enough to leave his home to go to Columbia University in New York. Without this stroke of good luck (good luck brought about by his own ability) it is hard to say what would have become of him. His mother, a woman of French origin, had first been married to a Danish planter of the Island of St. Croix and after she left him

187

had become the common-law wife of a Scotchman by the name of James Hamilton of St. Christopher, with whom she had moved to the island of Nevis where both Alexander and his brother James were born.

But in the year 1768 the mother had died and the father had gone into bankruptcy and the boy, as we have said before, had been left more or less to his own devices.

He had only been a short time in Columbia University when the Revolution broke out. He had offered himself as a volunteer and had shown so much ability for military life that within a very short time he had been made a lieutenant colonel on the staff of General Washington and for four years thereafter he had acted as that gentleman's confidential secretary and principal aide.

In the year 1780 he had married into one of the old Dutch families of upper New York State and had settled down to practice law and save society from that organized anarchy which was so dear to the heart of the out-and-out democrats. For such a policy he was eminently fitted because he himself was an immigrant. He was therefore without that strange allegiance to any particular state or country which made most of his native-born contemporaries first a Tennesseean or a Rhode Islander and only in the second place an American. What the people of that age called his "instinctive allegiance" must have gone out toward a small volcanic island in the West Indies which he had left when he was fifteen and had every reason to hate. As a result he was free from that dreadful affliction known as "local patriotism" and it was therefore quite easy for him to regard the United States as a nation and not as a loose combination of small and independent principalities, each one of which considered itself a little better than its neighbor.

Furthermore Hamilton had seen something of the world. One of the things that had made him so valuable to Washington was the fact that he spoke French fluently and for several years he had been engaged in international business and therefore knew that all commercial relations are firmly based upon that rock of mutual confidence which is known as credit.

The members of the different state legislatures, a good many of them farmers and accustomed to a simple form of barter, were only too apt to overlook this embarrassing fact. Ever since they were children they had been taught to hate and distrust the moneylenders of the big cities who at any moment might foreclose the mortgage and ruin the family. The actual and practical working of money, drafts, and checks had always been a mystery to them, something that was highly suspicious, an invention of Satan. Of course they liked to have money, a lot of it. It allowed them to buy things that were useful. It seemed that one could not fight a war without it. But once the French francs and the Dutch florins that had been sent to America as part of a national loan were safely in their possession and had done their duty as pay checks for the army and the navy, then their interest ceased. And so (if I may be allowed a very poor pun) did the interest that was to have gone to the foreign bankers who now grew eloquent upon the sad subject of what they were pleased to call "their risks," and wept bitter tears when they thought of such ingratitude.

To give these sons of Mammon their due, they had every reason to feel worried and to be disgusted. When Hamilton assumed the secretaryship of the treasury, the country was in debt to the tune of some seventy-seven million dollars, an enormous amount in those days. The greater part consisted of notes held by American citizens. Twelve millions made up the sum we owed to foreign banks and governments. And the states could add another twenty million of their own.

The money which was owed to Americans caused the greatest difficulty of all. For the people who held such notes were often in need of cash and then they were tempted to sell their claims to speculators for one-tenth or one-twentieth of their actual value. And if the government now were to redeem these notes (as it was proposed to do) the speculators would make millions and the original owners (who had been actuated by a most exalted and truthful patriotism when they trusted their savings to the care of Congress) would be left destitute.

At once there were two parties. One favored Hamilton's plan for complete assumption of all outstanding liabilities. The other, following Jefferson's lead, was against such a policy. In the end the usual compromise was brought about over the equally inevitable coffee cups of a copious dinner. Mr. Jefferson agreed to support Mr. Hamilton's plan for the debt and Mr. Hamilton said that he would aid Mr. Jefferson with his project for a new capital which was to be built on the banks of the Potomac, far away from the wicked contamination of the East.

But Hamilton was not contented with this first success. Until the finances of the United States were definitely placed upon a sound basis and the new nation had been made into a concern that could pay its way as it went along, the Republic could never hope to retain its independence. Hamilton's mind (more European than American in such matters) could not imagine a country without a national bank. Venice had become prosperous with its Banco di Rialto. The British government in times of crisis had depended upon the Bank of England. Sweden had had its Riksbank ever since the middle of the seventeenth century. Holland had done business through the Bank of Amsterdam as long as people could remember. But the United States were to be without a bank of their own—because the farmers, who could not possibly understand the working of anything more complicated than a grocery store, and who distrusted the idea of "all that money in one place," were against it.

Clearly this was preposterous.

And so in the year 1792 Hamilton, who was the brain and the driving force of Washington's cabinet, got his bank and established it in Philadelphia with a very modest original capital but enough for all immediate needs.

But a bank alone was not enough.

There also must be certain regular sources of revenue for the Federal government which was now called upon to perform the many services which formerly had been entrusted to the care of His Majesty's Parliament and was therefore in constant need of ready cash.

The idea of a duty upon foreign goods was not new. The Arabic origin of the word tariff (originally meaning "an inventory") showed that the institution dated back to the early Middle Ages.

Almost all other nations had a tariff.

Hamilton proposed that the United States should have one, too.

Again there was a storm of opposition from the direction of the agricultural districts in the South and in the West. A protective tariff, so the farmers and planters claimed, would only benefit the manufacturers from the seaboard and it would throw an additional burden of taxation upon the farmers.

But Hamilton had his way and for good measure he added a tax on whisky which in the remoter regions of Pennsylvania, where the people had just changed from rum to whisky and where they were in the habit of distilling whatever pleased them, led to a great deal of shooting and a disturbance which was not suppressed until President Washington had mobilized an army of fifteen thousand militiamen.

The United States were now, what in the eyes of all "sound men" (as President Washington loved to call them) constituted a decent and self-respecting nation. But those who did not care a tinker's damn whether they were called "sound" or "unsound" could hardly view this change from a league of independent nations to a highly centralized pseudo-monarchy without grave concern for the future.

And once again the old quarrel between seaboard and frontier, between moneylender and money borrower, between city and farm, between aristocrat and democrat, broke loose in full force. Only by now the two parties had rallied around a definite program and had been given new names. Those who were on the side of Washington and Adams and Hamilton—that is to say, those who believed in a strong central government conducted by the wellborn, the well-bred, and the well-to-do—were known as the Federalists. Those who revered Thomas Jefferson as their spiritual master—who hated the idea that the states should surrender part of their ancient sovereign rights to the newly established Federal government—who believed in the superior virtues of the lowly and the humble and the disinherited, were called Anti-Federalists. But as the Federalists were generally supposed to favor a return to a mild form of monarchy, the Anti-Federalists went one step further and called themselves by way of contrast the Republicans.

The quarrel which followed between those two groups after Jefferson had resigned from the cabinet in the year 1795 made the remaining years of Washington's official life very unhappy.

On both sides the campaign was conducted with an absolute disregard for the amenities of civilized society.

The people of the big cities, New York, Philadelphia, Boston, Hartford, Charleston, who hoped to see the United States become the leading manufacturing nation of the world, denounced Jefferson as a dangerous demagogue, a freethinker, a free-lover, a man who had lived too long in France and had become too enamored of French ideas to be a sound American patriot.

And the people from the frontier who hated all these supposed blessings of the East because they reminded them too much of those conditions in Europe from which they had at last escaped, retaliated with vigor and zest and bestowed upon Washington and his advisers a collection of personal epithets which the most scurrilous of our illustrated dailies would only dare to print in the form of dashes and asterisks.

All this was very unfortunate but it was only a beginning.

In France those same young men who only a few years before had crossed the ocean to place their sword at the disposal of the American rebellion were now faced by a revolution of their own. Their King had been decapitated. Their monarchy had been destroyed. Their country had been proclaimed a republic. And such of them as had not been killed were wandering abroad, trying to eke out an existence as teachers of the French language, as pastry cooks, or instructors of polite behavior.

The British monarchy had looked with scant approval upon the bestial cruelties committed by a starving and neglected people upon those whom they considered their tormentors. And Edmund Burke, the old friend of the American colonists, had gone so far as to preach a regular crusade against those monsters who had dared to rise against their legitimate sovereign and who in the fullness of their new idealism had purged the world of everything that smacked of the Middle Ages and feudalism.

Relations between the two countries had soon become so strained that war was inevitable. In the year 1793 France and England were in open conflict.

To the average Frenchman, the duty which was then thrust upon the people of the United States was a very simple one. Ten years before France, with a noble gesture, had come to the assistance of the hard-pressed American nation and had freely offered her gold and her blood that the colonists might gain their independence.

Now France was surrounded by enemies. And of course the Americans would hasten to reciprocate. But alas! The poor Frenchmen were to be bitterly disappointed. Nothing happened. The only gesture made in New York was a slight movement of President Washington's right hand by which he signed a proclamation which bade all his subjects to maintain "a strict and absolute neutrality" during the present conflict between the French Directory and King George and not to take sides, either in word or deed.

Such a decision seemed contrary to all the stipulations of that most solemn treaty which not only had proclaimed America the ally of France but had also placed upon the American people the duty of protecting the French possessions in the West Indies and had opened all American harbors to French privateers and their prizes while at the same time closing them against her enemies.

Such a proclamation of neutrality (to the average French mind) seemed a contradiction of all the ancient laws of honorable conduct. But it was the law of the land, as the French people were to learn soon afterward from

Washington

the reports sent home by their newly appointed diplomatic representative.

This amiable young man, by the name of Edmond Charles Edouard Genêt, arrived in America fully prepared to be a sort of second Benjamin Franklin and to repeat on the banks of the Hudson the success which the famous printer had gained along the shores of the Seine. Franklin had been given free rein to come and go as he pleased. He had been allowed to borrow money, to equip privateers, to address himself directly to the people of France in his efforts to enlist their sympathy for his friends in America.

Genêt, of course, was a great deal younger and could not count upon the personal following of the genial old Philadelphian. But the United States government still owed France millions of dollars. This money, so Genêt reasoned, would now be placed at the disposal of the French emissary to be used by him for a private little warfare upon England and Spain, and America would become a French base of supply in the west, just as ten years before France had been the base of supplies for those Americans who had carried the war into European waters.

In the beginning everything had gone without a hitch.

Genêt had landed in Charleston and the people of that region who had suffered greatly at the hands of the English invaders were loud in their expressions of devotion and gratitude to France. Genêt's trip to Philadelphia had been in the nature of a triumphal procession. But as soon as he had set foot in the temporary capital of the Union, his troubles had begun.

The proclamation of neutrality was not withdrawn. When he inquired what had become of that sacred treaty between his country and the United States, he was given to understand that the treaty had been made between the United States and the King of France and that, since the French people had seen fit to kill their king, the treaty had ceased to function.

When he asked for some of the money that was still owed to France "that he might use it for the sufferers of a slavery revolt in the West Indies" (in truth that he might equip a few filibustering expeditions against England and Spain), Mr. Hamilton met him with a flat refusal.

When his frigates took their prizes into an American harbor, the English minister got busy with lawyers and injunctions and prevented their sale, and when in sheer despair he addressed himself directly to the Senate and the House of Representatives (who in his eyes were the representatives of the popular will) the Secretary of State returned the document with a very curt and rude letter and sent word to Paris to ask the Directors to recall their envoy.

But that was not all. The next year the American government which, according to its treaty obligations (as the French interpreted them), ought to have been at war with England, sent Chief Justice John Jay to London with instructions to arrange for a treaty of amity, commerce, and navigation between the United States and Great Britain and allow the erstwhile enemies to become staunch friends.

When this was reported in the European newspapers, not only did the Parisian coffeehouses resound with abuse of the contemptible republic which seemed to place profit before friendship, but in America, too, there was such an outburst of anger as had not been witnessed since the early panicky days of the Revolution.

The House of Representatives even went so far as to ask for a copy of this singular document that was said to have been drawn up in London a few months before, only to be told that the power of making treaties was outside of the jurisdiction of the House and that the members of that august body would see it when they would be asked to discuss the provisions for its execution but not a day sooner.

In vain did Hamilton (who upon one occasion was almost killed by a mob of infuriated citizens) and the other advisers of the President try to persuade the public that the Jay treaty was an act of absolute necessity and that without it the complications and ramifications of the great European war might cause an outbreak of hostilities between England and America. The Republicans refused to be satisfied and the agitation continued until the year 1796, when the time had come for a new election.

Washington was asked to serve a third term but he refused. Not because he did not think it right for any citizen to be President of the United States three times, but because he was tired. He wanted to go back to his own home, to sleep in his own bed, to eat from his own table, to enjoy the few simple pleasures of being with his own family before it was too late.

He was sixty-four years old. During the last twenty years he had never known a moment of rest. These two decades had been one endless succession of campaigns and debates and meetings and misunderstandings and abuse.

Just before he gave up the famous coach and four of his high office he issued a public farewell, a sort of political testament for the benefit of the nation he loved so well and for which he had (within the limits of his ability and understanding) made such great sacrifices.

He urged his friends to think a little less of the state and a little more of the common country.

He bade them not to let mere partisanship influence them in all their decisions.

And then he warned them against the people of that vast European continent whom he had always distrusted and from whom he expected no good for his own country.

*Europe,* so he wrote, *has a set of primary interests*

*which to us have no, or a very remote, relation. Hence
she must be engaged in frequent controversies, the causes
of which are essentially foreign to our concern. Hence
therefore it would be unwise in us to implicate ourselves
by artificial ties in the ordinary vicissitudes of her politics
or the ordinary combinations of her friendships and en-
mities. And it is our true policy to steer clear of permanent alliances with any portion of the foreign world.*

On the fourth of March of the year 1797 John Adams
of Massachusetts was installed as President. Washington
attended the ceremonies. When they were over, he walked
out of the hall behind the new President and Vice-President, took a carriage, and drove to Mount Vernon.

Two years later he died, quietly, peacefully, almost as
deliberately as he had lived.

## Chapter Thirty-Three

# HIS EXCELLENCY PRESIDENT JOHN ADAMS
LEARNS THAT A REVOLUTION AND A REVO-
LUTION ARE NOT ALWAYS THE SAME

ACCORDING to the Concise Oxford Dictionary, the word
"revolution" means: "A complete change; turning up-
side down; great reversal of conditions; fundamental reconstruction, especially forcible substitution by subjects
of a new ruler or polity for the old."

If we accept this definition (and it seems to cover the
case thoroughly and impartially) then America between
the years 1775-1783 and France between the years 1789-
1795 passed both of them through a full-fledged revolution. In both countries there was a complete change, a
great reversal of conditions, a fundamental reconstruction, and a forcible substitution by subjects of a new
ruler or a new polity for the old.

What more reasonable therefore than to expect these
two sister republics to become fast friends?

They lived at different ends of the world.

The French Revolution

They were not business rivals in the strict sense of the word.

And furthermore, France had rendered very important services to America during the days of her rebellion against the mother country.

But it came quite otherwise. And the leaders on both sides of the ocean had to learn that a revolution may be a revolution and yet something quite different.

When such great events occur it is difficult for the contemporary observers to know what is actually happening. They are like soldiers on the field of battle. All around them there is confusion and smoke and noise. If they are lucky enough to survive they may be informed of the details of the encounter by some competent historian, fifty or a hundred years later.

Almost a century and a half have gone by since these events occurred. The cause of the ill-feeling between France and America which puzzled so many honest Frenchmen and Americans is no longer a puzzle to us.

In America the revolution had meant a change of sovereignty which had placed the power of the new state in the hands of the property holders, the aristocrats, the upper classes.

In France the revolution had meant a change of sovereignty which had placed the power of the new state in the hands of the disinherited masses, the democrats, the submerged masses of the slums.

In America the new government was composed of such respectable and highly solvent citizens as Washington, Adams, and Hamilton.

In France the men who took charge of affairs were the penniless son of a bankrupt notary public, born in a half-barbarous island of the Mediterranean; an impecunious captain of engineers; a broken-down nobleman who had turned adventurer; and a few other politicians of no special social or economic prominence, all of them slightly the worse for wear.

But also in the way in which the two revolutions had been conducted there had been a startling difference.

The Americans had been protected from their enemy by three thousand miles of water.

The French had lived next door to theirs.

The Americans, once the first few battles had been won, had had their hands free. The loyalists, without arms or armies, had fled to distant parts, to Nova Scotia and to England, and had almost immediately ceased to count as an element of real danger.

In France, on the other hand, plots on the part of the Crown, the nobility, the clergy, and the peasants had created a state of panic during which the people in a sudden attack of unreasoning fear had been guilty of the most terrible atrocities.

As a result, while both countries could boast of having done a very thorough job of housecleaning, they had grown so far away from each other that they could not possibly hope to understand each other.

The new government of America had moved into the front parlor of a substantial colonial mansion. While the French rulers, half dead from fatigue and loss of sleep, conducted the affairs of their nation from a couple of cellars and garrets in an old and ruined royal palace.

When Mr. John Adams and his distinguished wife (née Abigail Smith) enlivened their morning's coffee with a perusal of the letters of Mr. Gouverneur Morris, the American minister to Paris, and learned how that gentleman had failed in his attempts to let the King and Queen escape from the hoodlums and apaches of the suburbs, how that King and Queen had been treated like ordinary criminals by their former subjects, how these former subjects in their new-modish and absurd trousers (which reached to the ankles) and without any wigs at all, but with long shining bayonets on their guns, were now overrunning the whole of civilized Europe, proclaiming those monstrous doctrines of "equality" of which the unfortunate Mr. Jefferson (who really ought to know better) was forever prattling, and "fraternity"—then they could only shake their dignified heads and regret that an erstwhile respectable nation had so far fallen from grace and had become almost as shabby and as disreputable as the crowd of people who had supported the rebellion of that despicable Captain Daniel Shays.

And a little later when Mr. Adams had moved to the presidential mansion and discovered that several millions of his fellow citizens were actually hooray-ing for these murderers and thieves who now ruled poor, afflicted France; that Republican penny-a-liners were filling the newspapers with long harangues about the superior virtues of the French constitution, the bravery of the French soldiers, the devotion of the French women; then he was more firmly than ever convinced that the country was on the verge of civil war and that it was time (in the parlance of the press) to do something.

What this "something" was to be, neither the President nor his advisers could tell, but luck handed them a straight flush which they played with great dexterity.

Genêt's bumptiousness in America and Morris's pronounced affection for the Bourbon family had left the two countries without diplomatic representation. John Adams, however, knew how very badly the United States, after their long and exhausting struggle for independence, were in need of a rest and he positively refused to get involved in a war. Wherefore, with a pleasant gesture of "Oh, well, let bygones be bygones!" he sent John Marshall, Elbridge Gerry, and Charles Pinckney to Paris on a general mission of peace and good will. He did not expect that they would be able to accomplish very much but an outward semblance of cordial relations would serve both countries better than the present state of semi-hostility and unofficial bickering.

The three Americans arrived in Paris at a moment when France was smarting deeply under her loss of naval power and felt very badly about the hospitality which the American harbor officials were said to be extending to British war vessels with French prizes. Furthermore, as the French did not fail to point out to their transatlantic visitors, there seemed to be one law for the English and one for the French. For the French, just as soon as they laid hands on an American ship that was bound for England or one of the British colonies, were sure to be bombarded with angry letters from Washington. But no matter how many American merchantmen the English captured, the American government never even protested while the American minister in London continued to be on the most cordial terms with the British foreign minister and was not infrequently seen to take a friendly cup of tea with that haughty dignitary.

To this the American commissioners could have given all sorts of answers. They could have replied that the American government being without a navy was more immediately at the mercy of the English than of the French; that the American minister in London was forever complaining about the illegal acts which the British navy committed on the high seas, even if he occasionally dined with the foreign minister, and other words to that effect. But as they had come as harbingers of peace, they wisely refrained from starting a debate that would have led to no practical result and approached the directors with certain plans that would solve all of the pending difficulties.

And they might have been successful if at this inopportune moment they had been able to escape the attention of what the French call the "haute finance."

"High finance" is something different from ordinary banking and pawnbroking and thrives almost exclusively upon war. Governments suddenly find themselves in immediate need of large sums of money. Whole armies of international crooks then descend upon their capitals, besiege their ministers with preposterous offers of assistance, and surround these poor officials with such a network of intrigue that only the most hardy and cunning can hope to escape without being incriminated and besmirched.

The three American delegates now found themselves hounded by a quartet of very persistent "high financiers" who assured them that they had inside information and could be of great service to the Americans—for a consideration, of course. This was quite according to the rules of the diplomatic game as played in the latter half of the eighteenth century. An occasional tip to a foreign minister was the customary thing. Almost anyone could use a snuffbox in those days of lace sleeves and lace hankies, and if the box happened to be filled with golden ducats, well—that was very nice, for then the recipient could buy himself some prime "Rappée de Copenhague" and even save a little for carfare.

The American delegates knew this and it seems that they would have been willing to hand a couple of dollars to M. Barras, who was a man of influence and who was said to have rather expensive tastes. But when in addition to this private graft the Directors hinted that the United States should grant them a loan of several million dollars, they refused point-blank. Such a transaction would have meant a breach of neutrality, it would have caused an outbreak of war between England and America, and furthermore, no self-respecting government could allow itself to be blackmailed in quite so crude a fashion.

The details of the whole intrigue are not known to this day. But when the correspondence that had passed between the American envoys and the French go-betweens reached Philadelphia, the Federalist leaders recognized the wonderful political weapon which the Directors had so gratuitously placed in their hands. They published all the letters, omitting the real names and substituting the letters X, Y, and Z for the signatures of the implicated French officials. Then they turned to the Republicans and said, "See! That is the sort of people your friends over yonder are! Those are the men for whom you feel such profound admiration."

But they went further. In the excitement of the moment they passed a number of laws that should protect the country from any further outbreaks of discontent on the part of the Republicans. The first of these measures, the so-called Alien Law, increased the number of years during which one must be a resident of the United States in order to become a citizen and raised that period from five to fourteen; it gave the President the right to arrest or deport any alien whom he considered undesirable, and it allowed the Federal authorities to arrest or exile any person who belonged to a country with which the United States were at war.

The second one, the well-known Sedition Law, made it a crime, punishable by imprisonment or fine, to publish any false, scandalous, or malicious writings against the government of the United States, the President, or the Houses of Congress, or to stir up opposition to any lawful act of Congress or of the President or to aid the designs of any foreign power against the United States.

These laws had considerable justification in the campaign of vituperation which a number of Irish exiles were conducting in the American newspapers against the government of Great Britain, but they were much too drastic and they spread great dismay among a large class of the population. All the work of these last seven years spent to destroy the autocratic power of a central government seemed to have been undone by the stroke of a Federalist pen. The decrees of the new Star Chamber were signed *John Adams, President* instead of *George Rex*. Otherwise apparently nothing had changed, and contrary to the provisions of the Constitution the citizens of the Republic were now to be deprived of the right of free speech and the press was to lose its much vaunted freedom.

When here and there officious Federal judges began to sentence harmless citizens because at some obscure political meeting they had dared to question the Jehovah-like wisdom of the government and condemned editors to jail on account of editorials which criticized the expediency of some presidential decree, the anger of the more democratic part of the nation made itself felt in a concrete threat of agitation.

The center of this opposition was Thomas Jefferson. Since he had resigned from Washington's cabinet he had lived quietly on his estate near Charlottesville in Virginia and with almost Roman austerity had kept aloof from his favorite game of politics.

The shrewd old gentleman, however, possessed of that voracious appetite for letter-writing which was characteristic of so many of the philosophers and scientists of the eighteenth century, was in daily correspondence with all the prominent men among the Republican party. He guided every move. He inspired the editorials in the Republican papers and whenever the leaders of his party did not know what policy to follow, they invited themselves for a week-end to Monticello and over a glass of port (Mount Vernon served Madeira) they talked of ways and means to bring their aristocratic opponents to terms.

Therefore when the state legislatures of Virginia and Kentucky passed formal resolutions declaring the Sedition Law null and void as being in direct violation of the articles of the Constitution, everyone recognized Jefferson's fine Italian hand in those eloquent but dangerous "nullification" documents and many people said that this was merely a desperate Republican effort to rid the country of the ever-growing tendency toward centralization which was so dear to the hearts of the Federalists.

In how far these two laws and the dispute about nullification affected the coming elections, it is difficult to say.

It almost seems as if there were seasons in the realm of politics, as there are in the domain of nature and in the fields of fashion. Spring follows upon winter, long skirts succeed short skirts, a period of government by the rich makes room for a period of government by the poor; and try however they may, no farmer, no dressmaking establishment, no statesman has ever been able to alter this normal course of events.

At the elections of 1800 the Federalists were defeated and the Republicans were successful.

The moneyed classes predicted an era of anarchy.

The frontiersmen burned bonfires to celebrate the end of the "plutocratic reign of terror."

And Mr. Adams returned to Boston, while Mr. Jefferson packed his valise and wrote a note to the managers of Conrad's well-known boardinghouse in the city of Washington and asked them if they would kindly reserve a room for him early in March of the next year.

## Chapter Thirty-Four

# THOMAS JEFFERSON, PRESIDENT OF THE UNITED STATES OF AMERICA, AND THE EMPEROR NAPOLEON CONCLUDE AN IMPORTANT DEAL IN REAL ESTATE

"No STEW," so the old proverb says, "is ever eaten as hot as it was cooked."

And no radical political party is ever quite as radical, once it has been called to power, as it promised to be during the exciting days just before the election.

Mr. Jefferson out of office was against every form of official interference with the rights of the states and the individual. Mr. Jefferson in office soon recognized that no government can hope to survive unless it actually "governs."

Whether one drives to the Capitol building in a coach and four or goes on foot to deliver a message to Congress is after all a very small and negligible detail. Whether one prefers being called Your Mightiness or likes the less formal, "Hey there, Tom!" is largely a matter of personal taste.

But when the President of the United States, speaking *ex cathedra* (if I may borrow an expression from a somewhat older democratic establishment) when the President in his quality of President says, "This, my fellow citizens, is the law of the land as duly laid down by those legislative bodies which you have elected for the purpose and as solemnly signed by me," then he must either see that his will is enforced or he must go out of business.

Now Jefferson happened to be one of the best educated of our presidents—a man thoroughly versed in the history of the past—a widely read student of antiquity—a philosopher with a sense of humor who understood the common run of the American people as well as he did his own house slaves. And he knew—what every statesman from the days of Hammurabi on has known—that it is infinitely better to have a few very definite laws and enforce them thoroughly than a whole sheaf of decrees and regulations which are so impractical that they become a dead letter the day they are signed and are therefore openly flaunted both by the public at large and by the courts. And one of the first things Jefferson did as soon as he had assumed office was to get rid of as many of the Federalist laws and the Federalist officers as he could without running the risk of upsetting the entire political and commercial life of the nation.

The Sedition Act was, of course, repealed. The navy, in so far as it was reducible, was diminished to something resembling the absolute zero. Civil servants who were not indispensable were encouraged to find other jobs. Every effort was made to rid the country of its national debt.

The President even economized on shoe leather. For he kept strictly to his end of Pennsylvania Avenue and whenever he was obliged to make a communication to Congress, he sent his message by a messenger-boy.

All these measures, however, were as purely destructive as the impeachment of Judge Samuel Chase, a veteran of the Declaration of Independence, who suffered from high

206

blood pressure and who in his choleric wrath had used the Alien and Sedition Laws to turn his court into a private little Star Chamber.

They were destructive, and Jefferson was too positive a character to be contented with a negative program.

But when at last he began his policy of reconstruction, it became clear that this slovenly gentleman-farmer from Albemarle County (a somewhat nonchalant disguise worn to impress the populace with the superior virtues of Democracy as compared with the outward splendor of Federalist pomp), that this simple backwoodsman had got hold of a fact which somehow or other had always escaped the attention of the rest of the statesmen who had tried to rule the world and which made him understand that political improvement without a corresponding amount of economic improvement is absolutely without value and is not worth bothering about.

Take the case of France.

Before the Great Revolution the nobleman drove in a fine barouche. The peasant went on foot. Neither of them felt a sense of grievance. The nobleman, when still a child, had been informed by his grandmother and by his church that it was his part in life to drive in a barouche, and the peasant, from the days of his cradle, had been told by his great-grandmother (peasants usually live so much longer) and his church that he and his sort were expected to go on foot from the hour of his birth to the moment of his death.

Then came the eighteenth century which cast a doubt upon the wisdom of both the grandparents and the village priests.

"Why," so the Voltaires and Diderots and Rousseaus asked, "should one class of society always drive in a coach and why should the other always plod through the mud?"

The nobles might have avoided the subsequent crisis if they had been willing to compromise—give the peasant an occasional lift—let him keep enough money for a small wagon of his own. But the nobility had gone too long to the school of grandmothers and spiritual advisers to be able to learn anything new. A few of the brighter members of their class warned the others. They were called "dirty radicals" for their trouble and were thrown on their ear. And so the inevitable happened. There was a revolution. And by act of the legislature the peasant was made the equal of the nobleman.

But did that give him a ride in the coach?

No. It did not.

It told him that he could drive in a coach if he wanted to, that there wasn't a law in the land to tell who should drive in coaches and who should not. But in order to drive in a coach, one must first of all be able to pay for a coach. And the poor peasant with all his theoretical rights lacked the practical assets necessary for the acquisition and maintenance of even a single little donkey cart.

Instead of one class of society going on foot and the other driving in a carriage, both of them now waded through the mud of the neglected highroads. One class had lost everything and the other had gained nothing.

What Jefferson knew and what he was one of the first to put into practice was this: that there is only one way to give a man who has become politically free the true benefit of his newly acquired dignity and that is by increasing "production" until there shall be enough for all those who are willing to do their bit.

Production, of course, means hard work. But it also means that the average man will get a much greater share of necessities and luxuries than before.

Jefferson was not a lover of machinery and feared that the manufacturing system would only lead to an unnatural and dangerous preponderance of the cities. He believed that the future of the country lay with the farmers, that the true strength of the land was vested in the frontier.

He may have been right and he may have been wrong, but as long as he was left in peace and was not forced by the threat of war to out-federalize the despised Federalists in their desire for a strong centralized form of government, he lived up to his convictions and threw all the strength of the Republican party into his plans for the improvement of agricultural conditions.

In this he was greatly helped by outward circumstances. But then, he had always been a lucky fellow. If he had been more of a dogmatic Christian he would have approved of Doctor Calvin's ideas upon the subject of predestination. As it was, he quietly accepted whatever good things fate brought him and found solace in Marcus Aurelius and Don Quixote.

If we wanted to go really back to original causes (as it is sometimes claimed that historians must do) I would now have to tell you of the year 1100 when the ancient family of the Buonapartes left Florence and began that strange peregrination which was to carry one of their members via Sarzana and Ajaccio to the banks of the Seine and was to make him heir to the traditions of Caesar and Charlemagne. But this history being too long as it is, I shall take it for granted that you know all about the French revolutionary wars and that you are familiar with the European political situation of the year 1803.

Three years before Napoleon had by a secret deal with the King of Spain again got hold of that vast French colony called Louisiana which, as a result of the imperial and royal land-grabbing schemes of the eighteenth century had been ceded to Spain in the year 1762. But although he never learned to speak the language of his adopted country without an accent, Napoleon was a typical Frenchman in his lack of ability to look beyond the frontiers of his adopted fatherland.

His long training in reading military maps undoubtedly told him that the city of New Orleans had great strategic value as the finger that could be held on the great Mississippi funnel, and could stop the even flow of agricultural products from the western hinterland. But the word Louisiana meant as little to him as the name of Canada had done to the contemporaries of Louis XIV. And the same man who would abolish a thousand-year-old empire before breakfast and would change the entire map of Europe three times between luncheon and dinner allowed more than eighteen months to go by before he thought of making definite preparation for the occupancy of his new territory.

Meanwhile of course the transaction between Paris and Madrid had leaked out. Rufus King, who was *persona grata* at the court of St. James, heard of it in London and reported the rumor to Madison, who was Jefferson's Secretary of State. Madison told it to Jefferson and the President was greatly disturbed. Millions of acres of land west of the Allegheny Mountains had been occupied by his beloved pioneers. They depended for the export of their grain and their furs on the Mississippi River. As long as a weak power like Spain held the keys of New Orleans, all was well. If the worst came to the worst, the frontiersmen could march down upon that neglected fortress and clean out the hidalgos. But once let this terrible Napoleon person (who could defeat anybody and anything) get hold of this valuable spot and the entire West would be bottled up for good. It was indeed a very serious matter and there was no use asking for the sympathy of the Federalists. They did not believe in the West. Their true interests lay on the other side of the ocean and whenever their colleagues debated the point, "Be it resolved that it would be foolish for the United States to acquire more western territory," the verdict was sure to go to the "ayes."

Of course as a true democrat, a plain, simple, and straightforward man, Jefferson did not believe in secret diplomacy. But this question was so ticklish that he thought it better to handle it with a certain discretion. He therefore asked his friend James Monroe (also a native of Westmoreland County in Virginia) to go to Paris and see what could be done and whether the French, who like all warlike nations were forever in need of money, could perhaps be persuaded to sell their American interests to their friends in Washington for a consideration in gold. Monroe accepted the mission and took ship.

But ere he reached Paris, the sale had been practically completed.

For once the right man had happened to be in the right place.

Robert Livingston, the American minister to France,

was a born promoter. He had already begun an agitation for the sale of New Orleans and the surrounding territory to the United States and had furthered his chances of success by a widespread whispering campaign (if one can use the word "whispering" for the usual indiscreet conversation of the French salons) which pointed to the dangers of a new war between France and England and to the certain loss of the French colonies which would be the result of such a clash.

The Indian grave

"Wasn't it much better," so this cleverly worded propaganda asked, "to sell a few square miles of wilderness now and get some money for them rather than lose them afterward and get nothing for them at all?"

That the Americans set so much store by the possession of New Orleans that many of them were willing to go to war to get this city was another point which he might have made. But the French, as he well knew, were a proud race and therefore much stress was laid upon the commercial aspect of the case but the military side was not touched. By a stroke of great good luck, Napoleon's minister of finance was the son of a former governor of Pennsylvania and had lived for a considerable time in America. This worthy, by the name of Marbois, was just then engaged upon the difficult task of trying to collect a sufficient amount of money for the next war. When he heard that Monroe's ship had been sighted, that the American plenipotentiary was coming with a whole cargo of golden dollars, he hastened to his master, the first Consul, and explained certain plans of his own. As a result of this conference, Napoleon the next day told his minister of foreign affairs (no one else than our friend, M. de Talleyrand, the Mr. X of President Adams's revelation) to send for Livingston and to open negotiations for the sale of Louisiana.

Mr. Livingston accordingly called upon M. de Talleyrand and asked him how much he would take for New Orleans.

M. de Talleyrand answered by inquiring how much Mr. Livingston would offer for the whole of Louisiana.

This was a somewhat startling offer, even to so astute a man of business as Livingston. He asked for time to think. Meanwhile Monroe had reached Paris with the latest news from Washington. All day long the two American delegates talked about their next move. Then they went to dine and behold, just when the dinner was nearing its end, Marbois happened in for a cup of coffee. He was delighted to make the acquaintance of the distinguished M. Monroe and hinted that if the Americans came to his office later in the evening, he might be able to tell them something to their advantage.

When they arrived, Marbois told them that he had spent the previous day with General Buonaparte at the court of St. Cloud and that America could have the whole of Louisiana for one hundred million francs. Livingston answered that that was too much and offered less. After some further haggling, Louisiana was sold for sixty million francs or $15,000,000—going—going—gone!

By a stroke of sheer good fortune President Jefferson had doubled the territory of his country at an expense of four cents per acre. Not a bad bargain even for a Yankee. But the Yankees, confirmed Federalists, made a terrible to-do about the whole transaction. The Hon. Timothy Pickering of Salem, Massachusetts, then a member of the United States Senate, went so far as to talk of secession, suggested the founding of a new confederacy of New England states, exempt from the corrupt and corrupting influence of the democrats from the South, and he proposed to the Hon. Aaron Burr, then Vice-President of the United

States, to make him chief executive of the new nation!

Nothing, however, came of all this agitation. The Republicans had learned from their Federalist friends how to force unpopular measures through Congress, while the reflections which Mr. Hamilton cast upon the personal character of Mr. Burr (who was indeed a brilliant scoun-

Exploring the Northwest

drel and a sad bounder) led to a duel in which Mr. Burr shot Mr. Hamilton through the heart and thereby signed his own warrant of exile for the rest of his natural life.

On the twentieth of December of the year 1803 the French tricolor was solemnly lowered from the flagstaff of New Orleans.

In the spring of the next year, Meriwether Lewis of Charlottesville, Virginia, and William Clark of the same city, both of them well versed in the lore of the wilderness, left upon an exploring expedition of that territory which now as in the days of Columbus bore the legend of *Terra*

*Incognita.* They explored the Missouri River, crossed the Rocky Mountains and paddled down the Columbia River until they reached the Pacific, more than two years later. It was one of the most astounding voyages ever undertaken. The percentage of loss (only one man out of twenty-three during three years of constant danger) shows how well those simple Virginia boys knew their business. The country recognized the value of their services, and Lewis was made governor of the northern part of Louisiana territory. He now had to sit in an office and sign papers which he did with his usual devotion to duty until he could not stand the life any longer and departed for the happy hunting grounds of his Indian friends.

While Lewis and Clark were footing it through the northern part of the United States another soldier, Zebulon Montgomery Pike, a New Jerseyite, was investigating the sources of the Mississippi and was making a first survey of that vast stretch of land which still belonged to Spain and which was still considered a *Tierra de Ningun Provecho,* a land without any value.

The men of Jefferson's frontier were not much given to the reading of fairy stories.

They did not have to.

They lived them.

## *Chapter Thirty-Five*

## THE MOTHER COUNTRY PAYS A FINAL VISIT

GENERAL BUONAPARTE hastened to use his unexpected American windfall in true Italian fashion. He went on a debauch of glory, proclaimed himself the logical successor of Charlemagne, and with the grudging co-operation of Pope Pius VII and amidst more ribbons, pieces of gold lace, silks, and plumes than ever had been seen together in a single church, he crowned himself Emperor of the French.

When the other nations of Europe heard this joyful bit of news, they trembled. Every promotion in rank of this strange little man had been followed by wholesale slaughter. For once their imperial and royal highnesses of the North and the West decided to be prepared. They formed a coalition. The emperor of the French expressed his astonishment, and the fight was on.

The American government kept wisely out of this quarrel, and President Jefferson urged his compatriots to be good and not come too near to the conflagration. But very soon the new nation was to learn that our common earth is only a fifth-rate little planet and of such small dimensions that what affects one nation must necessarily affect all others. The method of neutrality made famous by the ostrich could safely be applied when the conflict was restricted to a couple of bushmen tribes in the Kalahari Desert. But a war in which France, Russia, Austria, Sweden, England, and two score minor states took an active part was bound to make itself felt from New Zealand to Hammerfest and from Baffin's Bay to Capetown.

As for Declarations of Neutrality and other such-like solemn documents, they were about as useful as a couple of insurance policies at a fire. The two contending groups in Europe were after each other in dead earnest, and heaven help the poor neutral sailors.

In this instance the situation was further complicated by the fact that the English sank the French navy at Trafalgar but that Napoleon sank the armies of the allies near Austerlitz.

The fable of the lion and the elephant had come true. England was master of the sea and France held sway over the land. From the high rocks of Boulogne the French sailors could shake their fists at the distant cliffs of Dover and from the poop deck of their sovereign's flagship the British tars could make faces at the little children who were baking mud pies on the beach of Barfleur. But neither side could get at the other. Napoleon could not leave dry land and the English could not go on shore. Under those circumstances they were obliged to change their technique of mutual destruction and they did so after the old and trusted habit of all big nations, by sacrificing the rights of the small ones.

To begin with in May of the year 1806 England declared the entire western half of Europe to be in a state of blockade. Napoleon answered this by a decree signed in November of the same year by which he from his side declared the British Isles to be in a state of blockade. Thus the neutrals, as always happens in a general European war, were given the choice between the French devil and the English deep sea and if they had not been so utterly helpless they would have used some big, bold words.

To make matters still more difficult for the hungry sailors of all the world, both France and England were loudly clamoring for the products of the American soil and were willing to pay fancy prices for grain and munitions of war. After all, the skippers of the United States were only human. Their war for independence had taught them to laugh at blockades. But a double-barreled blockade was something new in their lives and they proceeded very cautiously. Then England, which could not feed its people without assistance from abroad, offered a compromise and promised that American ships would be allowed to carry so-called contraband goods to France if they would first call at an English port and pay a tax and get a permit to deal with the enemy.

"Very well," answered Napoleon, "but in that case I shall be obliged to consider every ship that carries such a license as a hostile craft."

Both capture and confiscation continued with a most uncomfortable regularity and millions of dollars were lost by the honest American merchants and still more millions by the dishonest ones and some said, "Now is the time to declare war upon England," and others argued, "We must go and fight the French," and then they all went to Washington and asked President Jefferson, "Please do something!"

That, however, was exactly what Jefferson hoped to avoid. He was a man of peace. War seemed an absurdity to him. It might be necessary occasionally to fire a couple of broadsides into those Tripolitan pirate vessels which were trying to blackmail the American government, but for enlightened nations to spill the blood of their most promising children for some absurd purpose of gain or glory, perish the thought! And the President instead of preparing for war quietly allowed the remnants of the army and the navy to slip into such a state of neglect that both France and England ceased to worry any further about the United States and henceforth plundered their American friends as unconcernedly as if they had been the citizens of some small Scandinavian state.

But if they thought that this would cause no resentment on the other side of the ocean, they were mistaken. Thomas Jefferson was a philosopher but not a pacifist. And while refusing to go to war, his nimble brain was evolving a new and highly original scheme of dealing with these high-handed procedures, which if it had been given a fair trial would have brought both groups of his enemies to their knees.

Thus far all the interference had come from the side of the British and the French. Quite suddenly in the year 1807 the United States began to do a little blockading of its own. Jefferson and his ministers knew that both France and England were in desperate need of American grain. Therefore, in December of 1807, they ordered all American vessels to remain at home until further notice and sent word to London and Paris that not another bushel of American grain or bale of American cotton would be forwarded to Europe until these two governments had promised to behave themselves and leave the American traders alone.

Unfortunately the Jeffersonian idea of an embargo did not work. The respectable merchants were ruined in less than no time. The others (the vast majority) turned smugglers and piled up millions. The greater part of all this money, however, went into the pockets of neutral middlemen and meanwhile the farmers and lumbermen of the West and the bona fide sailors of the seaboard fell upon such hard times as they had never experienced before.

The outcry of this large and influential group of people

who saw themselves headed for the bankruptcy court was so loud and so persistent that the Embargo Act was repealed and was replaced by a Non-Intercourse Act which forbade all trade with England and France but allowed America to deal with the "neutral" European nations. But again a lack of knowledge of the true situation in Europe made Jefferson take the wrong step. These so-called "neutral" nations were sovereign in name only and had long since ceased to function as independent units. And so American commerce continued to be annoyed and bothered and American ships continued to be dragged into this port and to be detained in that and it became more and more evident to the people at home that the whole business would lead to war. Already upon several occasions while peace still hovered over the waters, the crew of an American square-rigger had undertaken to do battle upon a French or an English man-of-war and it had taken a great deal of diplomatic laundering to iron these difficulties out of the spotless linen marked with the crest of *Absolute Neutrality*.

Even at this late hour the difficulty might have been settled amicably among the diplomats of the three nations if it had not been for the ancient and far from honorable British institution known as the "press gang." Impressment was the popular name for a haphazard sort of conscription which was quite common on the European continent until our friend from Corsica made every man a soldier or a sailor and turned every nation into an armed camp.

The sovereign (according to the medieval conception of law) had the right to make war, therefore the sovereign had the right to provide himself with the instrument necessary for a successful campaign, *i.e.*, an army. As no one in his senses likes the idea of being killed and will refuse to expose himself to actual violence unless he himself is in immediate danger of attack, it was never easy to get the required number of soldiers. Hence the pleasant habit of His Majesty's tipstaffs of emptying the prisons and of raiding saloons and respectable beer gardens and dragging the occupants to the nearest war vessel to become jolly tars and lead the life of galley slaves until the re-establishment of peace.

Needless to point out that these pickpockets and footpads (not to mention perfectly peaceful tailors and clerks who had gone out for a bit of air and a mug of ale) did not make ideal sailors. By the time they had learned the difference between a backstay and a topping-lift they were apt to be dead from an enemy's bullet or from one of those forms of disease which the jailbirds carried to the fleet and which turned so many ships into floating hospitals. It was necessary therefore to get hold of a few real seamen and these were only to be found on the merchantmen. Hence the practice of waiting for all returning commercial vessels and depriving them of the greater part of their crew. And when the English merchant marine had been despoiled of man power (until some of the ships could not so much as hoist a single topsail), then His Majesty's officers began to board foreign bottoms, insisted that all likely-looking young fellows were in reality runaway Britishers and enlisted them (with the help of irons and chains) into the forces that were fighting the evil powers of despotism and autocracy.

This habit (for a habit it became) was most annoying to the American shipowners. A Danish or Dutch captain who was mustering a crew could easily tell the difference between an Englishman and a native but how could a Charleston skipper tell whether John Doe who came to him for a job was born in Salem, Massachusetts, or Salem, Jamaica?

There were his papers.

But has anybody ever heard of a sailor who bothered about such trifles as a birth certificate or a passport? No, there was nothing for the average American skipper to do but to take his chance, run away if his ship were the faster or submit to search when the English bullets began to knock the splinters from his bowsprit.

While ocean travel was in this sad, sad plight, the day came for Mr. Jefferson to pack his trunks and leave the national capital. Like Washington before him, the third President of the United States was more than willing to devote the rest of his days to his horses and his dogs. He was sixty-six years old and had spent the last four decades in the service of his country. Few had rendered such tremendous services to the new nation as this shrewd old gentleman from Virginia and few (with the possible exception of Washington) had been abused as scandalously for their supposed shortcomings. Jefferson's friends offered him a third term, but he declined. Henceforth he was to be a spectator. He returned to Monticello, devoted himself to the upbuilding of the University of Virginia, quietly preached his doctrine of common sense and personal independence and left the affairs of state to his good friend, James Madison, who had been his Secretary of State for eight years and who was therefore supposed to know foreign affairs better than anyone else.

James Madison, the fourth of our Presidents, was less of an idealist than his predecessors and his many years as Secretary of State had deprived him of most of his illusions about the lovingkindness of the human race. He had been obliged to submit to the insults of bullying British ministers (the first of the English diplomatic representatives to the new Republic had with rare tact been chosen from among the sons of an American loyalist family) and the next instant he had listened to their assurances of friendship; he had discovered the crookedness of the Napoleonic diplomats and had heard much about their undying admiration for the memory of the great Doctor Franklin and he knew that neither side cared a hoot about the rights of American commerce or would change its policy of Schrecklichkeit until forced to do so by the presence of a sufficient number of American cruisers.

That mere paper ultimatums would accomplish nothing he had learned on the fatal day when the British ship *Leopard* of fifty guns had stopped the American frigate *Chesapeake* (which was fresh from the wharf and had not even got her guns in position) had killed and wounded twenty-one of her men, had arrested four alleged deserters and then had joined the English squadron which, if you please, was taking in a fresh supply of water off Norfolk. This affair had of course been at once reported to London and the British Foreign Office had promised a full apology. But the work of telling the Americans how sorry their British friends were at this outrageous breach of neutrality, if not hospitality, had been entrusted to one of those top-lofty emissaries who since the beginning of our independence have been thought good enough for the post in Washington and who unassisted have managed to cause more ill-feeling between the two countries than all the coal men and the oil men who are usually blamed for the rivalries that exist between the two great democracies.

The period of talk and irritation continued for another four years, and what with Indian rebellions (instigated, so it was said and believed, by British agents) and pitched battles between English press gangs and American skippers and great political upheavals at home which brought into action a new and fire-eating party of so-called "Young Republicans," the administration of Madison was not exactly that era of peace and good will of which the founders of the Republic had dreamed.

As for the war which finally broke out between the mother country and her former colonies, that, too, caused many unpleasant moments to those whose memories reached back to the proud days of Saratoga and Yorktown.

There were dreadful dissensions among the different states. The New Englanders, of whose "mercenary spirit" and "lack of patriotism" George Washington had complained so bitterly as soon as he had assumed command of their armies, once more showed that they regarded themselves as a different people.

The Embargo and the Non-Intercourse Acts had not worried them. From the days of the old Plymouth Colony on, they had always been engaged in the smuggling business and they had experienced very little difficulty in evading those measures of Congress which forbade commerce with the English and the French. As soon, however, as war had been declared, they were forced to stop their illegal practices and to give a thought to the country. They now loudly blamed their southern and western neighbors for having brought about a war without a justifiable cause—their newspapers clamored for nullification—and at a meeting in Hartford the delegates from five New England states worked out a complete plan for the foundation of a separate New England Confederacy.

Under such circumstances it would have been foolish to look for anything resembling a brilliant military victory —for another storming of the citadel of Quebec—for another surprise at Montreal.

On the sea, where the sailors of the American merchant marine had been fighting against great odds for almost a dozen years, there were several encounters which ended in a victory for the United States.

But on land, one disaster followed another.

It was no doubt a proud day for all good patriots when young Mr. Henry Clay of Kentucky declared that the militia of Kentucky alone would be able to conquer Canada in less than a month. But when it was found that the militia either would not fight at all, or refused to leave its own territory in pursuit of the enemy, or insisted upon going home the day their term of enlistment was over (and all these things actually occurred), then even the ardor of the young War Hawks began to cool.

When in addition valuable American fortresses were surrendered without firing a shot (as happened in Detroit in August of the year 1812), when the American capital was left to the mercy of an invading British force (which set fire to the city and the White House and the other official buildings on the ground that "civilians had fired at soldiers"), when British marines were allowed to burn and plunder to their hearts' content in the very heart of Maryland, there arose such a storm of dissatisfaction with the unfortunate and ill-served President that nothing, not even Perry's much heralded victory on the Great Lakes, could prevent the collapse of his party.

And then it was Europe which mysteriously saved the American Republic from further humiliation. It happened in this way. The endless Napoleonic wars had completely exhausted Great Britain and the country was on the verge of a collapse. Finally in October of the year 1813 Napoleon had been defeated at Leipzig and had been

municate with the possessions in South America, an attempt was made to return to the good old days of the seventeenth century. And then it became apparent that something had changed after all and that a new social influence was beginning to make itself felt in a part of the world which thus far had seemed to be as completely set for the ages as Charleston, South Carolina.

I refer to the question of the Creoles.

The Creoles were descendants of white people who had settled in the colonies many years before and sometimes many centuries before. They themselves therefore were white but they had been born in the colonies and this fact in the eyes of the officials who had seen the light of day in the old world, bestowed upon them a slight social stigma of which they could never rid themselves. They were white, and before the law they were in every way the equal of their Spanish masters who hailed from Castile or Catalonia. But when it came to practical politics, they found themselves completely excluded from participation in the government of their native provinces. In short, they were the people who paid the taxes and were then invited to stand by and smile sweetly while one governor after another enriched himself at their expense.

Needless to say that they did not like this. But they were without political training and without political organization and they were divided into different clans which hated each other most cordially and so nothing was ever done to improve their situation and they remained what our English friends call "colonials."

Young Bolivar belonged to such a family and was the embodiment of all its manifold failings and virtues. He was brave, he was generous, he could stand enormous physical hardships and the day after he was beaten he was ready for another fight. But he lacked all the qualities necessary for the successful conduct of a highly complicated rebellion. Besides, his early training as member of a provincial aristocracy, accustomed to lord it over vast armies of half-breeds and docile little Indians, had warped his entire outlook upon life and had not made him an ideal man to command an army in the field.

In North America it had happened that the interests of the landed gentry of Virginia and the commercial classes of Boston coincided at least to a certain degree with those of the majority of the farmers and artisans and as a result George Washington and John Adams (typical representatives of their respective classes) had been able to render great services to the common cause. But in South America where the Spanish officials, the Creoles, the half-castes and the natives were each other's sworn enemies, the ideals of liberty, fraternity, and equality had about as much chance to take root as mustard seed in Greenland.

Notwithstanding those many and quite terrible handicaps, Bolivar in the north and San Martin in the south succeeded in creating a movement for political independence which swept across the entire South American continent and placed the power of government in the hands of the old established families.

Roughly speaking, this movement for independence began in the year 1811 with an uprising on the part of the Venezuelans and it ended in the year 1823 when Mexico threw off the Spanish yoke.

That was quite a long time, and of course the Spanish government did not sit idly by and wait for the erring children to return to the fold. On the contrary, the Bourbons did everything they could to reconquer the lost provinces, but they had lost most of their ships during the Napoleonic wars, there wasn't a peso left in the family treasure chest, and the ghastly guerilla warfare between the French and the Spaniards had been a terrible drain upon the country's man power.

But at this moment, when all seemed lost (honor included) salvation offered itself from the side of an unexpected friend.

Europe after almost thirty years of uninterrupted fighting was sick and tired of bloodshed and war.

"Peace and order at any price" became the slogan of the generation that survived Waterloo. Now peace and order can always be had at a price. As a rule that price involves the loss of self-government and the substitution of a professional policeman for the power of an elected parliament. When, however, conditions have become so utterly chaotic that business has come to a complete standstill, then large classes of society are invariably found willing to make the sacrifice. And that is what happened in the year 1815.

Their Imperial, Royal, and Serene Highnesses were left in undisturbed possession of the government. And the radicals of day-before-yesterday tried to forget that they had ever sported pictures of Robespierre on the walls of their sitting-rooms and by the exemplary loyalty of their behavior succeeded in making themselves useful and ornamental parts of a highly genteel and respectable society of dyed-in-the-wool conservatives.

A situation like that is never without a touch of humor. And during the great reaction which followed upon the downfall of Napoleon it was Russia which provided the indispensable comic relief.

The Little Father, who then graced the Muscovite throne, was a certain Alexander, the son of Paul. This young man, ever since the unfortunate day of his father's murder, had been a victim of what the vulgar world called "a bad conscience." Now for his sins he fell under the spell of a sentimental and middle-aged Teuton baroness, who saw spooks and was an adept at "New Thought." The "new thought" of the year 1815 was of course not quite like the "new thought" of the year 1927, but it was sufficiently vague and obscure to make a deep impression upon the troubled mind of such a second-rate citizen as Alexander Romanov. And as a result the autocrat of all the Russias proclaimed himself the servant of God's wishes (as revealed at convenient moments by old Frau Krüdener) and in his capacity of world savior he became the spiritual father of a curious political idea, the so-called Holy Alliance.

By the terms of this high-sounding and solemn agreement, the Emperors of Russia and Austria and the King of Prussia, in view of the blessings which Divine Providence had showered upon those states which placed their confidence and hope on it alone, undertook not only to be guided in the administration of their respective states solely by precept of Holy Religion, namely, the precepts of Justice, Christian Charity and Peace, but also to render each other reciprocal service, and having confessed themselves the fathers of their subjects and armies, they invited all other potentates to come and join them for the greater glory of the true Word of Life.

When a high-school fraternity or an obscure conclave of the Ku Klux Klan indulges in that sort of nonsense, the damage done is not very great. But when the Tsar of all the Russias, the commander-in-chief of three million horse guards, foot guards, life guards and Cossacks, begins to talk sweetly of brotherly love, it is time for decent people to look to their guns.

But the only government which at that moment seemed to suspect the danger that might arise from such an Imperial Trade Union was the English. As the British are not called upon to obey the written paragraphs of a constitution (since they haven't got one) they can do a great many things which are impossible to other nations who are always at the mercy of their political decalogue. For example, they can keep the management of foreign affairs within the hands of certain families who have enjoyed a prolonged training in that difficult field of simulation and procrastination, and who are infinitely better fitted for the job than the amateurs who aspire to such offices in other countries.

I do not mean to imply that all English ministers of foreign affairs have been brilliant statesmen and diplomats. But however limited they were in the gift of tongues or their knowledge of geography, they almost invariably understood the true nature of that half-dozen foreign and domestic policies upon which during the last five hundred years Great Britain has based her phenomenal commercial success. And never (with the exception perhaps of the Crimean War) have they allowed sentimental considerations to interfere with the well-known pursuit of pounds, shillings, and pence.

The high-sounding imbecilities of the Holy Alliance, therefore, could only provoke feelings of great irritation among the clever people who resided in Downing Street. And when urged to join, they dictated a polite letter of regret which was duly signed by the Prince Regent and which informed the Emperor Alexander that Great Britain, while in full sympathy with His Majesty's sacred maxims, preferred to keep aloof.

As for America, it is not known whether the Tsar ever contemplated sending a copy of the document to Washington. The Americans, it must be remembered, were either rebels or the sons of rebels and self-respecting rulers like Alexander refused point-blank to recognize them as fellow members of the human race.

Let us hasten to add that this attitude was reciprocal. Perhaps a few Americans had vaguely heard of the Holy Alliance, but it had failed to arouse more than a passing curiosity and was merely regarded as another expression of European noodledom and chuckleheadedness.

Then, however, came those terrible years during which the troops of the King of Spain were being driven from every part of the South American inland and were forced to take refuge in half a dozen fortresses along the coast. And to complicate matters still more, His Most Catholic Majesty himself had just been expelled from his capital by his too long-suffering subjects. Such an abrupt interference with the regular habits of Divine Providence the Holy Alliance could not allow to pass by unnoticed. The King of France was invited to proceed across the Pyrenees and restore his good brother to the throne of his ancestors. When that had been done, so it was said, His French Majesty would be urged to cross the ocean and reconquer the rebellious colonies of South and Central and North America.

The little plan in itself was disturbing enough.

But it was to be only a beginning.

The Russians who had established a colony in Alaska as early as seventeenth century were gradually beginning to explore the western shores of the Pacific Ocean and they had established themselves on the Farallones Islands, right off the bay of San Francisco and they had built a small fort a few miles from the Golden Gate. All that

The Monroe Doctrine

territory was still a sort of no man's land, although certain maps and atlases claimed it to be a part of Mexico. Strictly speaking, therefore, these Muscovite experiments in colonization did not concern the Washington government, but when the Tsar suddenly forbade all foreign vessels (including all American vessels) to come within a hundred miles of his American possessions, a good many people in New York and Philadelphia felt that a joke could be carried too far and that this was one of those cases where one must either laugh or fight—preferably the latter.

Soon afterward the papers reported that the English people shared this view of the situation. After the outbreak of hostilities in Chili and Peru, England had taken the place of Spain as general purveyor of all the daily necessities of life. If those rebellious states, now flying their pretty yellow and green and purple flags should be reconquered by the mother country, then the British merchant would suffer very serious losses. Plainly therefore it was

232

in the interest of Great Britain that someone should speak sharply to the founding father of the Holy Alliance and tell him to desist. For reasons of state, however, it seemed better that such a warning should not come directly from London. But the message which George Canning, the Secretary of State, whispered across the ocean (and whispered so loudly that it could be heard far and wide) was this:

"You go ahead and do whatever you can to prevent the Spanish from reconquering their former possessions and we shall be right with you and support you to the best of our ability."

In consequence whereof (and after due deliberation with his colleagues of the cabinet) James Monroe, President of the United States, speaking "officially" in a letter addressed to Congress (on the second of December of the year 1823), warned all European nations that the season for hunting disaffected American subjects was now closed and that, in so far as it was within the power of the United States, it would remain closed forever.

It was a bold step. The United States were in no position to enforce this drastic *verboten* sign.

If Russia or France had seriously desired to question the legality of this decision by the strength of their cannon, the outcome would have been very doubtful.

But President Monroe had other qualifications for his high office than those acquired as one of Washington's most trusted lieutenants and as the Colonel House of the Jefferson administration.

Sometime during his early career he had learned the advantage of a good poker face.

## Chapter Thirty-Seven

## THE NEW FAITH

As a faithful and orderly chronicler of past events I ought to have paid tribute to many important events which had taken place during the first twelve years of the nineteenth century and which I seem to have overlooked.

I ought to have told you of the sad demise of that very able Federalist party which had saved the Union by changing the insolvent heritage of the Revolution into a sound and self-respecting nation and which destroyed its own usefulness as soon as it had begun to rave about nullification and the right to secede during the panic-stricken years of the last English war.

I ought to have mentioned the name of John Marshall of Virginia, who as Chief Justice of the United States had elevated his court to the dignity of a semidivine institution, ready and often eager to make scraps of paper of such Congressional legislation as seemed to be in contradiction to the sacred stipulations of the Constitution. And I ought to have reviewed the adventures of that group of young Republicans who became the successors of Thomas Jefferson and his followers and who thereupon out-federaled the former Federalists in their enthusiasm for a strongly centralized national form of government. But somehow or other all these events seem of very little importance compared to those fundamental changes in the mode of living and thinking which came over the country during the twenty-four years between the reign of General Washington and the rule of General Jackson.

These changes, as we all know, did not make themselves felt very strongly in the East. They were restricted to the western and southern parts of the country, or, in the language of the modern historian, they were the product of the frontier.

And when this has been stated, there follows the usual hymn of praise about the spirit of adventurous enterprise which animated the pioneers, of their independence of thought and action, their rough and ready, but courteous manners, their sense of equality, their want of deference, their devotion to the principles of freedom of speech, their helpfulness to friend and neighbor.

No doubt these qualifications were all of them true to a certain extent. The settlers were adventurous and hospitable. They worked hard and they stuck to their own opinions and did not care a hoot what anyone else thought

234

about their ideas. But those qualities have also been characteristic of other people who have moved out into the wilderness, and yet in other parts of the world they failed to create that very definite philosophy of life which we call "American."

Then what was the difference?

I will offer an humble guess but I may be mistaken.

The English and Russian and French and Dutch *voortrekkers* who pushed into the unknown wilds of Siberia and India and Borneo and Africa remained essentially English or Russian or French or Dutch. They were the only white men in a community of black or yellow or dark-hued neighbors. The thread that connected them (however imperfectly) with the home country

The river steamer

was the lifeline that prevented them from being drowned in a sea of loneliness and despair, and they sacrificed everything to keep it intact. For they knew that once they had let go of it they would be lost and would degenerate into mere beachcombers.

The American pioneer had passed through a different form of social and economic development. The happy burghers of New Amsterdam or Philadelphia might pity the poor frontiersman and his isolation. But the frontiersman was not at all conscious of his hard lot. To be sure, life was not easy. The stumps were obstinate—the mosquitoes were more dangerous than wolves—there were too darn many stones all over the world—cows and sheep had a fool habit of catching diseases which no veterinary could

235

cure. But as for loneliness—no. Loneliness in the old-fashioned sense of the word he did not know, for his community was based upon something the world had never yet seen and which for lack of a better expression I would like to call "organized isolation."

The western pioneer was undoubtedly "isolated" in the strict sense of the word which means "to place oneself apart from the rest of the world." But so many thousands of like-minded people had done exactly the same thing at exactly the same moment, and had also "placed themselves apart from the rest of the world" and had joined him in his voyage beyond the Appalachian Mountains that the desert ceased to be lonely and the woods lost the terror of their mysterious silence.

As a result these pioneers, no longer beset by a thousand old fears, decided that they could do without the cultural lifeline that still bound them to the civilization of their youth. They took their axes, they cut the lifeline in twain and said, "Good riddance!" And next they began to work out a scheme of living which should be the perfect expression of their spiritual needs and their economic ambitions and in due time this primitive communal program became the unwritten law for all those vast acres of land which the energy and perseverance of this advance guard of civilization had subdued to the will of man.

If you accept this explanation of the development of the frontier spirit (which eventually became the American spirit) you will begin to understand why a philosophy based upon so many positive virtues continued to be marred by those strange and outrageous prejudices which were fast disappearing from the rest of the world when the pioneers incorporated them afresh into their own code of thought and behavior.

But that is the inevitable danger of a voluntary life of exile.

Every publisher, every librarian is familiar with those pathetic manuscripts that come to him from some distant village in the prairie; that appear to be the result of a lifetime of patient research and are found to contain information that has been available in published form for the last two or three hundred years. In such a case the actual damage is not very great. The publisher composes as tactful a letter as his secretary can devise and somewhere in the hinterland three or four days away from the big cities, a poor author who had eagerly looked forward to money and fame begins to prepare for his funeral.

But when the owners of all the grain and all the lumber and all the copper and most of the coal and oil set themselves up as the prophets of a new age and begin to insist that those standards of conduct and thought that were practical and inevitable in their own isolated communities shall henceforth be accepted as the basic laws of a world that has progressed to quite a different state of development, then the matter becomes more serious.

The frontiersmen who had fought with Washington, who had been the boon companions of Jefferson, and who had helped to hammer their thirteen little colonies into a single and powerful nation, had still considered themselves part of the cultural ideals of the world as a whole.

The new pioneers of the twenties and thirties, as I explained a few pages ago, thought of themselves in a different light. They, too, were eager to be good and loyal citizens. But they insisted upon being good and loyal citizens according to the ideals of "goodness" and "loyalty" that continued to prevail in a part of the country that had voluntarily cut itself off from the rest of the universe and that still preferred tallow dips to oil lamps.

They believed so strongly in the superior qualities of their own gospel that some day they hoped to carry the good tidings to all of their neighbors of the North and the East.

No new message, however, will make any headway without an apostle.

Thus far the propagation of the new faith had been left to the humble care of several minor prophets. The moment had come for a true Jeremiah of democracy.

He made his appearance in the year 1824.

He ran for President of the United States on a backwoods ticket and he was none other than our old friend, Andrew Jackson, the hero of New Orleans.

## Chapter Thirty-Eight

## DICTATORSHIP

JACKSON'S FIRST ATTEMPT at power failed and it failed by so small a margin that the followers of the new Messiah raised a most terrible cry of treason.

For since their candidate was the "choice of the people" and since the people, when expressing their will through a majority of the vote, spoke with the tongue of Jehovah, any measure that tended to upset their decision was considered a direct and personal insult to the glory of the Almighty Himself.

The terrific outburst of profanity and denunciation that followed the defeat of Andrew Jackson in the year 1824 made all the more impression because during the previous twenty-five years politics had threatened to become a respectable profession.

The first six presidents of the United States had been highly dignified gentlemen, graduates of well-known colleges and universities, well versed in the polite usages of letters and society, veterans of the old order which had founded the Republic and framed the Constitution.

None of them had ever been obliged to soil his hands with spade or ax.

Their personal tastes and their economic backgrounds had caused some of them to look toward the farmer for their political support; had forced others to close an alliance with the merchants and bankers and manufacturers of the seaboard. But whether they had been representatives of the aristocratic or the democratic ideals of life, they had all of them been animated by a desire for efficient and honest service and they had regarded the high office to which they had been called as a semiroyal reward that had come to them because (be it said in a spirit of great humility) their fellow countrymen regarded them as best fit for the job of being their temporary sovereign.

Some of them had insisted upon pomp and others had made a virtue of slovenly garments, but that had been as much a question of political expediency as an expression of personal taste, and I hate to think what would have happened to the boisterous young go-getter who had undertaken to slap Mr. President Jefferson on the back.

I am making this slight detour into the realm of etiquette because without a perfect understanding of the eminent respectability of the official life of our early Republic it is impossible to realize the profound horror with which President John Quincy Adams (the son of John Adams of Revolutionary fame) anticipated the arrival of his successor.

And yet to those whose political ears allowed them to hear and whose social eyes allowed them to see, the election of Jackson seemed absolutely inevitable. Not only was the center of economic interest beginning to shift from the East to the West, but Jackson himself was the ideal candidate for the party that was now coming into power. A man of great personal dignity (undoubtedly the most courteous President we have ever had) he yet was by birth and training a simple child of the frontier and remained so by preference when he was called upon to be the nation's chief executive.

The parents of Jackson had moved from Ireland to North Carolina in the year 1765. Two years later their son Andrew had been born and fourteen years later the infant had been sufficiently husky to enlist under the Revolutionary banner, to take part in a few skirmishes and to get himself into a British prison camp. The recollection of this experience remained with Jackson until the end of his days and he died as he had lived, an open and avowed enemy of Great Britain.

Meanwhile the young man had decided to escape from the drudgery of a Tennessee farm. An unlimited belief in the potential abilities of every child (male or female) was part of the code of the new West. Wherefore young Andrew improved his leisure hours by studying law and by preparing himself for a career in the field of politics.

239

In the year 1788 he received his first appointment. He was made prosecuting attorney for the western district of North Carolina. Soon afterward he rose to the dignity of a Federal Congressman and a United States Senator. During this part of his career he did not make himself conspicuous except for his hatred of everything that seemed to remind him of the old days of the monarchy, a dislike which found expression in his violent opposition to all the policies of General Washington and in his support of that very doubtful character, Vice-President Aaron Burr.

But once away from Washington and the other haunts of civilization, he lived an eager and busy life of his own. He helped frame the constitution of his adopted state—for several years he was a judge of the Supreme Court of Tennessee—and he was recognized as one of the coming men of the Republic.

These peaceful pursuits in the field of jurisprudence and administrative statesmanship did not prevent him from being a very peppery citizen and from fighting a large number of duels. Why and wherefore these dangerous encounters took place we do not know but in a society soaked in mint juleps a single word could lead to a quarrel, and a quarrel in the year 1800 was inevitably followed by "pistols for two."

In these encounters Jackson sometimes killed his man. Upon other occasions he was not quite so fortunate, and one wound, received in the year 1806, continued to bother him until the day of his death.

Then came the last English war and the uprising of the Indians in Alabama and Georgia. Jackson as commander-in-chief of a small detachment of militiamen followed the Creeks into the wilderness, and in the battle of Horseshoe Bend he defeated them so thoroughly that never again did they threaten the safety of the Southern states.

The success of this campaign got him a commission in the regular army. He stayed in the South where he was familiar with the lay of the land, occupied those parts of Florida which the English hoped to use as their base of supply against America, and saved New Orleans by his defeat of the British expeditionary force under Pakenham.

Then, as military commander of New Orleans, he defied all civil laws, banished a Federal judge who had undertaken to oppose him, and got himself mixed up in a case for contempt of court which led to a lawsuit that dragged on for almost thirty years. Then came another Indian campaign. The peninsula in Florida, nominally under the jurisdiction of Spain but badly administered and hopelessly neglected by the Bourbons, was used as a base of operations by a large number of native and half-breed marauders. Finally in the year 1818 a regular war broke out between the Seminoles (a remnant of the old Creek confederacy) and the settlers of southern Georgia. The Seminoles played their old trick. They withdrew from the jurisdiction of the United States and fled across the border into Spanish territory. To Jackson, a boundary line on paper meant nothing more than an unnecessary and irritating reminder of old-world diplomacy. He pursued the Seminoles across the Spanish frontier, took possession of Florida (although the United States and Spain were at peace with each other), he hanged two British traders whom he accused of having encouraged the Seminoles in their rebellion, and then got himself into a perfect fury when he was informed that this invasion of a friendly territory was not regarded favorably by his employers in Washington and that several reputable citizens of the East wanted him to be court-martialed for what they were pleased to call "the murder" of Arbuthnot and Ambrister.

In the end nothing came of this affair. Spain sold Florida to the United States for five million dollars, the charges were dropped or forgotten, and Jackson was appointed military governor of the new territory, a position which once more (as in his New Orleans days) got him into a violent quarrel with the Federal judiciary and with all those of his subordinates who sometimes tried to think for themselves.

It was this old fire-eater whom the general assembly of Tennessee nominated for President in the year 1822 and who found himself supported by such large numbers of honest democrats that he received the largest number of votes in the electoral college and stood first with ninety-nine votes against John Quincy Adams with eighty-four, William Harris Crawford with forty-one, and Henry Clay with thirty-seven.

To a mind which believed with pious implicity in the right of the majority to rule, overrule, and upon occasion to abuse the minority, it seemed incomprehensible that the presidency should be withheld from him on account of a mere paragraph in a paper document. But as none of the candidates had an absolute majority, the final decision was left to the House of Representatives.

It was then that Henry Clay asked his adherents to support his friend, Mr. Adams, and as a result Mr. Adams was sent to the White House. General Jackson accepted his defeat but he left Washington firmly convinced that he had been cheated and that the hated aristocrats of the East had once again defrauded the plain people and had deprived their representative of an office that belonged to him by the moral right of superior numbers if not exactly according to the written letter of an antiquated law.

Aided and abetted by several clever politicians from the East who worked upon the old gentleman's prejudices and strengthened him in his belief about the corruption and wickedness of all those who did not share his views, Jackson now returned to his "Hermitage" and prepared for the onslaught of the year 1828.

In that election he carried every state south of Maryland and west of the Appalachian Mountains. In addition (and through the clever management of his local henchmen) he received all the votes of Pennsylvania and a majority of the electoral votes of New York, with the result that he had twice as many votes as Adams and could proceed to Washington in the only role that really suited his temperament—the role of a dictator.

On the fourth of March of the year 1829 the cohorts of a triumphant democracy descended upon the national capital. More than fifteen thousand people came to listen to the inaugural address of their leader and as many of them as could afterward crowded into the narrow rooms of the White House to assure the people's hero with a hearty shake of both their hands of their wholehearted support and undying affection.

Jackson played his new role with his customary grace. He smiled upon his simple friends, he listened patiently to their speeches, he allowed them to trample down his carpets and his furniture, but when all the noise was over and the mess had been cleaned up, he assumed complete charge of affairs and for the next eight years he ruled the country by the grace of his own will and according to all the best examples of classical and modern despotisms.

For at heart he was a conservative. Not in the New England sense of the word. But a conservative in the true spirit of those isolated frontiersmen who rejected everything that was not of any immediate use to their own needs as useless and despicable remnants of an old and effeminate form of civilization, and who hoped to replace the hard and fast rules of a highly trained aristocracy by the intolerant canons of a new and untried democracy.

If there were those who had hoped that the Jacksonian triumph would mean a return to the happy old days when the states were superior to the nation, they were soon to be disappointed, for Washington, during the rule of Andrew Jackson, became more than ever before the capital of an empire.

If there were others who had foreseen the destruction of capitalism on account of Jackson's personal distrust of the United States Bank and his disastrous attacks upon that useful institution, they, too, were to suffer a rude awakening, for the tariff, although slightly modified, was not abolished and those agricultural states which proposed to rid themselves of this unwelcome burden by declaring the tariff null and void within the jurisdiction of their own isolated regions were at once threatened with a descent of Federal troops and were quickly forced to toe the Jacksonian mark.

And if there were still others simple-minded enough to believe that a pure democracy would henceforth entrust the management of the business of state affairs to those who were best fitted for the available positions, they were to receive the rudest shock of their lives when the entire fabric of Federal patronage was turned into a system of reward for political services, and when the doctrine "to the victor belong the spoils" (which had already made its appearance in several of the states long before the election of Jackson) was now made the official rule of conduct for the executive of the nation.

But all these disadvantages counted for very little compared to the great and lasting services which the Jacksonian dictatorship was able to render to the American world in general.

Many of the general's contemporaries, of course, spoke with great bitterness when they compared the abrupt and gruff methods of their new masters with the dignified manners of the previous generation. They were inclined to agree with the judgment of Thomas Jefferson that the far-famed hero of New Orleans was at once rude, malignant, and muddle-headed, and they denounced his followers in terms which the politicians of today reserve for their friends from faraway Moscow.

And they were dreadfully upset by the social clumsiness of these upstarts who smoked all over the White House (a most shocking innovation) and allowed an absurd quarrel about a woman's past to degenerate into a bitter personal fight which ended with the resignation of half the cabinet and caused an irreparable breach between the President and the Vice-President.

But all that was only one part of the story, and a minor part. The other half stood writ in that chapter of the book of progress which insists that no lasting progress is possible until we shall consider the interests of all the people and not that of a small group or combination of groups.

The emancipation of the black man, because it was accompanied by a costly and bloody war, has attracted a great deal of historical attention. The emancipation of the white man, however, is apt to be overlooked because it took place without any interference on the part of the executioner and his gallows. But in this movement to set the white man free from the last shackles of his ancient serfdom the new dictator played a prominent part—perhaps not a conscious one but a very important one all the same.

The people of the frontier might not care whether they had ever heard of Europe or not, but Europe was beginning to hear of them and the success of the great experiment in popular government in America encouraged them in their own efforts to shake off a yoke that had become unbearable.

First in England, where the feudal system had continued to hold sway with unabashed vigor, then in France where the Bourbons had revived all the most objectionable features of medieval absolutism, next in Austria and in Germany and even in faraway Russia attempts were made to substitute a representative form of government for the current system of autocracy. In France and England these efforts succeeded. In Russia they failed. In Austria and Germany they were partially successful. But everywhere they brought about a renewal of the forces of democracy. And part of their success was undoubtedly due to the existence in America of just that form of government of which the leaders in Europe had been dreaming for more than a hundred years.

The pioneer

This did not mean that the new masters were to be paragons of wisdom and virtue. Heaven forbid! The democratic ideal, in the hands of the wrong people, can do more damage in a shorter space of time than any other form of government ever devised by the ingenuity of man. Worst of all, it had (and still has) a terrible tendency to encourage mediocrity and to make a virtue of ignorance and inefficiency.

On the other hand, it is apt to set loose certain energies and enthusiasm which are doomed to eternal repression under an autocracy or a plutocracy, not to mention a theocracy.

Jackson was guilty of terrible blunders of conduct and judgment. When his anger or his suspicions were aroused, he could commit himself to policies that were downright disastrous in their ultimate effects upon the happiness and prosperity of the land. But at the same time he gave not only to America but to the entire world a lesson in practical politics which was badly needed.

He showed the people of the old and the new world that a popular form of government could manage an empire quite as successfully as a highly organized aristocracy. Not as smoothly, perhaps, or as decorously, or as efficiently, but it could make a fairly respectable go of the business of administration, and it could guarantee a greater return of happiness upon the average human investment of self-respect and independence than any other system then in practice.

In such questions it is, of course, impossible to reach a definite conclusion based upon the irrefutable data of statistics and blueprints. But the opinion of contemporary visitors is enlightening.

"Absolutely impossible," said Mrs. Trollope, bitterly remembering the painful days when she had been obliged to sell galoshes and hairpins to the graceless rustics of Cincinnati, and she could see absolutely nothing good in the great democracy of the West.

But Count Alexis de Tocqueville, who did not look upon the world from the uncomfortable angle of a debtors' prison and a smelly boardinghouse in Bruges, thought differently.

"There is something in this strange political experiment," he warned his friends.

And he was right.

## Chapter Thirty-Nine

# THE FRIVOLOUS JUGGLERS AND THE USELESS PLAYERS OF THE LUTE

POOR JUGGLERS!

They did not lead very happy lives and, truth to tell, they were not very amusing.

Their own contemporaries treated them with scant respect, and those who came afterward looked at their ponderous output, shrugged their shoulders, and said, "Quite interesting as a chapter in the intellectual development of our country, but pretty dreary stuff! Pretty dreary!"

In order, however, to be entirely just to the condition of art and letters in the new commonwealth we must go back to a period more than three hundred years before.

In another book I once compared great social and spiritual upheavals with the stones that Providence heaves into the tranquil pool of humanity. Such missiles cause ripples and those ripples spread far and wide to every nook and cranny of the pond. They grow fainter and fainter as they get farther away from the center, but they are never quite obliterated. They may not seem to cause much of a commotion, but they are bound to change the placid aspect of the waters to some degree, however infinitesimal.

The Renaissance which bade man turn his eyes away from the problematic joys of a very problematic heaven and fix them upon the actual possibilities of happiness on this most tangible earth had been such a disturbance.

It had had its origin in Italy. Then it had crossed the Alps and had enlarged its sphere of influence until practically every country of the old Continent had felt the touch of this new gospel of the Divinity of Man.

England, separated from the rest of the Continent by

the North Sea and the Channel, had been the last to come under its influence. And then, just when things were going nicely, when the poets and the musicians and the playwrights and the actors and the painters of Good Queen Bess were turning their tight little island into a mighty cheerful place, Doctor Martin Luther and Doctor John Calvin came along, heaved a ton of controversial bricks into the merry duckpond of the New Humanity, and caused an upheaval which has continued to this very day.

In short, before the Renaissance had had a chance to make a thorough conquest of the British Isles, the great big splash of the Reformation drowned the Renaissance out of existence and once more substituted the doubtful joys of being dead for the more positive satisfaction of being alive.

And by a strange turn of history, the class that had remained the most unmoved by the New Ideals of a Glorious Humanity and that afterward fell most completely under the spell of the Reformation was the very class that had migrated to the New World and that had been able to impose its own code of ethics and its own standards of taste and behavior upon the entire colonial community of northern America.

You may remember a little incident of the French Revolution. The terrorists had got hold of Lavoisier, the famous chemist, and were dragging him to the guillotine. His friends, with a rare display of courage, petitioned the president of the tribunal to spare the life of this man who was the greatest chemist of the age.

"Pshaw," answered that dignitary, "the Republic don't need no scientists. Off with his head!"

The Calvinist clergyman who ruled the Puritan realm with an iron rod had the same attitude toward those who devoted themselves to the useless pursuit of the arts and who did not work for their living in a factory or an office as behooved all decent and God-fearing citizens.

They did not decapitate any painters and sculptors and writers. They did not have to do so.

The poor devils stayed away of their own free will,

and in the field of arts, New England remained as sterile as that old barren land of Judea which served the founders of the Massachusetts Zion as their ideal and filled their hearts with the only enthusiasm that was not regarded as an expression of levity of spirit and wickedness of soul.

An exception ought to be made for some of the craftsmen. The humble carpenters and masons continued to build first-rate stuff. But then, architecture had always fallen within the pale of Calvinistic prejudices. Hadn't Solomon built a temple, the fame of which had penetrated as far as distant Abyssinia? Wasn't the book of Exodus full of specifications for pillars and boards and doors and bars?

As a result the hewers of wood were given a free rein, and the few surviving workers in copper and silver lost none of that cunning which had distinguished their particular trade in the old world.

But that was not all.

Literature in the broader sense of the word had become superfluous among a people who believed that the Bible was the last word in all the higher forms of literary expression.

Music, on the other hand, was too closely associated with the worldly pleasures of the theater and the dance hall to be tolerated for an instant.

The art of painting had never even penetrated to the simple homes from which most of the immigrants had come, while the stories they had heard of studio life during their long sojourn in the Low Countries had convinced them that both the brush and the palette were special inventions of the devil, and should be eschewed as assiduously as playing-cards and Christmas presents.

There remained the stage. And the stage had always been a particular object of hatred to those who hoped to preserve their souls in uncontaminated purity. They shuddered at the mere mention of the name of Shakespeare, and as for the other great Elizabethan playwrights, they were never mentioned at all. Of course, a life of hard work without a single appeal to the average normal sense of beauty was a very dull affair. But the bloodcurdling exhortations of the Sabbath morning, when women wept and children shrieked at the plastic description of the Great and Glorious Hereafter, offered a certain outlet for the pent-up emotions of the average man. While an occasional orgy of witch-hunting, with all its attendant frenzies and sadistic hallucinations, brought relief to those members of the community who insisted upon something a little stronger than mere hearsay about Sodom and Gomorrah.

With the exception of a few collections of homemade psalms, spelling-books, and the inevitable anthologies of dreadful clerical sermons, the American contribution to the sum total of the arts of the seventeenth and eighteenth centuries was less than nothing.

Such a state of affairs could not endure forever.

It had been comparatively easy to purge the Community of the Saints of all dissenting elements by hanging Quakers and throwing play-actors into the village jug. But when the youth of the country itself began to rebel, the game was up and the former dictators of man's conscience were driven into that destructive rear-guard action which has not yet come to an end.

Unfortunately, just when this emancipation of the soul took place, the center of our civilization was being shifted from the East to the West, and the pioneers, having voluntarily withdrawn from a civilization which did not suit their urge for freedom and independence, could not fail to regard the arts as a useless survival from the days when the world was ruled by soft-handed ne'er-do-wells and pretty ladies and satins and brocades.

It took years, therefore, ere those who had something to say ventured to give expression to their thoughts in the form of books and magazines, and most of the authors of that early time were too conscious of their inferior position in society to evolve a style of their own and (in the realm of letters at least) they were contented to remain transplanted Englishmen. They sometimes introduced American elements into their novels, but they wrote as if there had been no separation from what they still considered "the mother country." With all their endless appeals to a pure and undiluted patriotism, they were much less conscious of their American heritage than the unkempt frontiersman whose sterling virtues they lauded in their poems, but whose presence in their cities and legislatures filled them with sad forebodings of the future.

Some exceedingly fine bits of prose were actually written during this early period. The Declaration of Independence was undoubtedly the work of a man who had a true sense of the value of words, while the authors of the *Federalist* showed that they had not learned their language from the New England Primer alone.

These documents, however, were more an expression of political sagacity than a desire to contribute something new to the Treasures of Literature and it was not until a generation later that Irving and Hawthorne and Cooper and Lowell and Longfellow managed to give a satisfactory answer to Sydney Smith's uncomplimentary sneer, "Who reads an American book?"

Even then it was impossible for a man who was not possessed of independent means to make a living as a mere author. The respect shown to the Lowells and the Irvings and the Coopers was due quite as much to their excellent social and economic position as to any profound appreciation of the work they were trying to do. When at last a first-class artist made his appearance (a man who by his originality and his careful workmanship stood all alone) the mere fact that Poe was a wayward character, a fellow of loose and uncertain habits, was enough to condemn him to a life so pitiful and so forlorn that the like of it is hardly to be found in the dreary records of Grub Street.

Of course, no race endowed with so much original talent could live forever without some sort of an outlet for their surplus intellectual and artistic enthusiasms. Many boys found a chance to express themselves in the vast ventures of the West. Others put their soul into the construction of railroads or in the further development of their father's business. But, if these respectable methods of escape failed them, they invariably drifted into the one and only profession of a literary nature that was not absolutely closed to the red-blooded, double-fisted he-men of that period.

I refer, of course, to the realm of journalism.

What great and glorious things the world has expected of the newspaper profession ever since the first appearance of Caesar's *Daily Doings*—how the common people were to become enlightened—how frontiers were to be enlarged by making every man, woman, and child a citizen of one enormous common country—how democracy would be enabled to triumph over all the dark forces of ignorance and prejudice! Of course, these beautiful dreams came to very little. Eventually several of the news sheets developed into nothing more elevated than instruments for the wholesale intellectual stupefaction of the masses and became the open and avowed enemies of all dispassionate discussion and argument.

But before this happened (and the above passionate aside is written, as you will please remember, in the year of the tabloid 1927), the papers rendered some very useful service as a retreat for those who had something to say and who otherwise would never have been given a chance to bring their opinions to the attention of their neighbors.

Finally, since literature pure and simple did not offer one chance of a livelihood, there was one other method by which a few young men could escape the countinghouse and the factory and yet feel that he was devoting himself to some form of creative life.

That was the teaching profession.

The ordinary schools were still rather crude and the colleges continued to bear the stamp of their origin, which was that of theological training-schools.

Those poor creatures, therefore, who were cursed with a mind of their own were not the sort of teachers whose services were sought after by the seats of learning, as the Rev. Dr. Emerson and several of his most distinguished contemporaries could have told you from bitter experience.

This does not give you a very happy picture of the state of art and letters which prevailed during the early years of the colonies and the Republic. Life was cruel and harsh for those who dreamed that there were certain things in this world which could not be bought for money: that there were ideas more precious than the thought of to-morrow's bread and jam. But these uncomfortable conditions proved to be a blessing in disguise.

Almost all those who could beg, borrow, or steal enough money for an ocean voyage fled to other parts of the world where they came into contact with certain other forms of civilization which had never been touched by the deadening blight of Calvinism.

Most of those voluntary exiles returned, for the love of home was strong within them and once back among the fold of the faithful they continued the good fight, struggled for the right to think and speak and write as they pleased, defied the tyranny of the clerical witch-hunters, and tried to the best of their great abilities to turn their prosperous new land into a country that should be a fit dwelling-place for truly civilized people. As was to be expected, the majority of those excellent men and women received scant gratitude for their unselfish labors and the spiritual loneliness in which they were condemned to spend the greater part of their lives drove many of them to the insanity of drunkenness or suicide. A few of the hardier ones survived. And they were not among the least useful of our many pioneers.

It is true, they never cut down a single tree or cleared a solitary acre of land.

But they made little ideas grow on a barren soil which thus far had only been covered with the sterile rocks of theological prejudice and dogmatic arrogance.

And that, in itself, was no mean accomplishment.

## Chapter Forty

# PRESIDENT SANTA ANNA OF MEXICO LEARNS THE TRUTH OF THE LAW WHICH STATES THAT NATURE ABHORS A VACUUM

HERE IS A SIMPLE LITTLE PROBLEM in historical arithmetic.

If country A has 50,000,000 acres for which it has not any use and country B, which is situated next to country A, has great need of 50,000,000 additional acres, and if country A is weak and country B is strong, how long will it take before country B has country A's 50,000,000 acres?

For an answer read the story of the Mexican war.

A strange episode in the development of our country!

The Northerners felt so badly about it that once again they threatened to secede from the Union.

The Southerners pronounced it a holy crusade.

As for the Mexicans, I doubt very much whether most of them ever heard about it. They may have noticed the passing of a few bands of armed men. But that was nothing new. And a little shooting more or less, well, that was all in the day's work of that unfortunate country. For if ever there was an anomaly among the strangely assorted nations of this earth, it was the good land of Mexico. Other European colonies have at different times proclaimed their independence because they were disgusted with the despotism of the mother country. Not so Mexico. The Mexican Creoles had made a few feeble attempts at liberty about the same time that Bolivar and San Martin made their attack upon the Spanish overlords of South America. But those Mexican rebellions had never amounted to very much and they had been easily suppressed.

Then in the year 1814 the half-witted King Ferdinand VII, whose first act upon his return from France had been the re-establishment of the Inquisition and wholesale murder of all those who had opposed him, was forced by a revolt to regrant to his exasperated subjects the liberal constitution of which he had deprived them seven years before. The news of this step came as a very unpleasant surprise to His Majesty's officials in Mexico City and to the clerical gentlemen who owned the greater part of all Mexican real estate. Liberalism has always meant anticlericalism, an open and avowed hostility toward the bureaucracy of the state and toward the religious intolerance of the Church. And in the hope of maintaining the system of reaction and suppression which up to then had been so successful in the mother country, the ruling classes of Mexico together with the leaders of the Church declared their country independent and after some discussion about the new form of government, they bestowed the crown upon a young Creole, Augustin de Iturbide, who became Emperor of Mexico in 1822 and who shared the usual fate of all Mexican rulers by being shot to death two years later.

All that, however, has little to do with our own history. Mexico, after its reactionary revolution, remained an independent country and fell heir to certain Spanish possessions in North America which began somewhere near the Caribbean Sea and ended, no one knew exactly where, among the plains and the mountains of the far West. As for the number of inhabitants, that, too, was a matter of conjecture.

Anyway, there it was, an enormous tract of exceedingly rich land, left to the mercy of the Indian and the coyote, and right next to it, just on the other side of the Red River, the turbulent and restless domains of that new Republic in which people firmly believed that the possession of a piece-of-land-of-his-own had been guaranteed to every citizen by one of the articles of the Constitution.

Even if the Mexican government had wanted to keep the Americans out of its territory, it would hardly have been able to do so in view of its endless boundaries and its small number of frontier guards. But the Mexicans had no desire to follow such a policy. On the contrary, they heartily welcomed those weather-beaten immigrants and gave large grants of land to all such speculators as promised to bring in a definite number of white settlers.

For about a dozen years all went well, and then the Mexican government suddenly discovered that it was faced with the problem of a state within a state. Such a situation is apt to lead to very delicate and long-winded diplomatic negotiations and General Antonio Lopez de Santa Anna was not at all the sort of man to be useful in such a crisis. Panic entered his soul, and he hastily passed a number of measures which were meant to stem the tide of the American inrush and which caused no end of ill-feeling. All old land grants were cancelled, no new settlers were allowed across the border, and slavery was abolished. Hence great consternation among the settlers. The embargo on farm implements and the cancellation of the land grants hurt the prospective immigrants who had been persuaded by Moses Austin, their fellow Yankee, to sell their old farms in the East and prepare for their trip to the distant Southwest. While the decree against slavery came as a great shock to the Southerners who had hoped that eventually all this territory would join the Union and would strengthen the forces of the slave-holders both in Congress and in the Senate.

Not knowing exactly what to do, these farmers did what all good Americans have always done under similar circumstances, they organized.

They organized, and then remembering the stories they had heard as children, they adopted a set of formal resolutions, issued a Declaration of Independence of their own and called for volunteers.

Meanwhile ten thousand eager faces were looking across the border, wondering when they would be able to join their friends across the Sabine River. A hundred thousand others were hoping that at some time in the near future they, too, might leave for a nice little homestead in Texas, and ten million more or less peaceful citizens, raising tobacco and manufacturing cotton, were carefully reading the papers and were taking bets on the relative merits of Jim Bowie and Davie Crockett.

A few months later both these heroes lay dead with a dozen bayonet cuts through their chests. They had been murdered, together with a hundred other Americans. They had been murdered in cold blood immediately after the capture of San Antonio by the troops of Santa Anna and it was a pretty terrible affair. It made a deep impression upon the people back home and loud were the cries of those who preached a war of vengeance.

But ere anything official was done, the frontiersmen themselves had settled the difficulty. Under command of Sam Houston, frontiersman extraordinary, ex-governor of Tennessee, and a distinguished member of the tribe of the Cherokees, they defeated the Mexican army, captured Santa Anna, and proclaimed the sovereign Republic of Texas. Whereupon they asked to become (what they already were in everything except the name) an integral part of the United States of America.

The South welcomed them with open arms, but the North, dreading the prospect of yet another slaveholding state, was dead set against this idea and the New England states positively refused to ratify the treaty until the year 1845 when President Tyler at last signed the resolution which made Texas a part of the Union.

That, of course, meant that the American government now fell heir to all the outstanding quarrels between the Republic of Mexico and the former Republic of Texas, which were a-plenty.

This uncomfortable state of affairs was due in part to certain strange conceptions of distance which were so common among the people of the far West. When they made a claim to something, they did not ask for a paltry fifty or five hundred acres. No, fifty thousand was the least they would consider. And as the territory around the Rio Grande was still for the greater part untouched by the tripod of the surveyor, it was very difficult to say what belonged to whom and where and how and why. But the successful dictatorship of Jackson and the continuation of the Jacksonian principles under President Van Buren had given the inhabitants of our western states a feeling of strength and independence which made them

257

ready (and I am afraid somewhat eager) to fight anybody who dared to interfere with the sacred duty of all good Americans to carry their beneficent rules and principles to the farthermost corners of the continent, or in vulgar language, to take whatever they wanted.

Those who did not share this view (and there were a good many of them in the East) claimed that all this agitation for a greater Texas was merely so much political buncombe, that the eagle was being made to scream for the greater benefit of the slaveholders and their supporters in Congress and in the Senate. But in the simpler terms of the frontier all this land was of no earthly use to anybody else, it had been explored first of all by Americans, that Americans were the only people who had had courage enough to go and live there when it was a wilderness and therefore why, in the name of common sense, shouldn't it belong to America?

Which from their point of view was a perfectly good and reasonable argument.

Finally, as was quite unavoidable, considering the temper of the two contending parties, the annexation of Texas led to a war with Mexico. This war, although greatly prolonged by the unwillingness of the militia to enlist for more than one term, was won by the United States. It ended when Mexico (in return for a few million dollars) ceded a slice of territory almost as big as the whole of Louisiana and which reached from the Rio Grande to the Pacific Ocean.

Almost at the same time, our hold upon the far West was further strengthened by the peaceful acquisition of those distant western regions generally known as the Oregon country. So that after the peace treaty of Guadalupe-Hidalgo, the map of the United States looked twice as imposing as it had done in 1845 and America (as far as territory was concerned) had to be recognized among the most important nations of the world.

I dare say that the orators of the forties with their eternal references to the "manifest destiny of the American race" got on the nerves of a great many of their contemporaries. So did the Germans a few years ago with their dreary chant about "a place in the sun." But at bottom they were both talking about the same thing—they hoped to get something that really belonged to someone else.

In this matter, however, the Americans were much luckier than the poor Prussians. Our ancestors began their search for new homes when there was still a large geographic vacuum which clamored to be filled. The Teutons on the other hand started their career of expansion (robbery, appropriation, call it anything you please), when every available little spot of America, Asia, Africa, and Australia had long since been taken up by one of the big powers and when there was not anything left for the newcomers.

Wherefore America succeeded and Germany failed.

For in the world of politics it does not matter so much what we do as when we do it.

And within that field our country has always been most fortunate by following the simple but direct advice of "Do it now."

## Chapter Forty-One

## UNCLE TOM AND PUFFING BILLY

DISTANCE HAS EVER BEEN the enemy of empire.

And distance, a hundred years ago, could only be conquered by roads and canals. Wherefore, as soon as the national household had been established upon a firm and more or less solvent basis, the government turned its serious attention to the problem of direct and cheap communication and began to build roads and to dig canals as fast as a slender treasury allowed them.

During a good many years, however, the majority of these official highways resembled that famous esplanade of Ambrose Bierce which started as a noble boulevard and ended in a squirrel trail which ran up a tree. When that point had been reached (the squirrel trail), the wanderer was left to his own devices and could continue his peregrinations as best pleased him.

Even today, with dynamite and all sorts of steel contraptions that eat up whole wagonloads of rocks at a single gulp, the business of road-building is expensive and complicated. What it was a century ago, I leave to the imagination of all those who have ever tried to make a flivver-track from the main highway to their front door.

For a long time, therefore, the immigrants bound for the free farms of the West closely followed the rivers and the valleys and kept as far as possible from anything remotely resembling a hill. But when the number of these travelers increased, when the route through the Hudson and Mohawk valleys became too long and too circumstantial, sheer necessity blazed a trail across the mountains and began to exploit those gaps through which the Indians, since prehistoric days, had passed on their way from the eastern to the western hunting-fields and vice versa.

Once across the Alleghenies the immigrant who was still possessed of a couple of dollars left his troubles behind him. He got passage on board one of the flatboats that were carrying merchandise downstream and peacefully floated to his new home. Of course, if he had to go upstream, he was out of luck, for then he had to foot it.

As for the eastern part of the country, there the problem was less complicated for all the states of the seaboard had gone canal-crazy and were wasting millions of dollars on new waterways. But the average immigrant avoided the East and tried to go as far west of the Appalachians in as short a time as possible, and his difficulties did not come to an end until James Watt looked at his grandmother's teakettle and said, "There is an idea."

It would, of course, be more scientific to talk learnedly of the inventions of Hero and Thomas Savery and Della Porta and Denis Papin. But in the first place, no one ever knew less about machinery than I do and in the second place, it was James Watt who perfected the steam engine until it was of some direct and practical commercial value and therefore we will just casually bow to all his famous predecessors and proclaim James as the man who did more for the ultimate development of our country than all the assembled statesmen, generals, bankers, and ward-heelers of the last half of the eighteenth and the first half of the nineteenth century.

At first Watt had worked exclusively for certain English mine owners who were badly in need of a convenient engine that should work their pumps less expensively than it could be done by horses. The eighteenth century was a great era of inventions and as soon as a successful stationary engine had been produced, the people of almost every country began to try and hoist the complicated contraption aboard a cart or a boat that it might do the work formerly entrusted to men or women or other beasts of burden. As always happens, there were those who said that it could not be done, but there were many more who were willing to bet their bottom dollar that sometime soon people would move from place to place behind an "iron horse" or in a choo-choo vessel. Some of these, like John Fiske of Connecticut, did not fare well. They tinkered with boats and engines until they had concocted something that kept afloat and could actually make some headway against the currents of the Delaware estuaries. But they found themselves opposed by the sailing interests and as the merchants who used sailing vessels were practically almighty in the East, the banks would not grant these dangerous enthusiasts any loans upon such silly collateral as a mere "steamboat," and the would-be inventors either drifted into some other business or like poor old Fiske got disheartened and killed themselves.

Others like Robert R. Livingston (of Declaration of Independence fame) decided that it was better not to put the cart ahead of the horse (or the engine in this case) and they collected charters for the exclusive rights to ply steamboats on certain rivers and lakes and meanwhile waited with more or less patience for the day when the venture should have been made commercially profitable.

That long-expected day seemed to have arrived when the *Charlotte Dundas,* a Scottish tug, towed her first string of coal barges through a Scottish canal in the year 1802. But much to the surprise of the manufacturers of the *Charlotte Dundas* nothing happened and the event caused hardly any stir at all.

It is difficult to account for this indifference on the part of the promoters and the public. Perhaps it was due to the general and profound disappointment caused by the balloon.

When Joseph and Jacques Montgolfier sent their sheep, their cock, and their duck upon the first of all aeronautical voyages, grandparents solemnly addressed their grandchildren and said, "This is a solemn moment. We are on the eve of great things." A few years later (January, 1785) when the Frenchman Blanchard and the American doctor John Jeffries crossed the British Channel in one of those new-fangled "airships," the people of Europe hopefully predicted the end of all war and the coming of the brotherhood of man.

"For now," so they reasoned in their innocence, "we shall all be each other's nearest and dearest neighbors; frontiers shall disappear, and warships and armies shall become obsolete."

The answer to this prayer had come in the form of two solid decades of uninterrupted bloodshed. And the balloon, after having served as a movable post of observation for the armies of the revolution, was shortly afterward permitted to degenerate into a toy for the amusement of holiday crowds.

And after this experience the public at large had become very skeptical about all sorts of scientific novelties and it would take a great deal more than a sooty tug on the Clyde canal to convince them that a ship provided with an engine and paddle wheels could actually go forward without the assistance of sails.

There was one man, however, who took the *Charlotte Dundas* seriously. His name was Robert Fulton and he was a poor Irishman who lived in New York. Fulton had started life as a jewelry salesman. Then he had become a portrait painter (a pretty bad one) but in the year 1787 he had taken his savings and had gone to London to study with Benjamin West, one of the few Pennsylvania Quakers who ever turned his hand to art.

In England Fulton had dabbled in engineering and when at last he went to Paris to present that long-suffering city with a panorama (does anyone remember what they were?) he carried with him certain plans for an undersea craft which he expected would give France command of the ocean.

Unfortunately for Fulton (and fortunately for England) Napoleon was at heart a medieval *condottiere*. He had as much use for the modern methods of warfare as the late Lord Kitchener. Footwork had gained him his laurels, and the submarine torpedo with which Fulton blew up a small vessel in the harbor of Brest interested him no more than did the steam-driven scow which Fulton exhibited a little later on the river Seine.

In the parlance of the street, the Emperor could not "see" either of those two inventions. And he returned to Monsieur Fulton his blueprints and his calculations and graciously suffered him to return to his home on the Hudson.

Back in his own country Fulton at first repeated his experiments of the Continent. The government of the United States to whom he addressed himself was not interested in his ideas. He then looked for private support, got in touch with Robert Livingston, and began to work in all seriousness.

The hull of his vessel he constructed in America. The engine, however, he ordered from the firm of Boulton & Watt in Birmingham in England. It was a good little engine and it did its work so well that the *Clermont* (the name of the first steamer on the Hudson River) was a commercial success and in less than a year had grown too small for the number of passengers who wished to go from New York to Albany in the fabulously short time of thirty-six hours.

The long years of friction between England and the United States which followed immediately upon the launching of the *Clermont* and her sister ship, the *Phoenix,* interfered seriously with the further development of steam navigation. But in 1811 the *New Orleans,* built in Pittsburgh, made her appearance on the Mississippi River and in 1818 the *Walk-in-the-Water* proudly puffed across the waters of Lake Erie.

After 1815 the westward trip could have been greatly facilitated if steam-propelled vessels had been given a chance on the big rivers of that newly developed region. For not only could they beat the flatboats when going downstream, but they could actually go upstream at a rate of four miles per hour, something which the flatboat had never been able to do.

But it took a long time for steam navigation to become general. For during the first years, the big steamship companies were more interested in playing politics and in getting "exclusive rights" and "waterway monopolies" than in the business of developing trade. And it was not until the middle of the nineteenth century that steamboat traffic reached its normal growth and became one of the most important factors in the development of the West.

In the meantime, however, another antidote for distance had been discovered.

That was the steam locomotive.

This creature was a contemporary of the steam engine. Indeed, it was slightly older, for on Christmas eve of the year 1801 an engine constructed by Richard Trevithick had dragged its first load of passengers across the roads of Cornwall and three years later the same sort of machine, but set upon wheels, had propelled a heavy coal train at Pen-y-darran in Wales. Then in the year 1813 another English engineer, William Hedley, had delighted the world with his "Puffing Billy" and again a year later George Stephenson had improved upon "Puffing Billy" with a slightly improved iron monster that bore the more dignified name of "My Lord."

After that steam locomotives had come into general use in all the English coal regions until finally in the year 1825 the same Stephenson convinced the board of managers of a tram line that steam would do the work better and cheaper than horses and presented the world with its first full-fledged railroad.

These efforts to diminish the distance between cities with the help of "traveling engines" found some echo in the new world. Here and there little stretches of railroad were built. But they could only be used when the sun was shining, as the engine of that day skidded as soon as the rails were damp, and rather than run the risk of uncertain hours, the directors returned to the use of horses and sold their steam-machines for old junk.

In the year 1828, however, the building of regular lines of railroad began in all seriousness. On the fourth of July of that year Charles Carroll of Carrollton, the last surviving signer of the Declaration of Independence, laid the first stone of the Baltimore and Ohio railroad. Ten years later the country had over two thousand miles of railway and twenty years later the problem of transportation between the East and the West had been settled definitely.

James Watt had triumphed and the meanest immigrant was now able to travel with such a degree of comfort and luxury that many fainthearted people who thus far had preferred to stay at home took fresh courage, sold their rocky farms in New England, and joined their hardier relatives who a generation before had departed for the freedom of the woods and the prairies with a pack on their back and a gun across their shoulders.

But now that the problem of quick and cheap transportation for man and beast had been settled, there remained that other and equally important problem of transferring ideas from one place to another without too great a loss of time.

Curiously enough it was once more a painter man (this time a good one) who undertook to wrestle with the difficulty and who solved it.

Samuel Morse was a Yale man who during his college days had played a little with electricity. But although the son of a Congregational clergyman, the urge of art had been strong upon him and he had escaped to Europe to study in England and France. But when he had learned his trade, he came back to America and helped to found the National Academy of Design. And then in the year 1832, when he returned from a second visit to Europe, a chance remark in the smoking-room of his ship gave him the idea of the possibility of "transmitting intelligence instantaneously with the help of electricity." He actually invented some sort of a device that would do this but a dozen years were to go by before he found a hearing for his electric "far writer." Even then he met with disappointment after disappointment. He did his best to interest Congress, and Congress actually appointed a committee to look into the matter and then quietly adjourned. Thereupon he talked telegraphy to bankers and they told him of the vast responsibilities that rested upon the shoulders of the men who are entrusted with the care of other people's money and would not invest a nickel. Thereupon he decided to try his luck in London, but again he was laughed at for his trouble. He went to Paris, applied for a patent, met with a refusal, and as soon as he had left discovered that the French government was stealing his ideas without intending to pay him a cent.

But finally after years of worry and poverty he gained the good will of a New Jersey wire manufacturer by the name of Vail and a New York Quaker by the name of Cornell (who gave the world the telegraph pole and a university) and on the second of September of the year 1837 succeeded in sending a message from one room in the New York University to another across 1700 feet of copper wire.

The rest was easy.

Congress, with quite unusual speed, voted Morse the funds necessary for the construction of a telegraph line between Washington and Baltimore and in 1843 (only five years after he had asked for his money) Morse was superintending the building of the first electro-magnetic recording telegraphs, which soon afterward were to make Philadelphia the next-door neighbor of San Francisco and London a suburb of New York.

So much for our young country in its warfare upon

distance.

But there was another enemy, a traitor who had dogged the footsteps of humanity ever since that memorable day when man was condemned to gain his livelihood in the sweat of his brow, and his name was Hunger.

Those who believe that history is merely a record of man in search of his daily bread, some butter, and a little jam, are apt to regret that both the Declaration of Independence and the Constitution give so little evidence of that economic spirit which is supposed to dominate every phase of ordinary human development. And they claim that this was caused by the fact that the American rebellion was in many respects a rich man's revolution and that the founding fathers had almost exclusively belonged to the leisure class who had made it their business to disfranchise the majority of their fellow citizens that they might keep their hold upon "property" and keep the government of the Republic in the hands of "the good and the wise."

Such an opinion, however, is a little one-sided and not quite fair to the people who navigated the thirteen states through the great war of Independence. True enough that in many states only those possessed of a certain definite sum of money could run for office (from five thousand dollars in Massachusetts to fifty thousand in South Carolina) and only taxpayers were allowed the use of the ballot, but one cannot demand that one class of society commit suicide for the benefit of another and property having run this world ever since the days of Nebuchadnezzar, it would have been unreasonable to expect that a few planters from Virginia and merchants from New England should be gifted with those virtues in which even Moses, the founder of our moral law, seems to have been slightly deficient.

The Washingtons and Hamiltons and the Adamses and the Jeffersons were all of them representatives of the school of economics that prevailed during the latter half of the eighteenth century. They had been brought up in the belief that no stable government was possible when those who had nothing to lose were given the same rights and privileges as those who played the game with real money and they acted according to their lights.

But in addition to the lessons which they had learned at school, we must remember that those men belonged to a generation that was not obliged to think in terms of profit and loss as much as we are today. Life in the year 1780 was comparatively simple and not beset by the complications of the year 1880 (not to mention 1927). Every household was an economic unit of its own. People were their own butchers and bakers and candlestick makers. Their needs were few and luxuries and pleasures were practically unknown.

The farmers of the West were as a rule indebted to the bankers of the East for the original purchase price of their homesteads and for the horses and cows and wagons which they had taken with them when they said farewell to civilization and pushed into the wilderness. From the early days of our colonial existence on there had been a distinct social cleavage between the creditor class and the debtor class and the two had not infrequently called each other very unpleasant names. But the country was still so rich that there had been enough food for all the people in the fields and in the forests and on the high seas and few were those young men, who in the words of Thomas Jefferson (one of the original exponents of the theory about the red factory and the green farm) had been obliged to entrust themselves to the caprices and casualties of trade in order that they might make a living.

Gradually, however, the country had begun to fill up and the surplus population had been forced to hire itself out to those among the neighbors who were rich enough to afford one or more of the expensive tools of the new steam-driven age which went by the name of "factories" and which were as popular among the masses as a hand grenade in a freshly built dugout.

That was the beginning of that strange vicious circle which soon encircled the whole world and which has so greatly puzzled the philosophers of the last hundred years.

The output of the new and complicated tools (usually

called factories) was enormous. All sorts of people who thus far had lived in a state of almost prehistoric simplicity (a wooden house with a stone chimney, some clothes, sufficient food, and one or two pieces of primitive furniture) began to enjoy all sorts of things which in the olden days had only graced the homes and the tables of very opulent monarchs. They soon accepted these unaccustomed luxuries as something that was their due and clamored for more. But the more they got, the harder they were obliged to work, and the larger the number of mills and workshops necessary to supply their ever-increasing demands.

Meanwhile the few rich men who owned the modern tools, the factories, in order to keep their workmen busy all the year around and assure themselves of a steady flow of profit, must be forever on the lookout for fresh markets, for favorable openings in China and Africa and Asia, and must make use of every trick of politics to prevent their own particular industry from suffering even a temporary loss.

This sudden change from the simple agricultural system of the Middle Ages, which had prevailed until ten years after the founding of the Republic, to the highly complicated system of international economics which was then rapidly spreading across the face of the globe, caused a tremendous upheaval in the habits and manners of all nations. In the North and in the West, however, where society was almost entirely composed of white people, engaged for the greater part in farming, the revolution took place without attracting very much attention. It was slow and gradual. It was accepted as something inevitable. There was, of course, a great deal of friction, but except upon rare occasions it did not lead to bloodshed and it did not destroy the civilization of which it was becoming an integral part.

But the same cannot be said of that other region in the South where the leading men were trying their very best to escape the nefarious results of the dreaded factory system by keeping all mechanical improvements at a distance. The South had remained agricultural. And the landed gentry, who were dominant in the state legislatures of Virginia and Tennessee and Kentucky and the Carolinas, intended that it should remain so. Let the Yankees pollute the air with the soot of their puffing engines. As for them, they would continue to lead the lives of gentlemen and with the exception of an occasional gin mill they were not going to tolerate any evidence of the unseemly industrial scramble on the estates that had belonged to them since early in the seventeenth century.

But alas! It costs money to lead the life of a gentleman. And as everything in the rest of the world was becoming more expensive (what with strikes and rising wages and an increase in the price of raw materials) the Southern squires now needed a much larger supply of ready cash than they had done before. Which meant that they must plant more cotton and tobacco than before. Which meant that they needed more hands to work in their cotton and tobacco fields. Which meant that they needed a greater number of slaves.

Once more a vicious circle from which no one knew how to escape was to decide the fate of a nation. But in this case it was a vicious circle of a very particular hue. It was part white, part black and part chocolate-colored.

As I have remarked before, the historian should not try to turn moralist unless it is absolutely unavoidable. But please let those of us who were born beneath the Aurora Borealis cease to wring our hands in holy horror at those terrible Southerners who kept slaves, for the world had always kept slaves. They sometimes had gone by a different name but they had existed since man first learned to walk on his hind legs.

The sweet maidservant of the Ten Commandments was really a slave-girl. The Greeks besieging Troy were forever gambling for the possession of some particularly desirable and attractive slave. Caesar upon one occasion sold not less than sixty-three thousand Teuton prisoners into slavery. St. Paul regarded slavery as an indispensable institution. Magna Charta recognized the existence of serfs. In short, everybody everywhere and at all times had kept slaves. Gradually in the western part of Europe and the eastern part of America the institution had been abolished, partly because the world was getting less interested in the ideas of theologians and more in the ideals of Jesus and partly because it ceased to pay. Unfortunately the iron man and the black man had never been able to co-operate with any degree of success and in the land of Uncle Tom, Puffing Billy had always been regarded as a most unwelcome intruder and had been treated as a social outcast.

Hence an economic system that was fast becoming an anachronism in every other part of the world continued to exist in the states below the Mason and Dixon line and absolutely refused to let itself be dislocated.

"But," you will argue, "didn't the men who ruled the South understand the danger they incurred by such a policy of obstinacy? Didn't they know that slavery had been condemned for hundreds of years by all decent men and women—that in the long run it would ruin their prosperity?"

Of course they did!

A few of the less well educated Southerners like Andrew Jackson might see in slavery a semidivine institution, but the true leaders of Southern thought were dead against it. Only they thought it was useless to say so. They might insist upon keeping the words "slave" and "slavery" out of the Constitution because they did not wish to be reminded by their Northern neighbors that they were slaveholders. But for the rest they went ahead and ignored the problem because it was so intricate, so hopelessly interwoven with the entire social fabric of their daily existence that it seemed impossible to touch it without causing the downfall of a civilization which was very dear to their hearts. And they would have continued in this aloof attitude if they had not run afoul of certain economic laws, the existence of which they probably did not suspect but which were just as far-reaching in Dixie as in Vermont.

For just as their industrial neighbors of the North were forced to keep their factories going at all cost in order to outbid and outlive their competitors and find labor for their workmen or go bankrupt, so did the plantation owners feel themselves under a constant obligation to raise the largest possible crops that they might find suitable occupations for their slaves during the greatest possible number of days.

That meant that they must raise cotton and tobacco and still more cotton and tobacco and then still more cotton and tobacco.

Until in the end they raised so much cotton and tobacco that they were faced with overproduction.

Then they bethought themselves of trying to cultivate something else: rice, grain, sugar beets, heaven knows what not, and they went to the bankers who had the money which was necessary for the financing of their spring planting to discuss the change and ask for a loan.

But the bankers said, "No."

They would not be able to retain the confidence of the people who trusted them with their money unless they could guarantee their customers absolute safety. In order to guarantee them such safety they must know the sort of collateral upon which they were asked to extend a credit. They were familiar with cotton and tobacco. They knew the average yield of cotton and tobacco to within a couple of thousand bales. But rice and grain and sugar beets would mean experiments—chances, ruin, perhaps. And so the planters were forced to stick to their cotton and to their tobacco and to raise enough to give work to their unfortunate slaves who must not be left idle—because idle slaves (contrary to the habits of well-regulated engines) continued to eat and to clamor for coats and hats and lodgings.

This was really a very perplexing and rather hopeless state of affairs and what made it so much worse was the complete ignorance of the North in regard to conditions in the South. The well-to-do families of Virginia and the Carolinas were in the habit of sending their sons to Harvard and Yale and Princeton to be educated. But few New Englanders ever passed beyond that line by which the English astronomers, Charles Mason and Jeremiah

Dixon, had indicated the boundary between the possessions of the House of Penn and the House of Baltimore and which was now recognized as the frontier between the slave states and the free states.

Such information as came to them was apt to be hopelessly biased. Often it was incorrect. Then there followed incriminating articles in the newspapers and magazines of Charleston and Springfield and then, one fine day, the whole question was bodily dragged into the delectable realm of literature, and a well-meaning but hopelessly prejudiced Puritan woman drew so monstrous a picture of the conditions which were supposed to prevail in the slave states that the whole of the North seemed ready to go to war and wipe out this dastardly race of Simon Legrees and other slave-baiters.

But I need not go on.

As it is, I seem to have assumed the role of defender of an institution which I detest and hate as cordially as the most bigoted of abolitionists.

The point I wish to make is a different one.

The North accused the South of keeping slaves.

But in their eagerness for justice and righteousness, the people of the North overlooked one very important fact —that the slaveholding Southerners were themselves the slaves of the system that in turn forced them to keep slaves.

Now when conditions have become so hopelessly muddled that no one sees a way out, then there seems to be but a single solution.

In years to come, when we shall know a great deal more about a great many important subjects than we do today, we may be able to cure such ills by the peaceful application of reason and intellect.

Today, for all such afflictions of the human race (individually or collectively) there appears to be only one remedy. When it happens to you or to me, we call it an operation. But in case of a nation, it is known by the dreadful name of War.

## Chapter Forty-Two

## AN IRKSOME CONTRACT

IF I WERE ASKED to state wherein the history of the United States differed from the history of all other countries, I would answer, "In the influence which the art of oratory has been allowed to exercise upon the political and social development of our nation."

Republics were nothing new when the Americans decided to strike out for themselves. The representative form of government which the original founders of our country chose in preference to a pure democracy was as old as the hills of Rome. And federated republics could look back upon a record of almost a thousand years when the delegates from the thirteen little independent states at last decided to form a defensive union of their own.

But with the possible exception of the short-lived Greek republics, no people had ever paid the slightest attention to oratory. On the contrary, they had shared Hamlet's well-known prejudice and had been deeply suspicious of those who tried to solve the world's difficulties with "words, words, words."

There was, however, a perfectly good reason for such a one-sided development of the cultural interests of America. The ancient Jews gained great renown as authors two thousand years before, because literature was the only form of art in which they could express themselves. Jerusalem was a tenth-rate little country town, not to be compared with the glorious cities of the East or the West. The glorious temple of Solomon was so inconspicuous that no reputable author of antiquity ever heard of it and those glowing descriptions of the interior which are to be found in the Old Testament show us with painful precision how everything within that sacred enclosure had been sacrificed to a desire for gaudiness and glitter, and they make it clear why the Greeks with their highly developed sense of harmony and their insistence upon simplicity of line had always avoided this far-famed edifice and had gone for their inspiration to Memphis and Thebes.

Of course David had been a musician and had played the harp. But that tinkly three-stringed instrument was not the sort of thing to appeal to men of real creative ability and as the second of their ancestral commandments forbade them to paint pictures, there was only one field of artistic endeavor that remained open to the Jews, and that was the field of the written word.

The country lawyer
from Illinois

The Puritans who dominated the early civilization of America had most successfully dramatized themselves into the spiritual successors of the ancient Hebrews. They lived and ate and drank and hated and plowed and harvested and ruled their wives and children and manhandled their native neighbors according to the best examples of Deuteronomy and the Book of Judges.

Hence their complete and profound contempt for those more graceful expressions of the soul, which were supposed to be of pagan origin. Hence that all-overpowering distrust (mentioned before) of the painter and the actor and the musician and those other useless people who only tried to add something to the outward happiness and the inner beauty of contemporary existence.

The art of the orator had been the only exception to

this rigid rule. In the first place, it was of genuine Hebrew origin and therefore beyond reproach. And in the second place, it was one of the most powerful weapons by which the clergy were able to maintain their hold upon the common mass of the people.

Deprive a congregation of the solace of Bach and Handel and their starving souls will begin to find a distinct relief in the long verbal harangues on Hell and damnation with which they were entertained upon all seemly and unseemly occasions during the days of their youth. Oratory, therefore, was and had always been the favorite form of emotional expression of the American colonists, and when they moved westward it followed them into the wilderness and when they acquired independence the theological spellbinder was succeeded by the political sermonizer. And whereas all other and older republics had been conducted with a minimum of verbosity, whereas Venice and Iceland and Holland and Switzerland had managed to rule themselves and their colonies without any patriotic eloquence, the new American commonwealth celebrated every new occurrence (however unimportant) by a brilliant display of verbal fireworks.

The founding fathers, like all good aristocrats, had not taken much stock in these rhetorical outbursts. They had listened patiently (because it was good politics to listen patiently to their impassioned colleagues from the backwoods) but whenever they felt that they were really among themselves (as for example they did when they worked on the Declaration of Independence or on the Constitution, or some other document of real importance) they cut short on elocution and stuck to facts.

When, however, the field and the forest triumphed over the city and when the form of government of the United States was changed from a representative republic to a pure democracy (the one calamity which the founders had feared above all other things and against which remote possibility they had taken every possible precaution) then the torrents of bitter tirade of the earlier days grew into veritable cataracts and waterspouts—and not infrequently they threatened by their violence to upset the little craft which Washington and Jefferson and Franklin and Adams had so laboriously launched upon the turbulent ocean of international politics.

And then was born that strange delusion which was to gain such dangerous popularity during the days of the Jacksonian dictatorship, the conviction (held by millions) that a mere gift for words would make a man fit to conduct the affairs of state.

It was a period when the old-timers of the Revolution were rapidly disappearing. Their children, well bred, carefully trained, and philosophically minded, tried to continue the standard of conduct laid down by their parents. But serious-minded administrators were no longer wanted by the Republic. Conspicuous fitness for a job and a lifetime of preparation were beginning to be regarded as highly undesirable evidences of that strange quality known as "highbrow-ism" and foredoomed a candidate to failure.

Now the aristocracy which ruled the Republic during the first thirty years of its existence had many faults. Those stiff-necked gentlemen were absolutely blind to the possible virtues of less fortunate people who had worked their way up from the ranks, and in their fear of democracy they passed many highhanded measures which were to the interest of their own class and paid scant attention to the happiness of the public at large.

But most of them were possessed of a high sense of duty. Their integrity (with a very few exceptions) was above reproach. They had grown away from the tyranny of the existing religious opinions. They stood for a much greater degree of broad-mindedness than was held respectable by the majority of their fellow citizens and with a profound and skeptical distrust of pretty words, they had preferred to say little and do much.

The new class of political leaders hailed from a different part of the social and geographic world. They soon discovered that by appealing strictly to the vanity of those who took pride in calling themselves the "plain people" and to whom flattery was as indispensable as, yea, more so, than a plentiful supply of fresh air, they could turn politics into a profitable business for themselves and at the same time gain the reputation of being the saviors of the country.

All of which merely serves as an introduction to the remark (by no means original) that the period between the election of Andrew Jackson and that of Abraham Lincoln cannot be regarded as a happy era in our national history.

In the first place, the sound advice of the first of our presidents to keep away from all foreign entanglements was completely forgotten. The new school of politicians fully understood the value of "spread-eagleism" as a factor in national politics and they made the beast scream until in an outburst of aquilian hysteria it bit and clawed at everybody and everything and made a very great nuisance of itself.

In the two decades which followed upon the election of Van Buren (Jackson's man Friday and heir) the United States interfered forcibly in other people's affairs at the rate of once for every twelve months.

The Monroe doctrine was supposed to have made the claim that "America belonged exclusively to the Americans" while stating in emphatic terms that the United States had no quarrel and meant to have no quarrel with the existing order of colonial management in either part of the continent and desired to live in a state of peace and amity with all of its neighbors, both foreign and domestic.

But such an attitude of live and let live seemed entirely too tame for those who in their first flush of Jacksonian enthusiasm hoped to bestow the blessings of pure democracy upon every other nation of this earth. As a result American war vessels sailed to distant parts of the world and "opened up" China and the Hawaiian Islands and Japan and other exotic kingdoms of the East which for reasons of their own had thus far preferred to keep the white man at a distance.

Next there was a direct descent upon the enemy's territory when several American diplomats, gathered in the vicinity of Ostend's gaming-tables, drew up a grandiloquent manifesto which declared that in some mysterious way the island of Cuba was predestined to be part of the

United States and that unless Spain were willing to sell this ancient and treasured possession, America must take it by force of arms. As this document was the work of a man who had been promoted to be minister in Madrid because he was not wanted at home (a disastrous diplomatic innovation which was bestowed upon us by the admirers of General Jackson) it was possible to withdraw from the unpleasant consequences of this blunder by calling His Excellency back to his home in Louisiana and by explaining that there had been a slight mistake.

The gratuitous aggressiveness, however, and the offensive tactlessness which characterized the conduct of our foreign affairs was as naught compared to the violence with which the two contending parties at home attacked each other.

Civil war

For two definitely hostile parties there were with ideals and slogans all their own and all the fine phrases in the world could not hide the fact that the introduction of steam—the far-famed economic revolution for our economists—had caused a hopeless clash of interests between those states which "made" things and those which allowed God and their slaves to "grow" them.

There was the North which depended for its sustenance upon an ever-increasing number of factories operated by supposedly free white men and women.

There was the South which derived its prosperity (and must continue to derive its prosperity) from the products of the soil raised by the labor of erstwhile African potentates.

There was the North which demanded that it be given a monopoly of the American market by a rigid exclusion of all foreign goods.

There was the South which needed a system of free trade in order to sell its output of cotton and tobacco and rice to the nations of Europe.

There was the North which dreamed of turning the forests and fields of the far West into manufacturing communities.

There was the South which hoped to gain the support of the frontier districts by turning them into agricultural and slaveholding communities.

Both sides pleaded and argued and made a great showing of unselfish patriotism. But both sides knew that there was only one issue, that it was moral rather than economic and that the name thereof was slavery.

During those terrible periods of disillusionment which seem bound to follow closely upon all outbreaks of human enthusiasm, there are always a great many people who are heard to say that there is no such thing as "progress" —that "civilization" is only skin-deep—that at heart we are savages and quite as unconcerned for the well-being of our neighbors as our ancestors of the early stone age.

And yet—and yet—the line of improvement shows a steady upward trend. Not, I grant you, without occasional temporary setbacks. Not without long years of apparent decadence. Not without violent upheavals which suddenly remove the center of culture and thought from one end of the world to another. "But," as Galileo never said (but might have said), "the old earth moves all the same!"

And during the first half of the nineteenth century the collective conscience of humanity (if there is such a thing, and I believe that there is) had reached the point where it was decided that chattel slavery must disappear from the face of the earth. Twenty or thirty years before the founders of the Republic had still been able to sidestep the question. But even they had known in their heart of hearts that the institution of slavery was doomed. And if only they had been a little younger when they assumed command of the Revolution and had not been so completely worn out by the labors of seven terrible years, they might have found a solution for this difficult problem that would have been both fair and intelligent.

In the clumsy hands of their successors, small-town statesmen with bushy beards and exaggerated reputations, village elders and parochial favorite sons who treated every problem as if it were an independent phenomenon and not related to the rest of mankind, such a conflict of opinions could only lead to disaster.

One by one, between the years 1788 and 1864, the other nations of Europe and America abolished slavery and although in many countries the slaves represented enormous investments of capital, the change was brought about without the spilling of a drop of blood. There were growls and there were protests and the Old Testament was carefully ransacked for texts that should turn the unendurable bondage of black people into something eternal and semidivine. But it was impossible to check the rising tide of decency or to silence those who insisted that the Fatherhood of God extended its merciful pity to all of His children and contained no bylaws regulating their respective pigmentations.

That many of these latter-day crusaders in their holy zeal broke all the rules of polite controversy and were just as narrow-minded and bigoted as the worst of their opponents was regrettable but quite unavoidable, for men were stirred to the very depths of their subconscious selves and when that happens, reason is sacrificed to emotion.

And all the haggling about the admission of "free states" and "slave states," the disputes about this or that or the other parallel that should be the definite line of demarcation between "free" and "slave," all the excitement about "squatter sovereignty" and other temporary compromises which failed to compromise—all these endless words and words and words could not change one iota from the inexorable law that slavery, black, white, brown, and yellow, must be wiped from the face of the earth.

The real danger, however, did not come from the side of the enraged slaveholders or the equally enraged abolitionists. The real menace lay among that rapidly increasing class of citizens who regarded the Republic as a convenient boardinghouse, whose ambitions did not reach beyond the unholy wish to make as much money as possible in as short a time as feasible and who therefore insisted upon peace and safety, even at the price of national dishonor.

The introduction of the ruthless Jacksonian methods had given them an excuse to keep away from all participation in the national life. The hundreds of millions of dollars invested in human cattle made them fear that interference with the institution would cause a panic which in turn might be disastrous to the regular flow of their own profits. And finally, and let this be said in extenuation of their lukewarmness, there had not been a single individual among the crowd of loud-bellowing partisans who demanded their attention who thus far had been able to appeal to their imagination or who had explained the issue in terms that were really clear to them.

And so the war of mutual abuse continued during endless years and some there were in the North who spoke of breaking up the Union and some there were in the South who talked of forming a federated republic of their own, but neither side had quite the courage to take such a drastic step.

And it seemed that nothing was to be done for all time to come.

And then Nancy Hanks, the wife of Thomas Lincoln, gave birth to a son and hoped to God that the boy would take after her own folks and would not be condemned to spend the rest of his days helping his ineffectual father to make a living on a farm that did not raise enough for a single cow.

## Chapter Forty-Three

# AN UNKNOWN COUNTRY LAWYER FROM ILLINOIS OFFERS TO TAKE THE CASE

"WE THINK that we are pushing, and meanwhile we ourselves are being pushed." And again, "I claim not to have controlled events, but confess plainly that events have controlled me."

The men who near the end of their days summed up their philosophy of life in these short but effective sentences were contemporaries, but they lived at different ends of the social and geographical poles.

One was the son of a rich and ambitious father who hoped to gain enduring fame by the brilliant career of his precocious offspring. The other saw the dim light of day in the slovenly home of a peasant who was a professional failure, a third-rate carpenter and occasional farmer who could hardly spell his own name.

The elder was given all those advantages that money can buy, private tutors, universities, books, foreign travel.

The younger was forced to dig and scratch for every scrap of learning that he could afterward call his own and he spent the greater part of his childhood in a cold and uncomfortable corner of a roadless wilderness.

A strangely assorted pair!

But Genius—praise be to Allah!—is not interested in pedigrees, and lightly touching the forehead of Abraham Lincoln and Johann Wolfgang von Goethe, she bestowed upon both these favorite children the greatest honor that can come to the sons of men—she gave them life everlasting and made them into the enduring symbols of their countries' noblest aspirations.

As for the younger of the two men (Lincoln was twenty-three when Goethe died) his story has been told so often that it is (and of right should be) the common knowledge of every child born within the shadow of his mighty name.

The Lincolns were of English stock. They had come to America during the first half of the seventeenth century when they moved from Hingham in Norfolk to Hingham in New England. Once in the new world they had felt the influence of the prevailing wanderlust and from Massachusetts they had trekked to Pennsylvania, from Pennsylvania to Kentucky, and then, when Abraham was four years old, they once more pulled up stakes, left the barren farm in Hardin County, and moved to a more hopeful tract of black corn land in Indiana.

It was there that the boy of nine whittled the wooden pegs for his mother's coffin and looked on wonderingly when they took her away and buried her together with her secret.

For Nancy Hanks was not supposed to be of the common clay of those honest weavers and iron-founders, those slow-witted, plodding farmers with whom she had spent her days in this squalid and poverty-stricken part of the frontier. Unconsciously she had reached back to a few of the things that should have been hers by right of heritage, things far away in a world which she did not even suspect.

And she had reached back to good purpose—for fifty years later her son was master of the White House.

. . . . .

What of the years that really shape a man's future?

The years came in the ordinary course of events. The future, however, seemed vaguely distant, not to say hopeless.

Like all the other boys of Spencer County, young Abraham worked on the farm.

He learned to spell and to write and to do simple sums in arithmetic. Then Sarah Bush, his stepmother, took a hand in his education and explained the beauties of the printed word as expounded by Burns and Defoe and Shakespeare.

All of which was very fine, but the old man was still

alive, bungling his farm job as usual and offering grudging board for long, hard hours of work. The prospect of spending all his days as his father's hired man did not appeal to Abraham. He left home and in a very casual way he went in search of the even more casual dollar.

He hired out as a deck hand on flatboats—he did chores —he talked to people—he was agreeable to whatever living creature came within touch of his lanky hands—he told stories—he listened—and he smiled. Next he clerked in a number of shops of one sort or another, mostly the other sort.

Then there was trouble with the Indians and he enlisted. But the poor savages took to their heels before Captain Lincoln appeared upon the scene and for lack of an enemy he dropped his martial disguise and went back to storekeeping.

The new venture proved even less successful than the career in the army. The customers stayed away—a good-for-nothing partner drank up all the liquid stock—and the concern went under with such a splash that it took Lincoln fifteen years to settle his debts.

All this, I grant you, makes very drab reading for a story that is supposed to deal with one of our national heroes. It seems so futile. It borders upon the grotesque. And yet even this episode in the bankruptcy court had its uses. It served as a postgraduate course in everyday humanities. And as an investment in the knowledge of human nature, it bore rich fruit.

For now the young man had reached his twenties when the early handicaps of environment are beginning to be left behind, when other influences are apt to make themselves felt in the ambitious struggle for recognition.

This funny-looking giant, this ambulating clotheshorse, seemed to have a mind. A strange mind—a queer mind—a mind with funny quirks—with little wandering by-paths which seemed to lead with incongruous indifference from the ludicrous to the sublime—but a mind!

And this commodity being fairly scarce, it received due acknowledgment and together with its possessor it was somehow pushed into a law office and from the law office it was raised to the state legislature, and from there it was promoted to the House of Representatives in far-away Washington and was even asked to function at a time when thinking was apt to make a man suspected of high treason and cowardice.

Lincoln reached the national capital while the Mexican war was going on.

He did not like that war.

He said so.

Then he made himself comfortable in that unwieldy cape which he had bought for the great voyage to the metropolis and waited.

Another storm was coming.

This time he meant to be ready.

. . . . . . .

The country was rapidly drifting into a state of anarchy and civil war. Slavery or no-slavery had split the old political parties into strangely assorted groups of saints and highwaymen—practical politicians and sentimental idiots—which obeyed no leader, had no party program, and were being kept together only by a few common convictions and prejudices.

Until the slaveholding Southerners rallied around the flag of the party known as the Democratic one, while their opponents formed a group of their own which proudly called itself the Republican party and proclaimed the principle of an undivided Union and freedom unto all men.

It was then that Lincoln's past experiences enabled him to play a useful role and make himself a figure of national prominence.

He had spent some of his years in territories where they kept slaves, and he had lived in the states that were free. He knew the horrors of the institution of slavery and he hated to think back to the days when his boat was crowded which shackled human beings. On the other side he knew from firsthand observation that the economic system of an entire people cannot suddenly be changed at the behest of a few well-meaning outsiders. Wherefore he counseled moderation. Slavery must go. It had no right to exist in a nation of civilized people. The only question now before the country was this—could the change be accomplished without destroying the nation and if it could not be done that way, should the nation be sacrificed for an abstract ideal of justice?

Poor old crazy John Brown shouted, "No! It can't be done without bloodshed!" And he raised a fluttering flag of rebellion which a few days afterward was reverently draped across his coffin.

But South Carolina politely answered, "Yes." And quietly and unobtrusively the state slipped out of the Union and solemnly voted herself among the "free and independent nations of the earth."

. . . . . .

That happened in the month of December of the year 1860.

Three months later, Abraham Lincoln, President of the United States by the grace of the Republican party, once more traveled to Washington and moved his carpetbag into the big white building that stood at the other end of Pennsylvania Avenue.

Two days afterward he took the oath of office and, rising awkwardly to his full height, he told his assembled neighbors what he meant to do.

It was, alas, his duty to protect, preserve, and defend the Union. And now a good many of his fellow countrymen were threatening to destroy that Union which it was his duty to protect, preserve, and defend.

That was very foolish of them. God knows, he did not hate them. He wished them only well. He was willing to listen to all their reasonable suggestions. He would lend every effort toward a speedy and peaceful solution. But he had sworn to protect, preserve, and defend the Union and protect, preserve, and defend it he would.

His words were very simple. Indeed, they were so simple that the vast majority of his beloved fellow citizens completely failed to understand their meaning.

Wherefore they poked each other in the ribs and laughed, and said, "Huh! Did you see the funny hat he wore?"

*Chapter Forty-Four*

## THE CASE IS SUBMITTED TO THE JURY

IT IS CURIOUS that the Southern States should have been the ones who actually broke that solemn pact of the year 1787 and withdrew from the Union.

Thus far the danger had always come from the side of the New Englanders.

But their oft-expressed desire to "nullify" (a dignified word invented by statesmen who are about to turn a treaty into a scrap of paper) had been the result of a secret conviction that the people of Massachusetts and their neighbors were just a little too good for the company they were keeping and had better set up an establishment of their own in which they need not fear constant interruptions on the part of certain uncouth citizens who lived on the other side of the Berkshires and the Connecticut River.

The affair of the year 1860, however, was of a different nature and much more serious.

If the brutal truth must out, the South, ever since the days of General Jackson's dictatorship, had been in the habit of bullying the rest of the United States. It had not been able to do this alone, but by making a clever use of the crude but entirely sincere enthusiasms of the West, it had been able to treat the northern and eastern part of the Republic as a political dependency, a small sister-republic which had better behave itself or—

"Or what?" asked that strange, lanky old rail splitter, who was now blacking his boots in the basement of the White House.

"Or we shall refuse to play with you any longer!"

shouted the eager young bucks from Charleston and New Orleans and Savannah and Richmond.

And they went to their tailors and ordered themselves very natty uniforms, entirely unlike those worn by the soldiers of the Federal army, and they paraded before a new flag that looked quite different from the old and familiar stars and stripes, and they laughed loudly and heartily when they thought of the funny trick they had just played on the damnyankees, who, of course, would be much too busy running their old mills and their banks and their grocery stores to take a gun and go and fight.

. . . . . . .

In which, as they were to discover shortly afterward, they were surely mistaken.

Now in the olden days, when people went to war they went to war, and that was all there was to it. They might feel that the final victory had been due to the direct interference of Jehovah or the protection of Baal or the support of Jupiter, but they did not try to surround the preliminaries with a dignified nimbus of holy forbearance and inhuman patience.

They got mad about something or other and they killed each other until they felt better and then they sold their enemy's wives and children into slavery and went home with such plunder as they could carry on their backs.

All of which was low and bestial and savage, but at least it was an honest and straightforward manner of conducting an affair which by its very nature is bound to be low and bestial and savage.

The invention of the art of writing (not to mention the fatal introduction of the telephone and the telegraph) has changed all this. During the last two thousand years, as soon as hostilities have begun the participants in the conflict have hastened to their professors of history and have asked them to prepare a statement about the "antecedents" of this regrettable misunderstanding in order that the rest of the world might appreciate the complete and total innocence of party A (or party B) which has been unprovokedly attacked by party B (or party A) and has, therefore, been put under the unpleasant obligation of declaring a partial mobilization "for the sake of defending its good rights against a brutal aggressor."

In the case of the Civil War, the period of preliminary discussions and official alibis lasted about five months.

On December the twentieth of the year 1860, South Carolina seceded from the Union. In January of the next year, Mississippi, Florida, Georgia, Louisiana, Alabama, and North Carolina did likewise, and in February the state of Texas followed their example and bade farewell to the common country.

On the fourth of February of the year 1861 representatives from these states met in the city of Montgomery in Alabama. They formed a Republic of their own, called the Confederate States of America, and elected Jefferson Davis as their president.

Like Lincoln, Davis was a native of Kentucky. He had been Secretary of War under President Pierce and had brought about a complete reorganization of the army. When the rebellion of the Southern states occurred, he represented the state of Mississippi in the United States Senate. He was undoubtedly a man of sincere convictions and of some ability. But he lacked the one dominant quality which accounted for the phenomenal success of Lincoln. The President of the Confederate States did not have that beautifully patterned analytical mind which allowed the President of the United States to go straight to the heart of any question, without being diverted by a mass of nonessential details. As a result (for in conflicts of such nature, the analytical mind is bound to win out with almost mathematical surety) the United States survive to this day while the Confederate States have been relegated to the museum of historical curiosities.

But to return to the movement for secession. Virginia, Tennessee, and Arkansas soon afterward joined the other discontented states and then the two republics entered upon a series of discussions, or, to be more precise, President Davis suggested a form of compromise by which the continuation or the abolition of slavery in any given state should be a matter of local option.

But his rivals in Washington refused to listen to any such proposals until the Confederate States should have first returned within the fold of the Union.

Then an effort was made to save the situation by adding another amendment to the Constitution which once and for all should regulate the power of Congress over slavery. But the North fought shy of a plan which would have solved nothing at all and would only have tied the hands of the Federal government, while leaving the slaveholders free to do what they wanted. Wherefore, the amendment was rejected and the inevitable was allowed to happen, without a further waste of paper and ink.

During all these months there had been constant and wholesale resignations (or desertions) from the army and navy on the part of Southern-born officers. Most of these had offered their services to Jefferson Davis and, clad in a becoming gray, they were now drilling and marching the Confederate recruits, while the North stood by and did nothing.

At last, however, seeing the drift of things, Washington reluctantly decided to take some countermeasures and prepare for a state of war which might last all the way from six weeks to four months.

One of the few strong points within the territory of the South that remained in the hands of the United States Government was an old fort in the harbor of Charleston. It was called after Thomas Sumter, the last surviving general of Washington's armies. It was situated on a small island and was one of the three strongholds which commanded the entrance to the Ashley and Cooper rivers. Major Anderson, who was in charge, was a peaceful man but he was also getting to be a very hungry man, for his supplies were running low and an effort to bring him fresh beans and bacon early in January had failed when the steamer *Star of the West* flying the United States flag had been fired upon by a South Carolinian battery and had been obliged to return. But finally during the latter half of March the gallant major received word that another expedition was being fitted out at the Brooklyn Navy Yard and that his time of waiting had almost come to an end. The second expedition was supposed to be a deep secret, but everybody talked about it and, of course, the Confederate government, which had thousands of ardent sympathizers in the North, was fully posted upon the affair and waited for the U.S.S. *Powhatan* with ill-concealed impatience. But when the stage was at last set for an open outbreak of hostilities, both parties got slightly scared and so unwilling were they to assume responsibility for the unavoidable "overt act" that the departure of the little ship was officially mentioned in communications between the Federal and the Confederate Secretaries of War and it was explained by Washington that the *Powhatan* would not try to re-enforce the garrison of Sumter but would only carry foodstuffs and a few medical supplies.

Why the Confederates chose this moment to force the issue is still a mystery. No doubt the decision was the result of psychological rather than political considerations. The Southerners had ruled the country for so many years that it must have become increasingly unbearable for them to be consistently outwitted by a backwoods lawyer who did not know how to order a dinner and who, furthermore, had the reputation of being the blackest of all black Republicans.

And acting in a moment of mental panic and driven by the secret fear that Abe Lincoln might be up to another one of his old tricks, orders were telegraphed to General Beauregard (formerly U. S. A. but now C. S. A.), who was then in Charleston, to attack Fort Sumter if he should deem such a step necessary.

A few hours later Davis and his cabinet repented of their rashness. But the deed was done and although Anderson let it be known that he had only food enough for two more days and would then be obliged to surrender or starve to death, the Confederate batteries opened fire on him on the morning of April the twelfth of the year 1861 and after a bombardment that lasted twenty-four hours, the ardor of the cannoneers was rewarded by the surrender of the objectionable Federal stronghold.

Although there had been a great deal of smoke and noise, the actual damage was very slight.

Not a single one among the Federal soldiers had been either killed or wounded. And as for the Confederates, they had turned the affair into a fashionable society event and had bravely fired their ten-pounders amidst the plaudits of the pretty girls from Charleston.

All of which then seemed harmless enough.

But these good people overlooked one very important item.

It was they who had fired the first shot.

It was they who had hauled down the flag of the United States.

In short, it was they who had committed an "overt act" of war.

And by so doing they had given their clever opponent in the White House the one thing for which he had hoped and prayed all along, a loyal nation, ready to back him up in whatever measures he might deem necessary.

On the fifteenth of April of the year 1861 Lincoln asked for seventy-five thousand volunteers.

One day later the first Yankee regiments began to move toward Washington.

*Chapter Forty-Five*

## THE CASE IS DECIDED FOR GOOD AND ALL

No DOUBT it would be very agreeable if we could live on a little planet all by ourselves. But as things stand now and have stood for the last couple of billion years (and probably will continue to stand for several billion years to come) we are part of the so-called civilized world and whatever we do reflects upon our neighbors, and whatever our neighbors do bears a direct influence upon our own happiness and prosperity.

The United States, according to the view of the North,

was engaged upon the unfortunate but necessary task of repressing a rebellion.

According to the South, a number of sovereign states were fighting to maintain their independence.

According to Europe a war had broken out on the American continent between two small independent nations and that conflict promised to bring about the downfall and disruption of a hitherto strong and much feared Republic.

Let me remind you here that in the code of international relations there is no such word as affection. If you diligently search the pages of those curious volumes dedicated to that mysterious subject you may find "respect" and "admiration" and sometimes "gratitude." But the expression "love between nations" belongs exclusively to the vocabulary of our professional propagandists and is not a part of the sober-minded glossary of the more brutal (and therefore less dishonest) of our historians and journalists.

Officially at least, England had long since agreed to overlook the rebellion of her former colonies which had led to the establishment of a free republic. As for the war of 1812, it had been too inglorious an affair for both sides to be honored by popular remembrance. And in the sixties of the nineteenth century there were many people in England who were heart and soul for the cause of the abolitionists and who gave of their best to bring about the triumph of the North.

But there were many Britishers who regarded—and rightly so—America as the most dangerous menace to the uninterrupted commercial supremacy of their own empire. They had never quite dared to take up arms to destroy this uncomfortable rival. But if anyone else was found willing to do so—more strength to both his arms. And if one could oblige this unexpected ally with the sale of a few guns and warships and kegs of powder—would they please place their orders (together with certified checks) at the earliest possible moment and would they please remember their friends in their hour of victory?

And then, of course, there was the highly important social aspect of the case. To the upper classes of old Europe (and their influence in those days was much stronger than we sometimes take the trouble to remember) the fight between the North and South was a continuation of the old warfare between king and parliament, between country and court, between Puritan and Royalist. In this warfare the side of the Roundheads was represented by the shopkeepers and manufacturers of the North while the plantation owners of the South, as true gentlemen of the old-fashioned British school, had drawn their swords in defense of those ideals for which their cavalier ancestors had spilled their blood and their silver spoons on the fields of Marston Moor and Naseby.

But England was not the only potential enemy of the Union. There was the Emperor Napoleon. Not, of course, the great Napoleon, who now rested underneath a slab of red porphyry in the chapel of his Home for Old Soldiers. But a nephew—a strange young man who spoke the language of his subjects with a rich German accent, and who had hitched his little wagon to his uncle's star with such a shrewd display of Buonapartistic cleverness that he had been able to fool eight million of his contemporaries into voting for him as their executive head. His new imperial throne, however, was a very shaky affair and he was seriously thinking of providing his subjects with a little entertainment in the form of a war. And as the nation which he ruled had always been willing to upset the peace of Europe for the sake of some imaginary scraps of "honor" and "glory," the rest of the world was kept in a constant state of suspense and irritation.

True enough, for the moment France and the United States were still on a friendly footing with each other. But who could foretell when the priest-ridden wife of the sallow, sick man would deem it necessary to preach a crusade against her grandfather's people? And what the Empress and her friends wanted, Napoleon wanted, and what Napoleon wanted, a subsidized press could overnight revaluate into "the will of the entire French nation," and the moment that was done, half a million more men would be added to those forces which England was prepared to transport to Canada.

All this may seem highly fantastic to us in the year of Grace 1927. But it was part of a very grim reality during the first year of Lincoln's administration and it caused him and his cabinet quite as much concern and worry as the uninterrupted series of victories of the Confederate armies.

In the year 1861 the New Faith of the Frontier of which I spoke in a previous chapter had been accepted as gospel truth by the greater part of the people of the United States. And there were two dogmas which no one dared to doubt on pain of the social and economic displeasure of his neighbors.

The first of these stated that every man of good, sound common sense could handle practically any job that offered itself with the possible exception of a few highly technical trades as those practiced in doctors' offices and chemical laboratories.

The second was an unshakable confidence in the war-like spirit of all free-born American citizens—a belief, often expressed in glowing terms of self-adulation, that at a moment's notice a million Americans would spring forward to defend the righteous cause of democracy and armed only with cornstalks or broomhandles would lick the stuffing out of five or fifty times their own number of mere foreigners.

Let me dispose of the second dogma first. The volunteer system had never been a success. Washington's letters contain endless laments about the incompetence and the indifference of the majority of his badly trained militiamen who often deprived him of a deserved victory by their cowardliness, their lack of discipline, and their total disregard of what the general called "the first rules of true patriotism." If it had not been for certain natural advantages of a geographic nature and the highly valuable support of the French regulars and the German drill masters, it is doubtful whether the United States would ever have gained its independence.

During the war of 1812 the behavior of the militia had

caused a public scandal. Whole regiments of New York State soldiers refused to fight outside the territory of the U.S.A., which was very pleasant for the Canadians but not so pleasant for the Americans along the frontier, who were left to the mercy of the English and the Indians. Upon several occasions the militia had stampeded from the field of battle for no very apparent reason. Called upon to protect the national capital from invasion and destruction, these patriots had engaged in a scramble to the rear, which survives in our folklore as the well-known Bladensburg race, and had left the actual fighting to a handful of marines of Teutonic extraction.

As for the Mexican war, seven out of eleven of General Scott's militia regiments had informed their commander-in-chief that they were "one-year men," that they had not enlisted for "the duration of the war" and had left their chief when he was within four days' distance of Mexico City and had thereby delayed the capture of that important stronghold for almost half a year.

When President Lincoln had followed the bombardment of Fort Sumter with a proclamation for 75,000 volunteers, his appeal had found an eager answering among those who really felt sufficiently strong about the issues of the war to back up their opinions with their lives. But soon this enthusiasm had waned, as such enthusiasm is apt to do. Thereupon bounties of one or two hundred dollars had been offered to all those who were willing to enlist and enterprising businessmen had gone to Europe and had filled whole ships with Belgian and English and Polish immigrants who entered the army as soon as they set foot on our free soil and had divided their bounties with the promoters! And this profitable business had continued until the British government complained of it in such forcible terms that the Washington authorities were forced to take notice and forbade further enlistments on the part of these "contract soldiers."

A few months of this sort of thing had made it clear to everyone in the North that the army of the Union could only be kept at full strength by means of conscription. A draft bill was therefore drawn up and was duly passed and every one of the states was put under the obligation of providing the Federal army with a certain specified number of soldiers. If these could be recruited among the volunteers, so much the better. But in case there were not enough volunteers, the deficit must be made up by a draft. No one quite liked the idea of conscription which was felt to be un-American, but it was the only way to beat the conscripted armies of the Confederacy and therefore the system was harshly enforced. An exception was made for those more or less well-to-do young men who felt that their presence was so urgently needed behind the line of battle that they were not warranted in risking their valuable lives at the front. These were allowed to send a substitute if they could find some poor devil who was willing to risk his neck in exchange for a certain amount of cash. Those who could not afford to do this were obliged to go, whether they liked it or not, and when the Irish of Boston and New York showed a disinclination to take part in a conflict that did not in the least interest them, there was a very serious riot during which the regulars fired upon the mob and killed enough people to make the others eager to obey the law.

All this was held to be a great pity but then as now it was impossible to make war without causing a certain amount of bodily harm to quite a large number of people, and then as now this fact seemed to come as a painful surprise to those who were most vociferous in their hatred of the enemy and who were the most ardent champions of what they were pleased to call "civilized warfare"—a remark which was invariably followed by loud outbreaks of profane hilarity among the denizens of the trenches or the occupants of the gun turrets.

So much for the physical background of the conflict and now let me say something about dogma No. 1—the famous pioneering theory that any reasonably intelligent citizen can undertake anything his (or her) hand finds to do and can make a success of his (or her) job. Alas! There, too, great disappointment awaited the people of both the North and the South.

Neither Jefferson Davis nor Abraham Lincoln was

quite fit for the task which awaited him in the year 1861. They had to learn their new profession from the bottom up. It was a foregone conclusion that the Northern President, endowed with a much higher type of mentality than his neighbor from across the Potomac, should eventually beat his rival and should lead his part of the nation to victory. But three terrible years were to go by before Lincoln had mastered the rudiments of his job. And nowhere did he meet with more difficulties than in the field of diplomacy—a noble and subtle art held in deep contempt by all good democrats—a sort of fancy-dress party which might appeal to the soft-spoken aristocrats of the effete European Continent but no fit game for red-blooded he-men and their equally red-blooded she-wives.

The highly favorable exceptions to this rule might have taught the people at home that one skillful and highly trained diplomat at the court of an unfriendly nation could be worth more than ten profoundly wise politicians at home. But the populace was in no mood to ponder such questions and as a result both presidents got into considerable trouble with the rest of the world before either of them had been in office more than a couple of months.

To begin with, President Lincoln had followed his appeal for volunteers with an edict which declared that the coast of America from Virginia to Texas was in a state of blockade and that all vessels trying to enter the ports of the seceding states would thenceforth run the risk of being stopped and taken to a Northern port by the war vessels of the Union.

Unfortunately by so doing the Washington government had tacitly recognized the existence of a "state of war" between the United States of America and the Confederate States of America. That placed them in an uncomfortable position. On the one hand they denounced the Southerners as rebels and traitors, on the other hand they spoke of the "belligerency" of the Confederate States, and a "belligerent" in the language of Noah Webster, meant a "nation, a party, or a person waging regular war as recognized by the law of nations."

The British law officers, when they read this document, were somewhat puzzled and explained that much to their regret they must stand by the stipulations of existing international treaties and agreements. They could not (officially, at least) take cognizance of the fact that the word "belligerency" as used by the American President in his proclamation of the nineteenth of April of the year 1861 really was intended to cover something more closely akin to "revolution" than to "war." And so they gathered as many whereases and therefores as they could and gave fair warning to all Britishers that "whereas hostilities have most unhappily commenced between the government of the United States of America and certain states styling themselves the Confederate States of America, and that whereas Great Britain intends to maintain a strict and impartial neutrality, they therefore must warn all British subjects from entering the armies or navies of the belligerents or from helping fit out, equipping, or arming at home or abroad any vessel which is to be used as a transport, a privateer, or a man-of-war" and so on and so forth. The usual proclamation of neutrality.

This ukase was published as a mere matter of routine. Nevertheless when it was published in the American papers, the people of the North very generally believed that England had recognized the "independence" of the Confederate States. England had done nothing of the sort. The British government merely recognized their "belligerency," which was quite a different thing. But when an entire nation is in a state of panic, it is useless to invite them to a lecture on the terminology of international law.

The Washington authorities, however, were bound to take notice. On the front, everything had gone wrong. The first attempt of the Northern armies to get a foothold within the territory of the Confederacy had ended in defeat. On the twenty-first of July of the year 1861 the Northerners had been so badly beaten near the Bull Run Creek in Virginia that they could not possibly hope to be ready for another campaign until the spring of the next year. When news of this rout (for it really was a pretty sad business) reached Europe it caused general satisfaction among the many enemies of the United States and the friends of the Confederacy predicted that Lee would soon be able to hang his flag from the national capitol in Washington. The situation was uncomfortable in the extreme. And then, to make it ten times worse, there occurred one of those slight international incidents which, insignificant in themselves, have only too frequently led to an outbreak of hostilities between otherwise sensible nations.

Early in November of the year 1861 the U.S.S. *San Jacinto*, after a tour of duty along the African coast to prevent slave-running and now bound for home, happened to stop at Havana. There the captain, Charles Wilkes, the hero of a famous scientific expedition to the South Seas, got hold of a batch of American newspapers in which he read that James M. Mason and John Slidell, diplomatic representatives of the Confederate States, were on their way to Europe and were supposed to sail from Havana on the British mail-steamer *Trent*.

Captain Wilkes (a man whose career was a strange mixture of gold medals and courts-martial) decided to distinguish himself by one bold, rash deed and he succeeded beyond his fondest expectations. He left Havana, waited for the *Trent*, threatened to use his guns unless that peaceful craft surrendered her rebel cargo, and triumphantly carried his "contraband of war" to America.

During the first moment of excitement, Congress voted the gallant captain a gold medal, but the English people thought differently, and the London papers talked so bitterly of this terrible, yea, this unbearable insult to a sovereign British vessel that any statesman less skeptical and worldly-wise than Lord Palmerston might easily have been driven into war. Even so, His Lordship was forced to instruct Her Majesty's representative in Washington to ask for the immediate release of the two prisoners and, in case of refusal, to demand his passports and leave the country.

By advice of the Prince Consort, the Palmerstonian letter was made as conciliatory as possible, but the situation was regarded as serious in the extreme and troops were beginning to be moved in the general direction of Canada and the navy yards of the North Sea showed an unusual activity.

From the Northern side it could have been argued that as the United States government had never recognized the independence of the Confederacy, Mason and Slidell had continued to be United States citizens and that Captain Wilkes had merely done what British naval officers had done thousands of times during the last century when they boarded neutral vessels and removed all those whom they suspected of being Englishmen. But Lincoln, who was fast learning his new trade, knew that it was not the time to argue. He ordered Mason and Slidell to be returned to another outgoing British vessel and to be permitted to continue their voyage under the protection of the English flag and in this way the episode ended without causing any further bad feeling on the side of either country.

No sooner, however, had this point been decided than another difficulty made its appearance. Since the Confederates had been formally recognized as belligerents, it followed that they must be in the market for gunpowder and cannon and all sorts of war materials. And they were. They had boasted that their monopoly of cotton would soon show who was the real ruler of the North American continent and they now endeavored to exchange their cotton bales for muskets and field pieces in the markets of Paris and London. If this had been done and if the muskets and field pieces had been duly shipped to Savannah or Charleston, the United States government would have had no cause of complaint. The goods would either have arrived safely in their ports of destination, or they would have been intercepted by a Union war vessel and would have been confiscated. But now President Davis threatened to do something that was entirely new. He tried to turn the British Isles into a naval base for the Confederacy. He ordered British shipyards to build Confederate cruisers. He armed those cruisers with British-made guns. He manned those cruisers with crews either recruited or assembled within Her Majesty's domains and then let them sail from Glasgow or Southampton to prey upon Union commerce, and to return to British ports whenever they needed fresh supplies of shells and bully beef.

All this, of course, was known to Lincoln and his cabinet and those worthy gentlemen stroked their whiskers and said, "That won't do at all." Hence a series of protests. But it is never easy to decide at which point the sale of war material to a belligerent ceases to be a lawful business transaction and becomes a breach of neutrality. If it is according to international law to sell a belligerent a dozen howitzers, it is also right to sell him ten thousand. But if a government is allowed to place an order for five million dollars' worth of assegais and harpoons, why cannot that same government use those same five million dollars to buy and equip a couple of cruisers?

Fortunately, while this problem was being discussed, the workmen in the Lancashire and Cheshire cotton mills, who were now actually starving because they were without the necessary materials and all work had been suspended, came most unexpectedly to the help of the United States government and suddenly petitioned Parliament to keep Her Majesty's government from recognizing or giving any further aid to a government which kept three million human beings in a condition of cattle, or do so at the risk of their displeasure. And still more fortunately for us, the Union at that time was represented in London by a man who was not ashamed of his country and who remained loyal to the interests of his own people although several dowagers struck him from their dinner list and treated him really quite nastily.

Charles Francis Adams was the son of one President of the United States and the grandson of another. He was not exactly what one might call an emotional man. Perhaps this was just as well. It allowed him to retain his composure even after the defeat of Fredericksburg, when it really seemed that the North had lost the war; even after that tactful speech of William Ewart Gladstone (the eminent theologian) wherein this official member of Her Majesty's government suggested that England recognize "the nation which that great statesman, Jefferson Davis, has so successfully founded on the other side of the ocean," Adams did not lose his temper. On the contrary it encouraged him to that sublime moment in his career when he unbent sufficiently to assure the British Secretary of State that a continued policy of harboring and equipping Confederate cruisers in English harbors could and would lead to only one result, and that result as His Excellency undoubtedly understood was spelled W-A-R.

That icy bit of information seemed to clear the atmosphere. It never came to an open outbreak of hostilities. In the first place, there were too many people in England who detested slavery and were ready to go to prison rather than fight the abolitionists of the North. In the second place, England was never quite sure about that most uncomfortable neighbor, the Emperor Napoleon. And in the third place, England was forced to keep a watchful eye upon Russia, which only a few years before had been badly defeated in the Crimean war and which now had concentrated the greater part of her fleet in the harbors of San Francisco and New York, not out of any profound love for American democracy, but because she hoped, in case of a conflict with Great Britain, to use those ports as convenient naval bases against England.

But all these considerations were of minor importance. The real cause of the gradual change in the attitude of Her Majesty's government was not the result of a sudden love for the ideals of Abraham Lincoln. It was caused by a change in the fortunes of the American armies. It was due to the successful efforts of an obscure ex-officer of the regular army, a former clerk in a tannery in Galena, Illinois, a hopeless failure of a man known as Ulysses S. Grant.

When war broke out between the South and the North, it seemed that the career of this once brilliant young officer had come to an end, and all the ladies of the local W. C. T. U. shook their heads and said, "We told you so! Our poor brother Ulysses!" and they predicted a speedy funeral, followed by a moral lesson upon the dangers of strong drink and equally strong tobacco. They were somewhat disturbed when this broken-down captain was made the commander of an Illinois regiment and was given the right to lead their lily-white little darlings into action.

As for Grant himself, he never was a person of many words, and so he took whatever troops were entrusted to his care and went his own way and quietly but efficiently smashed the western front of the Confederacy and next by his invasion of Tennessee forced Lee to withdraw many of his best troops from the northern front to protect the western and southern frontiers of the territory that had been entrusted to his care.

This was good enough as a start. It was followed almost immediately by another unexpected victory which was of even greater importance.

The South was really very hard hit by the Northern blockade. What was the use of raising five million bales of cotton every year when you could not sell them abroad? Now and then, of course, it was possible to load a few thousand bales into a fast-going steamer and try and run the blockade until you reached one of the English or Spanish or Dutch or Danish possessions in the West Indies. But such small amounts hardly counted and it was necessary to discover a more successful way of breaking through the iron wall of Union ships.

The Confederates were not possessed of those manufacturing facilities which were so common in the North. But their engineers had heard of the iron-clad steamer with which all the nations of Europe had been experimenting since the war of the Crimea and they looked for a solution of their difficulties along that line. Who drew the original plans for the first Confederate armor-clad vessel, I don't know, but one of the members of Davis's cabinet had for years been chairman of the Senate committee on naval affairs and he must have had a certain familiarity with all the newest ideas upon the subject of armor-protected ships. The Confederates were rather hard up for material, but by building an iron roof over the hull of a half-burned old United States war sloop, they evolved a miniature dreadnought that could reach a speed of seven miles an hour and that was absolutely invincible in a fight with an ordinary wooden vessel.

This strange craft, the U.S.S. *Merrimac*, was re-baptized C.S.S. *Virginia*, and on the first day of her career sank two Union war vessels.

It was only a beginning, but if Stephen Mallory had been given a chance to build a dozen other *Virginias*, the road from Charleston to London would have been open to Confederate trade and their cotton might have proved mightier than the sword.

But alas! While the Confederates were sawing the top off the old *Merrimac* and were hammering iron plates to her sides, a Swede by the name of John Ericsson from Langbanshyttan in Wermland, a former captain in the Swedish army and as prolific an inventor as ever lived, was working on some blueprints of his own which were destined to blow all those Confederate visions of maritime supremacy into so much kindling wood and scrap iron.

Ericsson, who had built locomotives in England with which to compete against Stephenson's *Rocket*, and had invented the famous screw propeller for the use of naval vessels, had finally hit upon the idea of providing iron-clad warships with guns that should be placed in revolving towers. He took his invention to France. But the third Napoleon was as little interested in Ericsson's boat as the first Napoleon had been in the model which Fulton had paraded for his benefit on the muddy waters of the Seine and he refused to give the Swede any encouragement. Just then rumors were beginning to reach Europe of a strange new craft which the Confederates were said to be building, and so Ericsson traveled to Washington and showed his plans to the construction engineers of the United States government. They were in such a quandary that for once they were willing to listen to an outsider and a civilian and allowed Ericsson to construct his *Monitor* according to his own foolish notions, in which, to tell you the truth, no one took any stock except honest John himself. He worked with such fury that his vessel was ready for action in less than six months. A heavy sea prevented the *Monitor* from going south in time to prevent the *Virginia* from being finished. But a short encounter on the ninth of March of the year 1862 showed the complete superiority of the *Monitor* as an instrument of destruction, and the last hope of the Confederates of breaking the blockade came to an end.

With the help of further monitors and armored vessels, the Northern blockade was enforced with even greater vigor and the Southern cotton lay rotting on the wharves of Mobile and Norfolk while the European powers, who no longer had any reason to expect a Southern victory, remained deaf to all further pleas for recognition or credit.

Desperately the armies of Lee and Jackson fought to gain a little time, that they might force a stalemate upon their opponents. It just could not be done, and their enemy struck what they regarded as a despicable blow in the rear. By a proclamation of President Lincoln all those who still were slaves within the territory occupied by the Confederate army on the first of January of the year 1863 would be forever free. The document, however, did not abolish slavery in those states of the Union which had remained faithful to the North. It was a war measure pure and simple, intended to gain the support of the abolitionists at home and abroad who from that moment on must regard the war as a crusade for the liberation of the human race and could no longer deny it as an unholy quarrel about state's rights. But it did not settle the slavery question (which was only one of the minor causes of the Civil War, anyway) and it was not until the year 1865 that a new amendment to the Constitution (the thirteenth) made an end to this "peculiar institution" and banished involuntary servitude from the territory of the United States for all time.

As for the war itself, I can be very brief. Once the commandership-in-chief had been entrusted to a single man, the former shoeclerk from Galena, Illinois, the problem was solved with chesslike precision. The Mississippi valley was occupied. Admiral Farragut forced his way into the city of New Orleans. Lee almost destroyed a Northern army at Gettysburg and failed by some ten minutes and five thousand men to gain a sweeping victory. Sherman marched from one end of Georgia to the other, performing such miracles of wanton destruction that many decent Northerners felt slightly ashamed of this spectacular but somewhat exaggerated display of ferocity. And then, after the Confederates had in vain tried to gain peace by suggesting a combined expedition of the Northern and Southern armies against Mexico, the city of Richmond, the Southern capital, was besieged, was bombarded, and was taken, and Jeff Davis was wandering through the wilds of Georgia in a vague attempt to avoid that sour apple tree of which the Yankee troops had been so lustily singing for the last four years.

Georgia

After that debacle there was nothing more to do but to surrender with grace and to accept this surrender in great humility of spirit, as was done by Grant and Lee after their meeting near Appomattox Court House.

And then at last—when the case was settled for good and all—when it had been decided that the rights of the common country should forever stand superior to those of the individual state, then at last the time had come to repair the damage done by four years of destruction and disruption.

Some of the people of the North were ready to lend a helping hand to their former enemies. Others, of the blood of the true Maccabees, were as relentless in the hour of victory as they had been despondent in the years of defeat. More than ever the fate of the Republic seemed to depend upon that pathetic and lonely man who during four lonely and terrible years had learned how to fight without hating.

On the morning of March the fourth of the year 1865, Abraham Lincoln, elected for the second time to the presidency of the United States, laid down his ideas for a workable and practical philosophy of life—a short American gospel of kindliness and charity—an appeal for justice and forbearance—a good-humored admonition to be generous and bear no grudge.

Six weeks later, he lay dead with a bullet through his brain.

## Chapter Forty-Six

## THE LAST OF THE CONQUISTADORES GOES HOME—IN A COFFIN

POOR FELLOW—he might have known that he would come to grief.

He was a kind soul, an amiable prince, and he painted lovely pictures and played quite nicely on the piano and knew an awful lot about botany. But he didn't have much of a chin—no, he didn't.

Wherefore like all the other Habsburgs he wore funny sidewhiskers and tried to look ferocious and talked in great hollow phrases about God and Fatherland and duty and all sorts of solemn things. Even at such moments he was slightly ridiculous. And only for one moment did he reach the stature of his ancestors.

He had not known very well how to live.

But he died magnificently.

And so, much will be forgiven him.

This unfortunate prince who was to be the last of the Conquistadores was born in the year 1832 in the imperial palace of Schönbrunn, and his father was an Austrian grandduke and his brother was Emperor of Austria and his father-in-law was King of Belgium and he called half of the crowned heads of Europe his cousins. And because he could read and write and do simple sums in arithmetic, the other Habsburgs decided that he must be quite a genius and so they made him a viceroy in Italy and commander-in-chief of the Austrian army. But in a way he fooled them. For he really had quite a good brain and he was a hard worker and he did what few of his relatives ever thought of doing, he read books and he studied subjects with the help of blueprints and charts and maps and so in due time he came to be recognized as an authority on naval matters and when the Austrian fleet was reorganized, he was given free rein, and he built the ships with all the newfangled iron-clad novelties which, until the recent war, gave Austria the command of the Adriatic and the eastern half of the Mediterranean, and as viceroy of Lombardy he advocated certain reforms of so intelligent and liberal a nature that they might have saved Italy for the Habsburgs, but as no one else seemed to know what he was talking about, he finally got discouraged and he resigned and built himself a nice house near Trieste and collected fans and played Schubert's sonatas and got ready to spend the rest of his days leading the life of a well-intentioned and pleasant-spoken Austrian grandduke who did not have a care in the world and was possessed of a beautiful wife, an excellent cook and everything.

Meanwhile in the distant mountains of Oajaca in an old Aztec fortress there lived an Indian by the name of Benito Pablo Juarez. He had begun life in an adobe hut. A kindly friar who had seen some promise in the boy had given him a lift and had made it possible for him to study law. Then he had done a little fighting, for he wanted to enter politics. He had been made governor of his native province and finally in the year 1861 he had been elected to the presidency of the Mexican republic. A long cry it was from Schönbrunn to Ixtlán. But in the domain of history the impossible invariably becomes the logical and we now introduce the third person in this little tragedy.

The grandmother of Napoleon III had been a Creole lady from the island of Martinique. His father (if we are to believe the best contemporary authorities) was a Dutch admiral. His official papa, however, was a brother of the great Napoleon himself and his wife was the granddaughter of an American by the name of Kirkpatrick who was United States consul at Malaga where that excellent wine used to come from. And at the moment I need him in my history, he had just told Europe that his newly made empire spelled p-e-a-c-e and that he was looking for a few new continents to conquer.

And now back to our Indian friend.

Juarez was that very rare thing, an unselfish Mexican patriot. He sincerely believed in the future of his own Indian race, if only people would leave it alone. And in order to give his country a short respite from the eternal pressure of its manifold creditors and catch up with current expenses, he suspended the payment of interest on foreign debts for a period of two years. This caused great consternation in those queer little dark alleys of Madrid, Paris, and London which are generally known as "financial circles" and without delay French, Spanish, and English cruisers were on their way to Vera Cruz to ask for "redress" and insist upon the "rights" of the sorely afflicted European pawnbrokers.

The British government with its traditional respect for the realities of life soon sensed that this humble Indian was a person who meant business and who would repay every ounce of trouble with an ounce and a half of his own making. The English ships therefore were withdrawn, and the Spaniards took the hint and also departed. But Napoleon, who had filled his kept press with glowing accounts of a world that should once more recognize the supremacy of the Gallic genius, could not possibly back out of this unfortunate enterprise without losing a great deal of his prestige. Much against his will, he stayed in, and such of his soldiers as did not die of yellow fever fought their way to Mexico City and drove President Juarez into the wilderness.

Then came the great question, what next?

The Emperor Napoleon was a veritable parvenu among the crowned heads of Europe. Several of his fellow monarchs even refused to address him as their "dear brother." Wherefore he devised a plan that was as fantastic as it was shrewd. He would offer the throne of Mexico to a member of the proud house of Habsburg. Then there would be another self-made emperor in this world and the next time when the Emperor of Austria tried to snub the Emperor of France by reference to his lowly origin, he could turn around and say, "So is your brother!"

The Habsburgs (I have said this before) were not very bright, as princes go, but they were not devoid of a certain amount of primitive political cunning. Otherwise they would never have been able to maintain themselves on their tottering throne for quite as long as they did. And from the very beginning, Francis Joseph was firmly opposed to the idea which the French ambassador tried to explain to him in words of one syllable.

Maximilian, on the other hand, thought the plan wonderful. He was a product of the romantic school of art and literature. He could just see himself in a modest but becoming emperor's uniform, leaning on the broken pillar of an old Aztec palace, the moon shining brightly upon distant Popocatepetl and thousands of little brown subjects playing Beethoven on the guitar and singing songs about how they loved their good king.

To make this sad story as short as possible, he took the job.

He even believed the story about a plebiscite among the Mexican people who almost unanimously had proclaimed him as the successor to Montezuma. At the request of his prosaic but practical brother, he renounced all his rights to the throne of Austria and sailed for Vera Cruz.

These fanciful little schemes of the great French mountebank had not remained unnoticed by the authorities at Washington and several American ministers at European courts had politely inquired whether the courts to which they were accredited had ever heard of a certain message which a certain President Monroe had read to Congress not so many years before. Their Majesties and their Excellencies answered, "Yes," but circumstances altered cases and Monroe had spoken for the entire United States, but now there was no longer any "United States" but in its stead there were two small republics who were engaged in a bitter conflict and who seemed in a fair way to destroy each other.

In 1863 that seemed fair enough.

But within the next twelve months, the Confederacy came to an end and then the United States had its hands and its armies and navies free to come to the rescue of its trusted neighbor Benito.

It began its campaign by exercising pressure upon the Emperor Napoleon. It showed that gentleman the newspapers which contained information about the signal victories which a country called Prussia had just gained over the neighboring state of Denmark; it spoke of a person by the name of Bismarck who seemed to have a dream about reviving the ancient German Empire to the greatest possible detriment of France.

Napoleon was forced to confess that all that was true, quite true. And not being hampered by any conscience, he abruptly withdrew his troops from Mexico and left the poor synthetic Emperor to his own devices.

Maximilian, if he had been merely thinking of his own skin, could have escaped while the roads to the coast were still open. But he was at heart a very serious man with a high sense of duty and he now felt called upon to stick to those who had supported him in the struggle for his throne.

When all was lost, he tried to find death on the field of battle. Alas! No bullet took mercy upon him and the inevitable happened. One of his Mexican subordinates sold him out to Juarez and Juarez condemned him to be shot. Maximilian did not ask mercy for himself, but bravely tried to get a reprieve for those few generals who had been faithful to him until the last.

When news of his sentence was telegraphed abroad, the whole world stood aghast at the idea of an imperial

Austrian prince being executed by orders of a full-blooded Mexican Indian. Even the President of the United States addressed himself to his good friend across the Rio Grande and asked that clemency be shown. But Juarez answered that he could not interfere. It was not he who was taking the life of the Emperor. It was the Law of the Land.

After that there was nothing more to be done.

On the nineteenth of June of the year 1867, Maximilian was shot.

Six months later an Austrian battleship with an Italian name and flying the flag of His Imperial and Royal Apostolic Majesty, the Emperor of Austria and King of Hungary, slowly entered the harbor of Vera Cruz.

The next day the last of the Conquistadores went home in a box in the hold.


*Chapter Forty-Seven*

## A GOLDEN SPIKE IS DRIVEN IN UTAH

Two PEANUTS are two peanuts, and two elephants are two elephants.

But although they are both "two's" in the numerical sense of the word, two peanuts are not quite the same as two elephants.

This little problem in arithmetic is so self-evident that it does not seem to be in need of any further elucidation. Unfortunately there are a great many people who insist upon staring themselves blind at the term "two" but to whom the rest of the equation means nothing. To them, "two" is and always was and always will be "two" and never mind your elephants and your peanuts.

Now when the Civil War was over and the spook of foreign invasion via Mexico City had been laid for all time, the hour seemed to have struck for a complete and thorough-going examination of the economic and social difficulties connected with the reconstruction of the devastated Southern region.

The self-righteousness of the Puritan, a very dominant trait in the civilization of the North, with its eternal insistence upon justice before mercy, made this a very delicate and difficult task.

To the Northerners, who had lost more than three hundred and fifty thousand of their best young men, the South stood revealed as an arch-traitor and criminal.

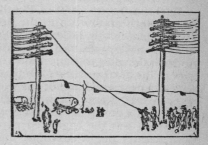

The East and West are joined

It was the South which had tried to force its will upon the entire Union in the matter of slaves.

When this had proved impossible, the South had seceded.

When this could not be done without the shedding of blood, the South had fired the first gun.

And all this on account of the queer Southern belief that the white man was by right divine the superior of his black neighbor.

No, there the good Northerners could not follow the rebels at all.

To them, two was two.

A black man was merely a white man with a somewhat darker skin and two darkies from the Mississippi cotton belt were quite as good as two Robert E. Lees from Virginia. A hopeless tangle and a costly mistake, for ere the North discovered that the laws of logic do not hold good in the field of human relationships, an entire people had almost been driven to the point of exasperation and ten years of peace had proved infinitely more costly than five years of war.

Yes—if Lincoln had lived!

But Lincoln was gone and his place as executive head of the nation had been taken by a man totally unfit for the office. He had been elected Vice-President because he was one of the few Southern politicians who had remained faithful to the cause of the Union and because the managers of Lincoln's party hoped to flatter the border states by giving a Tennessee Democrat a prominent place on a Republican ticket.

The murderous pistol of Booth had thus elevated this poor tailor's apprentice to the presidency. And now this disciple of Andrew Jackson, this professional stump artist from the backwoods, was called upon to guide the country through the most difficult period of its career. And a man, who in his heart of hearts felt that the South had suffered a great wrong and had not deserved the ignominy of such utter defeat, found himself obliged to make common cause with a group of New Englanders who believed that the North was the aggrieved party and that the former Confederates ought to count themselves fortunate that they were allowed to be alive at all.

The open and avowed hostility between those two divergent points of view eventually led to the impeachment of the President and to a long and futile trial which proved nothing and accomplished even less. But for the South, where all economic life had long since come to a complete standstill, this disastrous quarrel between the executive and the legislative branches of the government spelled disaster. It meant that the hundred-percenters of that day, the righteous avengers of the unspeakable system of human bondage, could now give full sway to their pent-up passion for oppression and revenge.

It meant a topsy-turvy world in which the black man (backed up by the bayonets of Northern regiments) lorded it with sublime ignorance and impudence over his former master, the white man. It caused the complete ruin of a social system that with all its faults had produced a great number of exceedingly capable men and had borne the lion's share of founding the independent republic of the United States.

Finally, it made a return to normal economic conditions so extremely difficult that it took almost two generations before the South was able to recover from this disastrous blow to her pride and her prosperity.

And then, as always in life, the unexpected happened. North and South had fought each other for the supremacy of the Union, and the West ran away with the victory.

What thus far had been merely a vague background suddenly became the center of the stage, and the old faith of the frontier was definitely accepted as their new religion by the people of the seaboard.

Indirectly the military and political emergencies of the early sixties had had a great deal to do with this change. It had been highly important for the United States to retain not only the friendship of the border states of the Middle West, but also to assure themselves of the loyalty of those Americans who lived along the shores of the Pacific Ocean. Unfortunately these were separated from the eastern part of the country by two thousand miles of mountain and plain, and it took at least six weeks ere a letter from New York could reach Sacramento by way of the Isthmus of Panama. But in the year 1860 the famous Pony Express was started between San Francisco and St. Joseph, Missouri. Those who were willing to pay five dollars for every ounce of correspondence could now send their letters from East to West in eight or nine days.

Next came the building of a telegraph wire across the plains.

But one great and dangerous gap remained, for one could not send soldiers by telegram or cannon by pony express. Besides, it was well known, indeed it had been well known ever since the days of Lewis and Clark, that these intervening stretches of land were highly valuable, a veritable farmers' paradise, and rich in all sorts of raw materials.

A self-respecting and careful government could not afford to let all this territory lie idle. Already in the days of Jefferson the mere rumor that Aaron Burr was planning to found a Mississippi empire of his own had been sufficient to drive the people of the East into a panic. And now the country was at war. The French were in

Mexico. English guard regiments had occupied the forts of Halifax. Of course the North expected to win, but one could never tell, and it would be sheer suicide to allow this vacuum in the rear to exist any longer than was absolutely unavoidable.

For a while the war had lamed all efforts at settlement. Those strong enough to carry spades and shovels had been forced to carry muskets and the horses of a few small regiments of cavalry were the only disturbing element amidst the endless silences of the prairie. As soon, however, as peace had been declared, the work of connecting the East with the West was taken in hand with all seriousness.

Thus far the railroad contractor had followed the pioneer. Now the railroad contractor himself turned pioneer. He no longer waited until there were enough settlers in any given part of the Union to make it worth his while to build an iron road and go after their business. He first of all provided a few thousand square miles of uninhabited territory with decent means of communication and then invited farmers from the East and immigrants from Europe to settle within reasonable distance of his depots and use his road for the transportation of their cattle and their farm products. And so fast and furiously did the surveyors work that ere long the entire Mississippi basin was covered with a complicated network of railroads and that the completion of the first transcontinental railway was only a question of years.

On the tenth of May of the year 1869 at Promontory Point in Utah, a golden spike was driven into the last four feet of missing rail.

East and West were connected and the first part of the program had been successfully completed.

The second part was more difficult.

The number of people who were prosperous enough to buy Western lands and move their families across the Mississippi was relatively small. The others were full of good will, but lacked the five or six hundred dollars necessary for a first installment upon their newly acquired farms. In order to facilitate the migration of this valuable

The golden spike of Utah

class of citizen, Congress passed a Homestead Law under which any fairly respectable citizen could take up one hundred and sixty acres of Western government land and could hold it as long as he worked it with a reasonable amount of industry.

This measure helped enormously in the settlement of the far Western regions. Only one other country has ever undertaken a task of such gigantic magnitude and that was Russia. But whereas in Siberia (I mean the Siberia of the pioneers and not that more notorious but much less important part of northern Asia used as a penal colony), whereas in Siberia the home government had to push the peasant by main force toward the rich grass fields of Tartary, the American authorities were obliged to act as a perpetual brake upon the unbridled enthusiasm of their prospective settlers. A few years of wholesale Western exploitation had definitely shown that King Cotton of the South was a feeble sovereign compared to the Imperial Majesty of Grain and Cattle who now held sway over millions of fertile acres in Texas and the Dakotas. Then there was no holding of the groups of eager hustlers who hoped to get their share before it was too late. In this mad rush for new grazing fields and fresh wheat fields, the last remnants of the Indians (who had been given this territory as a sort of conscience money when the United States occupied their ancestral possessions in the East), those poor savages were ruthlessly pushed out of the way or were cooped up in vast concentration camps where they were allowed to vegetate and to degenerate as mildly interesting specimens of the original local fauna.

But such cruel incidents seem to be an unavoidable part of the White Man's progress across the face of the globe. Theoretically the European and the American recognize the fact that black and yellow and copper-colored creatures also have the right to exist. In practice, however, they prefer such creatures when they "know their place" and shine their boots for them or do their masters' laundering. When one of the races which seem to stand between the pale-face and his immediate profits declares itself too proud to become a bootblack or a dishwasher, the Caucasian does not quite know what to do with him. In such a dilemma he gets nervous and begins to play with his revolver and nine times out of ten something happens and the gun goes off. If the poor dumb Injun happens to be in the way of the bullet—so much the worse for him. Why in the name of merciful heaven didn't he look out? And since he is dead anyway, suppose we bury him and forget about it?

This chapter in our history is not very flattering to our pride. On every page we read the records of greed and cruelty and of broken treaties, and the entire episode is steeped in the contraband rum of the prairie saloon. But what are ethical principles pitted against the laws of nature? The two million or more square miles of mountain and plains which the United States had bought, swapped or taken from the French, the Mexicans, and the English and which contained some of the richest deposits of gold and silver and lead and copper and oil of which the world had ever dreamed, were in the possession of a weak race which fought with bows and arrows and they were eagerly coveted by a strong race with rifles and cannon.

A German statesman with that disgraceful lack of tact which his people called "honesty" once stated that "this world is ruled by might and not by right."

We go to our little white schoolhouses and our pretty little white churches in Idaho and Wyoming and Montana and Nebraska and we sing our hymns and thank a merciful heaven that we are not like those brutal foreigners who publicly avow that the strong will inherit the earth and the fullness thereof and that the weak will be deprived even of the little that is their own. We detest such an idea. Impatiently we shout, "No!" It may be true of others, but our own people, we feel sure, were never guilty of such a thing.

I hope that my great-grandchildren may be able to speak in such a fashion without revealing themselves as hopeless liars.

For the moment, however, seeing myself surrounded by a world that either eats or is eaten—destroys or is destroyed—kills or is killed—I shall accept life as I find it and I shall abide by the dictates of a power which seems infinitely stronger than any expression of the human will.

Whereupon the shade of Carlyle gives a sad, sad grin and whispers, "You had better!"

## Chapter Forty-Eight

## THE DECLINE AND FALL OF THE THIRD CYCLE OF AMERICAN CIVILIZATION

WE HAVE ALL OF US HEARD the complaint of our elders that this is a jazz age, that we live too fast, that our civilization is in too much of a hurry.

But old people are always complaining and comparing and so our infants just say, "Yes, sir," very politely and pay no attention to these laudations of bygone days.

Tomorrow grandpa will have found something else to worry about and then we will have to listen to a new set of lamentations about the "lack of respect on the part of the younger generation," or "the shocking plays that are now being given on the New York stage."

Nevertheless (although I hate to make this confession), it does seem as if the form of living had been very definitely influenced by the recent introduction of steam and electricity and that western civilization (white man's civilization, Christian civilization, anything you like to call it) is moving forward (or backward, it is hard to say which way it is going) at a rate of speed which was totally unknown fifty or five centuries ago.

Think back for a moment to the days of the Egyptians and the Babylonians and the Greeks and the Cretans and the Romans. A small number of people, more intelligent or energetic than the rest of their neighbors, would get hold of a small piece of land that offered economic advantages. Then there would be a prolonged period of slow growth, during which the newcomers painfully learned the rudiments of civilized behavior. After that, and usually under the leadership of half a dozen great men, there would be a so-called "Golden Age" when the country suddenly went on the warpath—grabbed all the trade in sight—burst forth into song and poetry—studied the heavens—explored the distant seas—investigated the behavior of the human body—turned lumps of marble into fine pieces of statuary—built pyramids and temples —dyed woolen garments a pinkish purple—and carried the blessings of its own culture to the farthest corners of the earth.

Such a Golden Age, however, never lasted very long. It was too careless of human energy. The flame of enthusiasm and joy was allowed to burn a little too brightly. Soon exhaustion set in. Then a weak and careless generation began to live upon the accumulated national capital. Decline set in and the rest was merely a question of time. If the ancestors had stolen enough wealth (and as a rule they had) and had built their social structure with great care (as the Romans had done) then it might be a thousand or fifteen hundred years before one could write: "Finis."

Even then, the spiritual inheritance of some particularly intelligent nation, in the hands of total strangers, might continue for five or six other centuries and might create the illusion that the patient had never died at all.

But on our own side of the ocean that rule did not seem

to work. We were able to do in fifty or sixty years what it had taken others forty or fifty centuries to accomplish. When the white man came to the northern part of the American continent he stumbled upon a large number of native Indian civilizations, some of which were very crude and some of which were of a very high order. But the sort of people who came here first of all were not the sort of people to be interested in such problems. They slew and hacked and burned and shot and hanged and generally destroyed everything the natives had built as rapidly as they could. Incidentally they borrowed certain things from their victims which allowed them to survive and to maintain themselves upon these inhospitable shores when their own white stock of forest-lore threatened to give out. But they were too thoroughly convinced of their divine mission to bother about that aspect of the case. They killed the Indian, they took his land, and native American civilization was relegated to the bead shops of Albuquerque and to the Wild-West laboratories of Hollywood.

Then the white man set his house in order and we got the second cycle of American civilization, that of the colonists. This lasted, roughly speaking, from the beginning of the seventeenth to the latter half of the eighteenth century. In the field of the arts and sciences, it contributed practically nothing. The domain of international letters was enriched by a few collections of execrable sermons and by some highly interesting travelogues, the work of several of the Jesuit missionaries in Canada. All the same, these small groups of Europeans, left more or less to themselves on the outskirts of a vast wilderness, had a chance to do some highly original work in the field of self-government and in due course of time they might have stumbled upon certain novel ideas of a political nature which would have been highly interesting and not without great value to the rest of the world.

The Revolution made an end to this famous experiment.

And then began the third cycle of American civilization, that of the Republic. This lasted from the year 1776 until the year 1865, from the beginning of the rebellion against the mother country until the end of the Civil War. During this period, the colonials willfully and willingly cut themselves off from their friends and relatives in Europe, turned their back upon the East, and boldly set forth to develop a new culture of their own, a form of living and thinking that should be the noble incarnation of their newly gained sense of freedom and equality.

It is easy enough to laugh at this new dispensation, for the first fruits of this glorious experiment were disappointing enough. Stuffy platitudes, the resounding reiteration of bucolic verities which the rest of the world had discarded half a century before. All the same, this was no mere period of placid stagnation. There was conflict. There was life. For the first time in American history the voice of the prophet was heard. There were people with a new vision, people who dared to stand up for their own ideas, fight for them, even suffer for them. No, we can't just discard this Jeffersonian and Jacksonian era as if it had been merely a period of ugly furniture and ghastly chromos and bewhiskered Websterian statesmen with tremendous stovepipe hats who delivered endless harangues upon endless subjects for which no one any longer gives twopence.

During those ninety years, there was an undoubted striving after something a little better than what the world had thus far produced—an effort to solve at least part of our problems by giving the average man a better chance than ever before—an attempt to approach a certain degree of economic happiness along certain roads that had never been opened to the general public. And all this was done in the name of America. Humanity was not forgotten, but it was America that was to set the world free—it was America that was to lead the way out of the desert—it was America that was to give our planet certain new and enduring systems of great spiritual value.

It was one of the most interesting human experiments of the last five centuries. And it is a terrible pity that it should have come to such an ignominious end.

Why did it?

That I don't know.

The science of history is still in its infancy. And we have never studied such problems with that degree of thoroughness which is bestowed upon the boll weevil or the plague that threatens the potato crop.

But as usual in such cases, there were several causes for the sudden downfall of this last and most typical form of a purely American civilization. And chief among these was the sudden annihilation of the best elements among the younger generation. The military leaders of the Civil War were terrible butchers. Those poor devils who were not killed in battle were often destroyed by disease or fell victims to one of those forms of official neglect which the war contractors and their political cup bearers told the public to be "unavoidable" during such a period of great national strife.

Anyway, they were dead and gone.

And who were left to take their places?

The slackers, the young bloods who had waited until they were sent for, the "indispensable" young legal and commercial luminaries who had bought someone else to do their dying for them while they remained safely at home. Especially in an issue where ideal values were at stake, the spiritually minded were the ones to suffer most severely and the practical boys and girls were predestined to survive.

In the year 1865, therefore, both the northern and the southern half of the United States found themselves deprived of those who had been best fitted to carry on their particular form of civilization. And this happened at the very moment when the domination of this world by members of the human race (homo sapiens) was threatened by the rivalry of an inanimate competitor known as the iron man or the machine.

Europe, which left its wars to be fought by small groups of professionals, was able to ward off the evil day a little longer.

But America, deprived of its most valuable line of defense, surrendered almost immediately.

Our country thereby gained great riches.

But at the same time it lost something which it was never quite able to recapture—the wholehearted support of the younger generation.

Youth is apt to be generous.

But can any healthy boy be really interested when he spends his days in a little iron cage, counting other people's money or goes forth to sell his neighbors something which they really do not want and most certainly don't need?

## Chapter Forty-Nine

## ELLIS ISLAND AND PLYMOUTH ROCK

HENRY ADAMS was the grandson of one President of the United States and the great-grandson of another. His father was minister to the court of St. James during the difficult years of the Lincoln administration. If ever there were a man who could lay claim to the name of American, it was the old sage of Lafayette Square.

Yet of the period following upon the Civil War he wrote: *The result of this great upheaval upon a survivor from the fifties resembled the action of the earthworm; he twisted about, in vain, to recover his starting point; he could no longer see his own trail; he had become an astray; a flotsam or jetsam of wreckage. His world was dead. Not a Polish Jew from Warsaw or Cracow but had a keener instinct, an intenser energy, and a freer hand than he, American of the Americans, with heaven knows how many Puritans and patriots behind him.*

A hopeless cry of despair—a futile regret at something that could not be helped—and as ancient as the slopes of Mount Ararat.

For there had been Henry Adamses in Babylon and in Thebes, in Cnossos and Damascus. Not to mention Rome. Lamentations of that sort had been the common form of literary expression during the entire fourth and fifth centuries of our era.

Then, what had happened?

It was really very simple.

A small group of exceptionally enterprising people, living under the most favorable economic and social circumstances, had founded a state and had occupied an empire, out of all proportion to their own numerical strength. They had wasted themselves in warfare and exploration. They had grown rich. They had sacrificed the graces of a civilized existence for the pursuit of material comforts. They had acquired the means for a comfortable existence and had lost the art of living.

In short, they had ceased to feel that "touch of the soil" which alone can give us enduring strength.

And now they were the masters of vast acres of land.

They owned more mountains and lakes and rivers and mines and grain fields and pastures than had ever been the share of mortal man.

But rivers and forests and fields and mines are of no value unless there be someone to work in them—to bring their treasures to light—to exploit their shores—to reap their harvests.

And who were to do this?

"Our children," said the pioneers.

But the best of their children lay dead on the fields of Gettysburg and Antietam. And the survivors, for some unknown reason, seemed unable or unwilling to perpetuate themselves.

It is a sad thing to confess but the old stock was no longer willing to tend to the daily tasks of the farm and the factory.

It remained behind as a class of professional landlords, the vassals of a new economic age.

And it asked for eager workers, for serfs and scullions, for anybody and anything with a lusty pair of strong arms.

The number of local applicants was insignificant.

The spoils had been so great and the number of people called upon to divide them had been so small that only the laggards had failed to get their share.

In short, it was the old, old story of a ruling class and no one to be ruled.

Under the circumstances the Americans did what the Babylonians and the Egyptians had done three thousand years before—what the Romans had done during the first two centuries of our era—they opened the gates wide to the foreigners—they let down the barriers—and broadcasted a general invitation to all mankind to come and make itself at home.

In the beginning, such a policy seems always harmless enough. The barbarian with his strange tongue, his uncouth garb, his general social clumsiness, his backward economic aspirations, does not look like a formidable opponent.

He is given a hovel to live in. A school is built to teach his off-spring respect for the institutions of the overlords. He is allowed to worship his own gods as long as he agrees to keep them out of sight of the respectable native deities. And provided he knows his "place" and acknowledges himself as slightly inferior to the ruling classes (be they Babylonian, American, Egyptian or Chinese) he is treated with a certain consideration and given so much more to eat than he has ever had before that he does not dream of rebellion. Instead he is patient and docile and obedient and praises his masters as great and good men and worthy of his loyal confidence.

But just as soon as he has been sufficiently fed to regain the use of his sluggish brain he begins to ask questions.

He has been told again and again how happy he ought to be that he has been allowed to come to this wonderland of the Civis Romanus (or Civis Americanus or Civis Graecus) and that he has been permitted to live in a stone house instead of a plastered hut—to eat meat seven times a week instead of once—to wear shoes instead of going barefoot—in short, to partake of all the blessings of a newer and richer civilization.

And being slightly bewildered by his new surroundings, he has said, "Yes, sir," and has convinced himself that he is really a mighty lucky fellow. Until the fatal hour when the serpent enters his little Paradise and whispers, "Who is growing rich at your expense? Whose roads do you build? Whose copper and coal do you dig out of the soil? Whose railroads do you run? Whose houses do you build? Whose subways do you blast out of the hard, unyielding rock?"

And then there is trouble.

Not as a rule with the first generation. Trained in a philosophy of life that has taught them obedience and discipline and has cautioned humble subjects not to ask too many questions, the first generation touches its cap, is profoundly grateful for many hitherto unknown blessings, and willingly confesses itself slightly inferior to the native aristocracy.

The second generation, however, fails to share the prejudices of the parents. Those young men and women have never seen the strange lands from which their ancestors hailed. They only appreciate the here and the now. And the here and now does not satisfy them.

Incessantly they are told that they are helots—the children of savage tribes—that their fathers and mothers were permitted to enter the hallowed precincts of the empire as "coloni" or bondsmen, as hewers of wood and carriers of water, humble folk who never expected to associate on a footing of equality with the old "land-seated" nobility.

But what they see around them belies this statement.

During the previous eighty years the first settlers had been able to hold their own. They had children and grandchildren to support them in the labor of social repression. But after the seventies of the last century, they began to run behind.

They were obliged to open the ranks to the newcomers. What was worse, they must give some of them commanding positions for they were younger and stronger and more intelligent than many of the natives.

And that, as far as the supremacy of the pioneers was concerned, was the beginning of the end.

If you think that I am too pessimistic, read what happened in western Asia, in northern Africa, in the Mediterranean, on the slopes of the Ural Mountains, a hundred or a thousand years ago.

In America, where all our issues are forever befogged

by a haze of rhetoric—by lovely words about a common brotherhood—by a vague belief in the equal chances of all men—in America it is much harder to follow such a movement than in Rome or Syria or in Greece or in Russia.

But the mysterious laws which control the historical development of the human race hold good for all time and all places and all ages.

The descendants of those who two centuries before had landed on Plymouth Rock, basing their claims upon the divine right of having been "first on the spot," demanded that they be regarded as the legitimate masters of the newly founded empire. They insisted that their language should be the language of the land, that their God should be the God of all the faithful, that their ideals of morality should become the accepted standard of conduct for all those who settled down within their domains at a later period.

But "government is force" and all the fine phrases in the world will never be able to change this. Government is force. Not necessarily in the sense of something brutal, of Cossacks and gallows and secret dungeons, but an intelligent and reasonable force that is capable of making itself felt—that leads others with the assurance of a ship's captain who knows his business and unconsciously expects others to obey him because it is the most reasonable thing to do. And when a constantly dwindling minority loses this delicate gift for leadership and is contented to sit back and invest its surplus funds and let others do the real work, then that small group of professional descendants will sooner or later be deprived of its power by those who only a short while before dug its ditches and blasted its tunnels.

During the first half of the nineteenth century the Mexicans had learned the ancient lesson that nature abhors a vacuum and that, given a weak race in the possession of a rich country and a strong adjacent nation in dire need of more grazing grounds, the strong race will inevitably overrun the weak race and will take the rich lands for themselves.

During the second half of the nineteenth century the conquerors of Santa Anna were given a taste of this biological dogma. That they hastened the process of conquest by their self-interested encouragement of wholesale immigration is neither here nor there. No doubt this was a mistake, but it was a mistake as old as the valley of the Nile—or older.

At a belated hour a few hasty efforts were made to save what still could be saved.

The breaches in the walls were more or less filled.

A mighty citadel was built in the path of the advancing hordes of "barbarians."

But the whole world lies strewn with the remnants of ancient Ellis Islands.

The ruins of the great Chinese wall tell us of the futility of such last-minute energy.

The little one-man bridge which connected Deshima with the mainland of Japan whispers a story of self-inflicted seclusion which ended in economic ruin and a complete reversion of all the old policies and there seems little hope that the history of our country will prove different.

The "polyglot boardinghouse" of which President Roosevelt used to speak with such intense bitterness has probably come to stay.

In due time it will be a little less polyglot but that will not change the fact that the days of the Anglo-Saxon as the ruling class of the Republic are numbered.

To some of us that may appear in the light of a terrible disaster.

To the Roman of the year 500 the advent of the Goth and the Burgundian seemed little short of a calamity.

He knew that their success was due to his own lack of interest—to the faltering courage of his own children—but that knowledge did not make it any easier for him to accept his defeat.

He predicted the decay of the Empire, the fall of the human race, the end of the world.

And behold, a thousand years afterward, the admixture of West and East had given birth to a new form of civilization, superior in every respect to the narrow culture of the old imperial days.

The mills of the gods grind slowly.

Perhaps we had better let them grind on for a little longer.

For as a rule they grind best.

## Chapter Fifty

## THE RULE OF THINGS

ACCORDING TO A POPULAR BELIEF which still has millions of adherents there had not been any organized government in the happy days of Adam and Eve. Each family had been a unit in itself and kings and princes and emperors had been unknown.

But as the world became more and more densely populated, it was growing increasingly difficult for the weaker members of the race to survive. They had, therefore, organized themselves into small groups and had elected certain strong men to be their leaders.

These leaders in due course of time had become full-fledged potentates, able to wield almost absolute power and to govern the tribes as if they had been their private property. This, however, had not changed the basic nature of the principle which underlay all forms of government and which consisted of a full-fledged "contract" between the king on the one hand and the subjects on the other by which the king promised to act as the "hired man" of his people as long as they wished to retain him, which gave the subjects the right to dismiss their monarch the moment they were displeased with his services.

That was the general theory still popular among the educated classes of those who lived in the days of Washington and Jefferson. But during the last fifty years we have done some serious digging in the broad field of social research and what we have discovered rather upsets the old idea that government began with the people and that potentates were invented at a later date for the benefit of their delighted subjects.

It is true that during certain happy periods of history when a large number of the subjects had attained such wealth that they could hire armies they not infrequently forced their will upon their rulers. Occasionally even, after a considerable display of cannon and muskets they were able to force them into signing some sort of document by which His Majesty confessed himself merely the first servant of the state and bound by a definite set of rules, duly enumerated in this sacred contract.

But originally the method of founding a state was the exact opposite of the process described so eloquently by M. Rousseau and accepted as the gospel truth by his many followers.

It was not the people who came together and formed a group or a state and then said, "Now let us choose a strong and husky and intelligent man to be our master."

It was some strong and husky and intelligent young man who made himself the leader of a small gang of ambitious cutthroats, who organized them into his bodyguard, and who then set out to conquer as many villages and cities and countries as he could possibly administer with his faithful henchmen and hammered them, by main force of their bludgeons, into a compact little state.

He would then call together all the village elders and would speak about as follows: "You low curs, behold your master! And if you love your life you will remember that from now on you are my subjects. You ask me why? Because I command a very experienced and hard-fisted band of bright young gangsters who will obey my every command and who will flay you alive should you so much as squeak when I issue one of my ukases. I am, however, a reasonable sort of a person. I want to live in comfort. I desire a nice house for myself and my faithful liegemen and for my horses and women and cows and sheep. As such an establishment will cost some money, I shall expect a certain annual sum from you in the form of taxes. But please look at the advantages of such a system for yourselves! In return for this slight trouble to which I must most unfortunately put you, I promise most solemnly to protect you against all your enemies. Not only because I love you so dearly but also because it is to my own direct interest to do so. For the richer you are, the more plunder I shall be able to collect from you. That is all and I thank you."

In due course of time the crude outlines of this agreement were considerably softened. Soon the priests came to the rescue of their sovereign and made a silent bargain by which the wielders of the spiritual and the worldly power promised to support each other in all matters that affected their common interests and that was a great help.

From then on the king became an anointed and sacred person and the favorite son of heaven. While the reverend clergy assured themselves of the royal good will (and the royal bodyguard) in case of trouble with their congregations.

And, of course, all those who had something to lose in the world, quickly recognized the advantages of a scheme that guaranteed them a much greater degree of security than they had ever enjoyed before and they came to the palace and were much pleased if they were allowed to fill the royal cup with wine or hold the royal stirrup when the master went forth to hunt.

Unfortunately in matters pertaining to the human race nothing ever runs quite according to schedule. Sometimes the king and the priesthood fell out among each other and upon other occasions it happened that the king and the rich merchants came to blows while the priests took that side which seemed to have the best chance of victory. But generally speaking and with the exception of those short periods when the dominant groups were at odds with each other (usually over division of the spoils) the propertied classes (the king, the priests, and the merchants) were each other's staunch friends and by a policy of intelligent co-operation assured themselves of a leading position in the community which the foresight and industry of their ancestors had founded among the weak

334

and helpless tribes of this or that or the other part of the world.

This theory does away with the more flattering aspect of the case as taught in the days of the French and the American revolutions.

That seems a pity, but it cannot be helped. As long as the world is composed of people of highly varying degrees of intelligence and courage, there will be those who rule and those who must allow themselves to be ruled. It may be to the interests of the ruling class to hide this fact. Democracy depends much more than any other form of government for its continued success upon the application of an elaborate system of flattery. Often, therefore, it may be deemed advisable to let the average man believe that he really is the source of all power, that there have been "social contracts" since the beginning of time and that "we the people" means something more than a polite phrase used in the preamble of certain official documents of state. As I have said before, it may be to the interest of the ruling class to maintain this fairy tale. But history has very little to do with fairy tales and so we can bluntly state the fact, borne out by every page of our ancient and honorable chronicles, that every period and every country has had its more or less sharply defined class of rulers and its equally sharply defined class of subjects—and that the laws which dominate the relations between the rulers and the subjects hold as good today along the banks of the Potomac and the Red River as they did four thousand years ago in the valley of the Indus or the Euphrates.

But we have discovered several other things about the relation between ruling-class and subject-class which are also of prime importance if we care to understand what is happening around us at the present time. Most important of those is a paragraph of the social-biological code which explains the strange modern worship of inanimate possessions, and which reads as follows:

*Those in power will invariably try to revaluate their own worldly interests into a system of spiritual ideals for the benefit of those who are not in power.*

335

In plain and sober words: *Those on top will always do their best to convince those at the bottom that whatever law is to the advantage of the people in the palace and the temple is really a part of the moral law of the land and that obedience to such a sacred statute means obedience to the revealed will of the gods.*

This sounds rather complicated and I had better give you a few examples.

Take the case of Egypt.

In Egypt, the "Man in the Big House" depended for his continued happiness and the continued happiness of his court and his priests upon the close co-operation between a river and several million little brown men. Nothing must be left to chance. Shiftlessness on the part of one village might mean disaster to a hundred others. When the river began to rise, the water must be let into the irrigation canals at such and such a time, and not a day sooner or later. Hence a form of discipline which made the Pharaoh into the captain of a ship, a tyrant whose wishes must be obeyed without an instant's hesitation. Hence the belief held by the general mass of the people and duly encouraged by the priests of the land, that implicit compliance with even the most absurd whims of the ruler was part of the divine law and that the worship of the person of the ruler of the land (the captain of the ship) was agreeable in the sight of the gods who controlled the flow of the life-giving tides.

But all those virtues were of a decidedly civic nature. For Egypt enjoyed comparative safety from foreign attack. On both sides of the narrow, fertile valley stretched a wide expanse of desert and few were the enemies who would dare to cross that hot and ghastly region of bleached bones and dead camels. Hence the military virtues were not necessary, and as a result, the military caste was held in slight regard.

The ideal of the good life in Egypt was the life of the farmer. And the soldier came at the bottom of the social ladder.

But now move from Egypt across the Mediterranean to Sparta. There the continued existence of a small, landlocked state, called Sparta, depended entirely upon the strength of its armies. No one cared an iron penny for the virtues of the plowman. But from childhood on the people were brought up to regard the "Spartan" virtues of discipline and physical hardiness as the qualities that were most agreeable in the sight of the gods.

Then go across the plains of Syria to a small country called Judea. The Judean state was built around a single town and that town would have lost its reason-for-being if it had ceased to be the center of an active religious life of a widely scattered populace and the place of worship for all those who recognized a particular west-Asiatic deity, called Jehovah, as their God. Too weak to maintain themselves by force of arms and without the opportunity to excel in agriculture or trade, the priestly rulers of Jerusalem, if they hoped to survive at all, were forced to make piety the main virtue of their subjects. The Judeans could be indifferent soldiers and no one cared how they tended their few meager acres of land. But they must be strict in their obedience to the religious law, for without such loyalty the country could not possibly hope to survive.

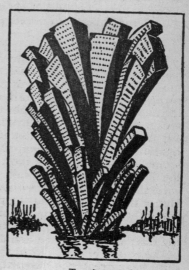

Top-heavy

Therefore all young Jews were taught that strict attendance at the temple and abject obedience to the wishes of the high priest were highly desirable qualities in all good little boys and girls. And a virtue which in Sparta and Egypt counted for very little was regarded in Jerusa-

337

lem as the cornerstone of a desirable civic conduct.

Then go a little farther toward the west until you reach a country called Phoenicia. There everything depended upon a favorable balance of trade. Sidon and Tyre were commercial republics. They had no need of farmers and they were rich enough to hire soldiers whenever they needed them, and as for religion, it played a comparatively small part in their lives. They existed by and for and through commerce. Hence the rich merchants (who ruled the city) preached shrewdness and diplomacy as the highest virtues to which any citizen could aspire and cheerfully neglected the body and the soul which meant so much to the Spartans and to the Jews.

By this time I am sure that you know what I mean. Rome turned the whole western world into a vast colonial empire. To exploit those possessions successfully, it was necessary that a large number of Roman citizens should be well versed in the business of administration and in the rudiments of jurisprudence. The cool and aloof patrician, the solitary soldier in a lonely tent, able to make quick decisions at a moment's notice, ever ready to sacrifice himself and his followers for the good of the state, that man was held up to all Roman children as the ideal after which they should aspire if they hoped to amount to something in this world.

In the course of time Rome ceased to be the head of the political world and became the center of the spiritual universe. Then there was a shifting of ideals. The new rulers needed competent clerics. Reading and writing and the pleasant gift of persuasion took the place of the sterner virtues of soldiering and administering which had been in such high regard during the republic and the empire.

In America during the first half century after the establishment of an independent commonwealth there had been so much free land that millions of people had been able to live happily and wastefully without calling any man their master.

Such short interludes, during which there exists an almost absolute economic equality, have occurred occasionally during the history of the last fifty centuries, but they have never lasted very long. And by the middle of the nineteenth century the world of Jefferson and the first Adams was as dead as the era of Asshurbanipal. Conditions were returning to normalcy, which meant that the people were again beginning to be divided into two distinct classes, a small one that dispensed credit and a large one that needed credit. And as soon as that had occurred, the ancient law which I mentioned a few pages ago once more went into force and the rulers quite unconsciously, but just as determinedly as if they had set out to do so, established certain definite lines of conduct which were to be held up to all good citizens as the ideal after which they and their children and grandchildren should strive.

In this case that ideal consisted in the worship of wealth. That, of course, was nothing new. Florence and Venice and Augsburg and Novgorod had been commercial republics centuries before America was discovered, and their citizens had been trained to regard the accumulation of riches as the greatest (because the most useful) of all civic virtues. But never before, in the history of the human race, had there been such an opportunity to acquire such great possessions in so short a space of time as now presented itself to those who were fortunate enough to come to the North American continent before the middle of the last century.

In consequence whereof the purely physical world acquired a degree of solemn respect which thus far had been strictly reserved for the spiritual claims of the medieval Church.

After the end of the Civil War and with Maximilian safely out of the way, the United States was no longer in any danger from foreign attack. A small but efficiently handled navy was enough for all our defensive needs and when there was some house-cleaning to be done (as was the case in the year 1898 when the continued Spanish mismanagement of Cuba forced the United States to give that unfortunate island a government of its own) it could be left to the marines and to a few regiments of regulars. Generally speaking, however, the military virtues were no longer necessary for the safety of the nation and they were quickly allowed to fall into abeyance. The same held true of those characteristics of self-reliance and freedom which for almost a century had been an indispensable part of life along the western frontier. They retained a sentimental value and were given great prominence in elementary books of history and patriotism. No one, however, took them very seriously, for they implied a degree of economic and spiritual independence which would have been disastrous in people who depended for their daily existence upon the good will of their bankers and employers.

No, the new code had no longer any use for the old virtues of the independent frontiersmen and the new masters of the earth looked eagerly for a different set of rules. As a result they began to explain the world in terms of property. They proclaimed the sacrosanct nature of inanimate matter. And finally they created a new deity which should henceforth rule the Republic and which they called "Success."

But that was not all.

The old maxims of the "good life" as it had been lived among the happy-go-lucky brethren of the frontier were discarded as no longer of any practical use.

A new gospel was written and it proclaimed thrift, economy, regular hours, regular habits, regular ideas, loyalty to employers, submission to the will of the majority, meek submission to popular views, to be the highest of all civic virtues.

And this was done so cleverly and so quietly that soon the old slogan, "Be true to your own personality and you will be happy," was completely discarded for the new doctrine, "Forget that you have any personality of your own and you will be rich."

This new philosophy of life was at once reflected by the political development of the country.

During the first half of the nineteenth century, the Presidents of the United States had been men of outstanding characteristics. Not all of them had been profound scholars, or students of statecraft. But each in his own way had been possessed of a definite personality. A few of them, like Polk and Pierce and Fillmore, had been people of rather mediocre ability. But even such minor prophets had represented certain definite ideas. They had got to the top by fighting. They had been men among men. One either liked them very much or disliked them intensely. And even their worst enemies could not accuse them of being negligible quantities.

Therefore when little boys grew old enough to ask questions, they were told that if they worked hard and studied industriously they might aspire to any office in the great country to which they belonged—yea, they might even hope to end their days as President of the United States, the greatest office in all the world.

But all this was changed during the second half of the nineteenth century.

Little boys were no longer urged to start their career in the general direction of the White House. They were taught that a lifetime of mediocre conformity might make them rich. Inanimate objects were dangled before their expectant eyes and they were told of the rewards that went with the successful accumulation of things.

The men who now went to Congress no longer went there as representatives of ideas, good ones, bad ones, indifferent ones—but ideas. No, they traveled to Washington as the plenipotentiaries of some particular group of interests. They spoke for "lumber" or for "coal" or for "synthetic gin." They took their orders from a board of stockholders. They thought of the common country in terms of a workshop. And the country retaliated and thought of them in terms of material success.

Those pioneers who had moved farther westward, who had settled down on the farms of Wisconsin and Kansas and Wyoming and the Dakotas and had not lost trace of the old frontier independence, sometimes tried to break through this barrier of inanimate matter and not infrequently gave expression to their discontent in the form of a new political party. But they never had a chance. They were laughed out of court. Or if ridicule failed to defeat them, they were outlawed as enemies of the new Dispensation and they were starved and embargoed into abject submission.

And ceaselessly the mills of the gods kept grinding on.

Coal, iron, lead, water power, oil, silver, gold, inanimate objects without end, were being exploited to add to the national wealth.

Immigrants by the million were scooped up by the gigantic machine of progress, were dumped upon our shores, and were set to work for the greater glory of the God of Success.

Until man was completely enslaved by the iron monster which he had erected to assist him in his manifold labors and became the servant of his own slave.

Once in a very long while a voice would be raised against this demoralizing process of a general dehumanization. One man, accidentally called to the high office of President, fought valiantly to show his fellow countrymen the folly of a policy which impoverished the human soul while it filled the human purse with golden eagles. But either the task was too difficult for him or Theodore Roosevelt was not given enough time to realize his ideals. For no sooner had he been eliminated than everything went on as before and the Republic continued what he had so bitterly called it, "A polyglot boardinghouse, a polyglot workshop, a polyglot savings bank without a soul."

Even genius, most independent of mental manifestations, accepted the dictatorship of the Inanimate and put its services at the disposal of the new national deities without a single word of murmured protest.

Under such circumstances the only chance of salvation could have come from the Hills of the Land of Letters. As a rule the satirist is more powerful than his rival, the political reformer, and one old goose quill is as powerful as a battalion of machine guns. In this case, however, literature was completely routed. A few of the more important critics of the reigning social system were cajoled into submission. Those who refused to submit to the new dictatorship of Things were trampled under foot. The others lost courage and remained behind to sing hosannahs.

That was the situation until a dozen years ago. Far removed from the rest of the world, protected on the east and the west by wide stretches of water, the country was practically impregnable. It could afford to dictate to its southern neighbors without the slightest fear of any unpleasant consequences and not infrequently made use of this pleasant prerogative.

It could dictate its will to all those within hailing-range of its battleships and whenever such a policy seemed advisable, it did not hesitate to interfere with a very drastic and often unnecessary display of force.

And then, quite suddenly and unexpectedly, Fate took a hand and asked an absurd question.

"You have," so this deity (who is not deprived of a sense of humor) remarked, "you have been accumulating more wealth than anyone has ever done before. You have built larger factories than anyone else and more of them and faster trains and more of them and higher houses and more of them and your bank deposits run into the billions and your per-capita national wealth is greater than that of any other country since the days of Moloch. But now that you have got all that, 'What,' in the words of one of your wittiest compatriots, 'are you going to do with it?' "

And when we came to think of it, for the life of us, we did not know!

## Chapter Fifty-One

## WANTED: MORE AND CHEAPER RAW MATERIALS

ONE OF THE REASONS why the exiled Puritan community in the Low Countries left their homes in Leyden and Amsterdam and went to America has already been mentioned in a previous chapter.

A short time before the English dissenters came to the Low Countries, the Dutch and the Spaniards had concluded a truce and had promised not to fight each other for at least a dozen years.

That truce was to come to an end in the year 1621 and then not only would the Puritan young men run the risk of being called to serve in the army, but in case of a Spanish invasion they would be exposed to the same danger as their Dutch hosts. Wherefore they departed before hostilities were resumed and left their Protestant brethren in Europe to save themselves as best they could.

The war begun in the year 1621 lasted until 1648 and it became part of a general European upheaval afterward known as the Thirty Years' War.

The Thirty Years' War was a direct outcome of the activities of Martin Luther. The religious revolt which he started had divided the German country into two irreconcilable groups. After the year 1517 Germans no longer felt as Germans. They were either Protestants or Catholics and the slender thread of a common fatherland was completely annihilated. The Thirty Years' War, which was the outcome of this deplorable state of affairs, destroyed the empire, reduced the population to one quarter of what it had been before, and set the clock of German progress backward by at least two centuries. That is the important part of it for the purpose of our present chapter.

During that important period in history when the big racial groups of Europe divided the outlying parts of the world among themselves, Germany was too weak to ask for her share.

Spain fought with Portugal and Portugal fought with Holland and Holland fought with France and England fought with all of them for the possession of Africa, Asia, and America and when their fury abated, they retained as much territory as they could safely hope to develop with their respective resources in men and money.

Then came the nineteenth century and a smallish giant by the name of Otto von Bismarck, a rough fellow from the Prussian frontier, took hold of affairs, made himself boss of the House of Hohenzollern, and hammered his distracted fellow countrymen into an exceedingly powerful and strongly united empire.

From the point of view of the average European and American this not inconsiderable achievement had one great disadvantage. It came exactly two hundred years too late. The available supply of coal and iron and oil had been parceled out long before when there had been no one to contest the claims of the white man except a few defenseless Injuns and Negroes. But now all the coal lands and the iron lands and the oil lands belonged to some strongly armed white country which was dependent upon them for its own welfare and would protect them against foreign attack by every means at its disposal.

Therefore if Germany really wished to get hold of her share of these raw materials (as she said she did) it would mean war, and war was about the last thing that those debt-ridden European countries could afford.

But once again the practical politicians of that age saw all their plans upset by certain mysterious economic forces which worked regardless of emperors and presidents, armament rings and peace societies.

The worship of the Inanimate had not been restricted to the American continent. All other countries had fallen a victim of the new gods. Everywhere the machine ruled supreme. But a machine is a voracious creature. It insists upon being fed every few minutes and it is very particular in its diet and asks for enormous quantities of coal and iron and copper and lead and other indigestible stuff or it won't do any work at all. And as soon as the point has been reached where the greater part of a nation has come to depend for its daily maintenance upon machinery, then the government of such a country must make sure of an uninterrupted flow of raw materials or it will expose its subjects to the dangers of almost immediate death by starvation.

That is exactly what happened in the case of the rejuvenated German Empire.

It appeared upon the scene two hundred years late and

then tried to make up for lost time by a display of such bumptious energy that all other nations were apprised of some vague future danger and began to take measures to protect themselves and those colonial possessions which their ancestors had bestowed upon them.

In view of what had happened during the previous three centuries, it was only natural that the opposition to the German plan should have centered in London. One after another England had defeated her rivals for world domination. Spain, Portugal, Holland, France, had all of them been forced to surrender part of their foreign holdings to the British Empire.

How or why the Germans ever expected to be successful in such a singlehanded combat when they knew what had happened to all the other enemies of Great Britain, is more than I can tell. But they were never very good at the game of politics and they were entirely too familiar with books to understand men. On the other hand, it is not difficult to find the reason for England's uninterrupted succession of victories in all colonial wars and enterprises.

The management of foreign affairs in England is today (and always has been) the private affair of a small and highly compact group of people. Such a policy has one enormous advantage. In the field of international politics, the English are the only people who really know what they want and who year in and year out can go after the things they want with a singleness of purpose that is entirely lacking in most other nations.

All of which Germany discovered, to her great mortification, in the year of Grace 1914.

The issue, of course, was so terribly befogged by the professional ballyhooers of both sides, that the strangest rumors were soon afloat about the original cause of the conflict. But the war was not brought about by the murder of an Austrian grandduke or the violation of a solemn treaty or the love of England and Russia and France for the rights of small nations. Austrian granddukes had been shot before and nothing had happened. Treaties had been violated regularly once or twice each year and no one had said a word about it. And as for the love of England and Russia and France for the rights of small nations—why, the subject is almost indecent in its hilarity.

No, that war was bound to come, and intelligent historians might have predicted it on that memorable day of the year 1871 when the halls of Versailles resounded with the first hurrahs for the newly re-established German Empire.

The immediate cause might have been anything—a fishery concession in Greenland—a tariff on hogs in Serbia —a third-rate coal mine in the valley of the Meuse.

The real underlying cause was the belated attempt of the unfortunate Teutons to get their share of the world's spoils, to find a cheap and abundant supply of raw material that was not controlled by another nation.

And because the United States of America had more coal and iron and oil than any other land, it was inevitable that the people of America should be dragged into the turmoil.

They did not take down their guns until the European rivals of Germany were on the very brink of ruin and defeat. Up to that moment, all the fine speeches of all the impassioned war orators, all the atrocity stories, all the blue books, the green books, the purple books, explaining the nobility and sacredness of all the different national causes had left the greater part of the populace only mildly interested.

But the moment the average man began to feel somewhere in his subconscious soul "This thing is going to hit us, too. If the Germans are successful and defeat England and France as they have already defeated Russia and Roumania and Italy and their other enemies, then we shall be next on the list and because we have more of the raw materials the Germans need to keep their machines going, they are going to come after us and they will try and grab what we need for the sustenance of our own iron monsters." The moment the average citizen became dimly aware of the fate that awaited him and his children if Germany broke through the cordon of the besieging European nations, then at last the American people were ready to enter the war on the side of the allies and when that happened, the fate of Germany was sealed.

For this was no longer a struggle between men, as wars thus far had always been. It was a clash of Inanimate Matter.

It was a struggle, the outcome of which could be foretold with a fair degree of accuracy by any competent statistician. And America, which during the last sixty years had concentrated upon one single purpose—the wholesale production of Things—now poured the output of her countless workshops upon the great European conflagration and she did it with the precision of an experienced fire chief who has unlimited reserves at his command—whose colleagues have localized the flames to a single city block—and who can set to work to drench the afflicted area at his leisure with the absolute certainty of ultimate success.

On April sixth of the year 1917 President Wilson called out the first of the engines. A few weeks later they made their appearance upon the soil of Europe. A few months later they were ready to start work. After that their numbers steadily increased. Ceaselessly they poured their tons of extinguishing material upon the burning heart of the old continent. Within a very short time the walls of Germany and Austria began to crumble.

With a terrific crash, the roof came down.

Two years later, the fire was over.

The engines went back home.

But then the government of President Wilson showed itself less competent than the fire departments of our big cities.

After a conflagration, however small, a fireman is delegated to watch the premises for several days and sometimes weeks.

This may seem an unnecessary precaution.

But the insurance underwriters will tell you the reason why.

A fire in itself is bad enough.

But infinitely greater perils hide among smoldering ruins.

Those heaps of ashes look innocent enough. All danger

seems removed. That is the moment when glowing bits of cinders begin to burrow their way deep down into the rubbish pile and set fire to some adjoining cellar. And before anyone has clearly realized what has happened, the red plague has spread far and wide and has touched parts of the city that thus far had been considered safe.

A solitary fireman, twiddling his fingers and reading last week's comics and apparently doing nothing in particular for days and weeks at a time may seem an absurd waste of money and energy. In the end he may prove to be a highly economical investment. With a single bucket of water he is able to prevent the repetition of a disaster which otherwise might have destroyed the entire community.

## Chapter Fifty-Two

## A WORLD UNSUSPECTED

COLUMBUS CROSSED THE OCEAN to find a short route to the Indies and stumbled upon a continent, the existence of which no one had suspected.

Four hundred and twenty-five years later, America returned the visit and went to Europe to save what was vaguely supposed to be an old and respectable form of civilization, and discovered instead a complex social structure which was totally out of keeping with the high-sounding ideals preached so eloquently by the war prophets of the different groups of belligerents.

And when I say this, please remember one thing. The average man is not historically minded. Especially in our own country where the domination of Things militates against the free and healthy development of ideas, a consciousness of the historical inevitableness of all human experience is frowned upon as a waste of time and as a manifestation of that skepticism which the guardians of Ellis Island are supposed to keep out of the confines of the Republic.

A fairly profound knowledge of a great many subjects is apt to make a man see all the sides of every problem. That in turn leads to a certain hesitancy of action and to a profound modesty of the soul. Both those characteristics, as any old drill sergeant will tell you, are bad for the morale of an army and since it was the avowed purpose of those who wished to dominate American life to organize the populace into a well-drilled civil army of commerce and trade, anything that might tend to upset the mental discipline is frowned upon and if possible is removed from the curriculum of the schools and universities.

Such a policy is not without certain distinct advantages. The younger generation is not encumbered with too much useless mental ballast. But on the other hand it has not prepared them for the role which they have been suddenly called upon to play.

When the young men of our country enlisted in the war—generously—enthusiastically—they were filled with an unselfish ideal of service to humanity.

What was really a struggle for raw materials between two powerful nations became a clash of devils and angels. On the one side Magna Charta and Joan of Arc and La Fayette and democracy and on the other side "Schrecklichkeit" and Nietzsche (whoever he was) and the despotism of a demented tyrant.

Indeed, the issues seemed so simple and so clearly defined that no one deemed it necessary to ask for a bill of particulars or to demand a definite program for the future settlement of such difficulties. When an honest fellow sees a ruffian attack a little boy and knock him down and rob him of his pennies, he does not stop to discuss the merits of the case. He pitches in and knocks the brute down. This image had been so consistently held up before the eyes of young America that several million men hastened to the other side to perform what they considered a most holy duty.

The moment they landed the disappointment began, and soon they learned that Europe was a strange land, inhabited by strange people—a universe in itself and for and by itself—which had never been successfully explored by the American mind.

And when the war came to an end, when half a dozen empires were overnight wiped off the face of the earth, when that outward form of European civilization with which the Americans had been more or less familiar was suddenly destroyed by the exasperated masses of the hungry and the disinherited, the glowing enthusiasm of the year 1917 made place for the chilly disillusionment of the year 1918.

During the administration of James Monroe, a presidential message had warned all foreigners away from the premises of the New World.

During the latter half of the presidency of Woodrow Wilson the overwhelming majority of the American people added an amendment of their own to the Monroe doctrine and decided that henceforth no American should participate in European affairs.

Once was enough, and never again!

For the hitherto unsuspected Europe—the Europe of the small, quarreling units and the large despotic groups of nations—was not at all to the taste of those who had unconsciously learned to think in terms of a continent.

The sudden realization of this fact—the gradual awakening of certain old traditions, vaguely remembered from a day when America meant a state of mind rather than a successful form of economic exploitation—these produced a mental and spiritual shock which for a moment at least caused us to revise all our current creeds and beliefs and make a serious search of the innermost recesses of our national soul.

In the lives of almost all great men there has been a crisis—a moment when some outward event forced them to face their career in the brutal light of complete self-revelation.

Up to the year 1916 we were merrily jogging along the commonplace road of prosperity with no thought of tomorrow. The Iron Men who worked for us performed their daily tasks smoothly and contentedly. We were all of us comfortable. If we worried about anything at all, it was about the new regulations for rural free delivery or the incessant desire of the people of Haiti (or of Chicago) to do murder upon each other—all of them negligible details that could be settled in a jiffy if we ever really paid some serious attention to them.

Then came the great upheaval that destroyed the older forms of European civilization and wiped away the accumulated wealth of an entire continent.

Suddenly the truth of the situation dawned upon us.

Europe, too, had worshiped before false altars.

Europe, too, had made the accumulation of Inanimate Matter the highest of all civic virtues.

And the end was—what we had just seen.

Chaos.

Chaos, complete and absolute.

Thus ended America's first participation in a European war, and what had been meant as a great and glorious crusade developed into a painful and disheartening voyage of discovery.

Evidently something was wrong with the world. By an accursed turn of luck the American people were called upon to set it right.

By an accursed turn of luck, or by the grace of a merciful God. We can take our choice.


*Chapter Fifty-Three*

## THE NEW ROAD FOR AMERICA

WE DID NOT KNOW it at the time—we did not even suspect it—but the end of the first World War also meant the end of America's happy and carefree existence as what we might call a "bachelor nation." After that conflict, our independence and freedom of action were gone. I do not mean to imply that we had actually gone so far as to commit ourselves publicly, had exchanged rings and were keeping regular company with one of our former partners. Being unusually rich, we had bestowed largesse upon all those who had been on our side and even upon those who until then had been our enemies. Therefore it could not be said that we had actually exchanged vows ourselves but neither were we the happy and carefree people we had been during the first century and a half of our existence, and that loss of our former freedom, as I see it, was perhaps the most important result of the Great War as far as we were concerned.

I shall therefore write this final chapter from that angle. Outwardly no great changes had taken place and the majority of our people probably never realized what had taken place. They were delighted that this most unwelcome interruption in their daily affairs had at last come to an end. The campaign in France which had started as a noble crusade had fizzled out (if I may be allowed quite such an uncomplimentary expression in connection with so good a cause) into a most depressing squabble of mutual recriminations. The same doughboys who only a few months before had sailed eastward with such high purpose to avenge a dreadful wrong and to make the world safe for democracy came limping back with far from tender feelings for their recent associates. Mademoiselle from Armentières had not at all come up to specifications. She had worn a ragged woolen petticoat, her wooden shoes had shown a prolonged familiarity with cow dung, and she had been less than articulate except in the matter of her personal finances. The mayors and shopkeepers, too, of the villages in which the boys had been billeted had shown a very decided gift for penny-pinching in those transactions which became inevitable when thousands of lusty youngsters with healthy appetites for fresh chicken and *vin du pays* were suddenly removed from farms in Iowa and Arkansas to remote hamlets in Auvergne and the Pas de Calais. And even the higher-up authorities seemed to be much more interested in the extra sums that could be wrung out of an official deal with *Les Américains* than in the more immediate problem of gaining the good will of their generous saviors.

Fortunately the barrier of an unknown tongue had protected the Americans from a too clear and direct understanding of the insults to which they were being constantly exposed, but in the case of their other allies, the British, there had been no such safety valve. Then both sides had known only too well what the other fellow meant to imply when he referred to the somewhat doubtful antecedents of the gentlemen with whom he happened to be discussing the relative merits and demerits of the republican form of government vs. that of a monarchy and *vice versa*. And this unity of languages, instead of contributing toward a better understanding of the allies (a prospect which had greatly delighted the hearts of all those who expected Peace on Earth from Esperanto or Volapuk) had often led to bloody and painful encounters between the humbler subjects of the King and the sovereign fellow citizens of the President.

To make matters worse, after the collapse of the imperial armies and the flight of the *Oberste Kriegsherr* to Holland, it had been the duty of the American troops to occupy a great deal of German territory. The peaceful villages of the Rhineland and those of the Moselle, with their neatly kept streets and their orderly houses and their well-behaved children and their smiling Gretchens and their non-overcharging hotel keepers and their obliging burgomasters (obsequiously trying to gain the friendship of the conqueror)—they had come as such a contrast to the simple-hearted boys from across the broad Atlantic that their entire view of the conflict had been pulled out of its true perspective.

*Those Heinies in the Old Country,* so they used to write to the folks at home, *are exactly like the old bearded fellows who used to sing at their Sangverein fests when we were small boys, and their Fraus treat us right and their daughters help mamma in the kitchen and they are all right! What is all this stuff we heard about atrocities and their being barbarous Huns? Why, they gave us apple dumplings for supper last Sunday and in France, what did we get?* And so on and so forth.

They forgot (what in most instances they had never known) that the merry inhabitants of the richest wine districts in the world—the gay and carefree Rhinelanders

—were an entirely different kettle of fish from the overbearing and bullying creatures who occupied the sandy wastes of Prussia and who, being more Slavic than German, had always been a highly emotional element in the nation, ready to explode at any moment and fill the world with the clamor of death and destruction.

Since the Allies had made the grave mistake of not occupying Berlin (an error for which they were to pay most dearly afterward), our young men had only seen those parts of the Reich where the natives had a liberal admixture of Gallic blood in their veins and by confusing them with the true Germanic type of the dark hinterlands of the East and the North, they had quite naturally reached a conclusion that was as far from the truth as if they had undertaken to judge the modern Japanese by studying the charming landscapes of Hokusai or Korin.

Small wonder that when they returned they were completely disorientated—that few of their reactions were still the same as on the day they had set foot on European soil and that they were more than ready to give the Old Continent up as a bad job—as a hopeless mess of absurd little nationalities, all of them incurably selfish and so hopelessly jealous of their own supposed rights and privileges that they would never be able to reach a common ground for any kind of spiritual or economic co-operation.

With millions of our people in such a mood, it was to be foreseen that President Wilson would have no easy time with his plans for a League of Nations in which the United States of America were to play an immediate and most important role. Here we should remember a point, rarely stressed by our historians, that Woodrow Wilson, an historian and a pedagogue, had always been much more interested in the more theoretical aspects of such a war than in the actual fighting. In this respect, he was the exact opposite of his successor who presided over our destinies during the second World War. For Franklin Delano Roosevelt is still as much interested in ships and sailors and soldiers as he was during the years he functioned as Mr. Wilson's assistant secretary of the Navy and when one reads his Atlantic Charter, one has the feeling that he and Mr. Churchill composed this document because it was the sort of thing the people at large expected from a couple of statesmen who were supposed to be not merely engaged in winning a war but also in making some preparations for the world-of-tomorrow by keeping the Germans under strict military control. But no one who has ever taken the trouble to study Mr. Wilson's Fourteen Points can have the slightest doubt about the man's utter sincerity and his deep concern about a future state of affairs in which such things as world-wide wars would no longer be possible because the awakened conscience of humanity would know how to take the necessary steps to prevent them and would be able to do so by an appeal to our ethical convictions and to those alone.

Since mankind, ever since the beginning of recorded history, has never bothered greatly about its conscience whenever its emotions or interests were stirred, it would take a professor to lay down such a noble-sounding program for future action and then expect that it would work. Unfortunately the vast majority of our doughboys were not exactly professors, a term which would have made them fighting mad if one had dared to apply it to one of their own kind. And after they had reached home, they had hastened to inform their families and neighbors that all this highfalutin nonsense about Justice and Equality among the countries of the Old Continent were merely a waste of good American time and money and that the sooner we over here washed our hands of the whole European muddle the better it would be for all of us.

President Wilson, however, was not merely a scholar but he had also been a college president and college presidents are not accustomed to being contradicted. It irks them to find their plans opposed, especially on such occasions, when they feel sincerely convinced that they are fighting on the side of the gods. And had anyone ever laid more careful plans for the future happiness of the human race than Thomas Woodrow Wilson, Presbyterian and twenty-eighth President of the United States of America? Of course not and to interfere with his grandiose project was absolute sacrilege.

"Oh, yeah?" the ribald veterans answered back and prepared to bury the Fourteen Points of their former commander-in-chief underneath such a mountain of vituperation that they would never again be either seen or heard. If Europe wanted a League of Nations, then let Europe get itself such a league and good luck to the Poles and the Czechs and the Albanians and the Lithuanians and the Hungarians and the Roumanians and the Bulgarians and the Spaniards and the Portuguese and even the Germans, if the others would let them in, which seemed highly doubtful. But as for the sovereign, free-born Americans, let them beware and remain aloof or they would discover to their everlasting regret that they would be allowed to do all the dirty work and would be left holding the bag, just as during the late unpleasantness when they had been charged rent for the very trenches which they were supposed to hold against the Huns.

The League of Nations might be a magnificent edifice but it was much too foreign to please most Americans.

I am here mentioning the old and familiar yarn about our paying rent for our trenches because it was so typical of our post-war attitude toward our former allies. The story was not true but practically everybody believed it and in history it does not matter half as much what is really true as what most people happen to believe to be the truth. A study of the methods of Adolf Hitler reveals him to be a brother underneath the skin of several of the most outstanding mass murderers of the last fifty years. But as long as there are tens of millions of Germans who consider him the incarnation of all Teutonic virtues and who are firmly convinced that their Führer was sent to them by Almighty God to lead their nation into the Promised Land of World Domination, the latter opinion is the one with which we have to reckon, and the former may be safely discarded, for it will not change the mind of a single Nazi slavey. And it was therefore quite futile to argue that from an ideal point of view, the League of Nations was exactly what the world needed if it were to avoid another disaster. The majority of our people did not want it for reasons which seemed entirely reasonable and adequate to them at that moment and therefore President Wilson was foredoomed to a terrific disappointment. The failure of that which was closer to his heart than anything else in this world proved too much for his physical resistance. He suffered a stroke and during the last month of his presidency, he was a physical wreck. He had failed to read the minds of his fellow men correctly and to fathom the depth of their distrust of everything "foreign" and as a result one of the noblest careers of our political life came to a sad and lonely end because once more a man in a highly responsible position had failed to understand that the highest wisdom of politics lies in the faculty of doing "that which is feasible."

As for the country at large, it either felt sorry for the leader who had come to such an ending or if one belonged to the ranks of the irreconcilables, jubilated in a most indecent and unbecoming way over the fate of one who only a few years before had been considered the savior of the human race. But with the exception of a few small groups of people who were farsighted enough to realize that modern means of transportation had made the United States an integral part of the world at large, America went back to its favorite practice of accumulating as many material goods in as short a period of time as possible and of establishing a standard of living which promised to guarantee every citizen two chickens in every pot and two cars in every garage and of doing this without giving a thought to the rest of the world. Here and there a few unpopular citizens mumbled ominous words of warning, declaring that such an orgy of indiscriminate spending and speculating could only end in disaster. But they soon discovered that one cannot possibly fight a million dollars and as everybody (except themselves) had at least a million dollars, those doleful pessimists were rudely trampled under foot and the merry procession hastened eagerly on its way to the poorhouse.

For the pessimists (as has happened so often in history before) had understood the situation better than the optimists. There was a slight rumbling among the rafters of the Stock Exchange, but nobody paid any attention. Next pieces of plaster began to come down. Then the walls were observed to show very serious cracks, and finally, with a thunderous crash, this whole edifice of folly and make-believe and wishful thinking came tumbling down upon a multitude which had not been in the least prepared for such a catastrophe. Then and only then did the American people realize what had happened during these many years when each one of them had been looking exclusively after his own interests, leaving the rest of the world to the devil and its own devices. And then it understood—what until that moment had been clear to only a few unpopular writers and other professional observers—that the United States were as much part of the rest of the world as any building in a modern city is a part of the rest of the town. Let all the other dwellings for miles around it fall to pieces and even the strongest of skyscrapers will show signs of damage.

That is why the history of the America of the last twenty years cannot possibly be understood unless we also know what meanwhile happened in every other part of the planet. And as behooves a faithful reporter I shall now give you a short resumé of the events in Russia and Turkey and Greece and Germany and Libya and Ethiopia, that you may be able to follow me when I add up these unfortunate incidents and then come to the conclusion that they were bound to give us a sum total of "minus zero."

Ever since the beginning of time, history and sickness have had this much in common—that no one can exactly foretell what they will lead up to—something entirely different from what even the brightest commentators had anticipated when, with persuading eloquence, they had endeavored to foretell the shape of things to come.

In the days of our great-great-grandfathers, people had enthusiastically danced around the Tree of Liberty, feeling that the Great French Revolution was on the point of carrying the principles of Liberty, Fraternity, and Equality into every nook and corner of both the Old and the New Continents. Twenty years of slavery at the hands of an ill-mannered little Corsican gangster had taught them the dangers of such rash prognostications. The liberal revolutions all over Europe in the forties of the last century, instead of leading to a government by the people, had merely opened the road to the reactionary forces of the Hohenzollerns and the Habsburgs and had made it possible for a third Napoleon to establish himself on the moth-eaten throne of his famous uncle, the first and most famous of the Buonapartes. And when the Great War, that had been started to make the world safe for democracy (in other words, to continue the *status quo* of the old imperial organizations) came to an end, who came out on top? Let us confess it! It was an unknown Russian revolutionist—an obscure fellow by the name of Nikolai Lenin (which was not even his real name for he had been born Nikolai Ulyanow) who carried away the victory, for he made one sixth of the world safe for Marxian socialism and that was about the last thing the old-time democracies had expected and the last thing they had wanted to come about.

This is the way it has always happened and probably will continue to happen until man shall become a logical animal, which for the moment seems to be still a very long way off. And therefore when I read books and articles about the world after the war and listen to speeches about our preparations for peace—even when I am invited to read a solemn Atlantic Charter—I feel inclined to raise a mild voice of remonstrance and to warn the eager enthusiasts, who assure me that this time the boys are being killed to put an end to all this nonsense of war, that the present conflict will undoubtedly be followed by a great many more and that in spite of all solemn treaties, mankind will only muddle through until finally and at last some genius will arise to show us how to run a nation as if it were a successful business concern, run by competent and honest managers, instead of being a political organization, dominated by people whose only qualifications for their high office consist of an efficient set of vocal cords.

Ever since the Greeks started their memorable experiment with self-government, the world has known that oratory has been the most dangerous enemy of democracy. For the rhetorical genius is closely akin to the musical genius in general and there is no more reason to suppose that a *prima donna* or *primo signor* of the political podium would be able to administer a complicated modern nation than to expect a similar miracle from one of the leading tenors of the Metropolitan Opera Company or the pianist or fiddler who packs them in at Carnegie Hall. But we are still under the spell of Demosthenes, whose magnificent flow of words, not backed up by any concrete plan of action, persuaded his fellow citizens to indulge in a policy which led to the definite elimination of Greece as an independent national unit.

However, as we are now as much under the spell of the word "democracy" as the people of the Middle Ages were under that of the Church, I am afraid that nothing much can be done about it. We were given our chance to observe a Demosthenes in action when we watched the sorry spectacle of our own William Jennings Bryan trying to qualify as a statesman. Here was the unrivaled elocutionist of the last fifty years, the man whose deep-booming voice had held an entire nation spellbound for almost two generations, but the moment he was given a post of responsibility as one of the practical leaders of the nation, he carried us not only to the brink of disaster but also to the verge of the ridiculous, which is apt to be even more fatal to the prestige of a powerful country. And we had to let him go, because even we, the best-natured and most patient and long-suffering of all the people gathered together on this planet, were finally obliged to come to the conclusion that a lyrical larynx is not a true qualification for the job of running an intricate industrial commonwealth of the middle of the twentieth century.

Why this excursion into the realm of theoretical politics? Because in a final chapter to a history of America, one might as well try and do a little constructive work. Some day this war will be over and then, if we leave the re-establishment of peace once more to the kind of people who have been doing that sort of work during the last hundred and fifty years, we will have another mess on our hands before the ink on the document is dry. The Founding Fathers, those shrewd and crafty disciples of eighteenth-century liberalism, knew what they were doing when they tried to leave the election of the President and the Vice-President of the Union to a small and independent body of carefully selected men who were not apt to be swayed by fine-sounding phrases, hiding hollow arguments. But no sooner were they in their graves than the forces of destruction must reappear upon the stage and undo all the work of the Washingtons and Jeffersons and Madisons by throwing politics back into that arena of wildcat fighting where the loudest *me-ow* is apt to be considered an evidence of a gift for leadership. And ever since it is there in that arena that the fate of mankind has been decided. With the result that the world has hardly known a day of peace since the Great Orators came into their own—until finally there appeared one of such monstrous ability to sway his fellow men by the mere flow of his words, that he set sixty million people in motion, persuaded them to do his bidding, regardless of all consequences, and finally pitched the whole civilized world into a witches' cauldron of hate and cruelty and death and despair, from which we can only hope it may ever be able to extricate itself.

But let us not be too haughty in our condemnation of

Hitler. It was only by a stroke of great good luck (though I hate to call murder anything "good"), that we escaped our own potential little Hitler, but a next time we may be less fortunate, for we shall never have a chance at a world based upon scientific facts and reason and horse sense (a most desirable goal) until our parliaments shall outlaw fine oratory in their debates as mere rhetoric has long since been banished from a gathering of scientists who are trying to find a new formula for saving human life. But, if I am not mistaken, I was led astray from the beaten track of my arguments by this unexpected but most welcome chance to take a short canter on my pet hobby horse and it is time for me to return to the point from which I started. I was then going to give you an abbreviated account of the circumstances in the old world which led to the almost catastrophic events which in America led to two stray cats in every garage instead of the promised limousines.

Of Russia I have already spoken. Had the allied nations understood the true nature of the wave of discontent which had spread across the Slavic lands, they might have saved the Czarist empire from that complete collapse which made possible the rise of the Bolshevists. Here, as in practically all subsequent cases of misunderstanding, the diplomats were at the bottom of the trouble. Their Excellencies of the Extraterritorial Brigade are a queer class of people. Other officials, in case they have committed a serious blunder, are held to a strict accounting and are dismissed, and even death may be the punishment for their lack in insight and foresight. Diplomats, on the other hand, when their gross incompetence has led to disaster, are provided with a special police escort, are given a special train and presented with a bunch of farewell posies, and are then sped to the frontier amidst much bowing and scraping on the part of their fellow officials of the now hostile country. After which they return to the home country, refuse to give any explanation of their errors of judgment ("we are bound to secrecy by the Department of State"), pay a courtesy call to their superiors (informing them no doubt about the shooting at Herr Goering's hunting lodge and what became of the dear little countess in Podolia who had been a Miss Whoozis from Detroit) and dissolve into space unless they decide to write their memoirs which, with Napoleonic finesse, they use to cover up their own blunders and put their opponents into the worst possible light.

Let us give the devil his due. During the first twenty years after the war, the diplomats were very busy but they still acted as if nothing had happened since the days when Metternich ruled the world by means of his far-flung network of international intrigue. They failed to realize that a great change had come over Europe since the days of the Holy Alliance and that the methods of endless conferences, which had been so successful in the period of the Great Reaction could not possibly be repeated in an era when radio and flying machines had annihilated both time and space and when a country's population no longer consisted of pious and obedient little peasants, but of industrial laborers whose professional training had given them great proficiency in the handling of a machine gun.

And while the statesmen of Versailles tried to bring back a world which long since had become a museum piece (and not even a very interesting one), Hitler moved on and these estimable fossils might just as well have been legislating for the planet Mars. They still saw the world as a sort of vast holding company, managed by a board of directors, and they themselves constituted that board of directors.

First of all they decided to put Russia's house in order and they subsidized a number of expeditions, led by former Czarist generals, in the hope that these ill-disciplined and irresponsible bands of *condottieri* would promptly drive out the wicked Bolsheviks. Even America, in an ill-guided moment, decided to participate in this futile attempt to set the clock of time back and to bestow upon the hapless Russians the renewed blessings of the Romanov regime of a hundred or more years ago.

After the leaders of these expeditions had been shot by

the victorious Communist armies, the elder statesmen (and their younger colleagues from the shores of the Potomac) decided to refrain from further armed interference with Russia's internal affairs. They would now try a sort of *cordon sanitaire*—an economic blockade which would speedily bring the wicked Bolsheviks to their knees. When that, too, failed to achieve the desired purpose, they bethought themselves of certain services the recently re-created Polish state might render to the cause of civilization. Joseph Pilsudski, a former Socialist agitator and a former leader of the Polish movement for independence, was encouraged to start a war against his fellow Slavs of the East. The dream of a Polish Empire reaching from the Vistula to the Dnieper made all the Poles ready for the Great Sacrifice. Aided by a staff of brilliant French officers under General Weygand the Poles waged a victorious campaign against the Russians and no doubt—for a short space of time at least—they succeeded in preventing the Communists from contaminating the western part of Europe. But in the end, nothing was gained, as the Poles who had marched to the banks of the Dnieper were forced to march back again to the banks of the Vistula. And the only concrete result was to show up Poland's inability to rule itself as a modern democracy. Old Pilsudski was much too shrewd to make himself dictator of the new state. Outwardly the forms of self-government were maintained, but America—in so far as it took any interest at all—shrugged its shoulders and said, "The same old stuff!" and withdrew even further from the European muddle of backward countries and selfish and irresponsible politicians.

As for Russia, the bloodthirsty terroristic methods put into practice by the Communists to make their part of the world safe for Communism, so greatly disgusted the average good-natured American that more than ever he would never have anything to do with these cutthroats who spouted Marxian maxims while they were firing Maxim guns into the backs of those who had dared to oppose the triumphant progress of the Communist party and who were now being exterminated with the same efficient violence with which a health officer goes after typhoid-fever microbes.

Meanwhile strange rumors were coming to us from across the Alps. In Italy, which had made terrific sacrifices in the war and which at Versailles had gained practically nothing, there had been a widespread outburst of Communism. As the Italian Parliament appeared to be unable to handle the situation, the inevitable happened. There is one thing for which no nation will stand, and that is chronic disorder. All trade and commerce had come to a standstill. The entire country had been turned into a vast debating society. Before Italy had been completely submerged in this sea of useless oratory, there appeared a man who had a definite plan for reconstruction and the re-establishment of law and order.

Most Italians did not trust this former Socialist agitator who up to the outbreak of the Great War had spent considerable of his time in one jail or another. But placed before the choice between an orderly kind of existence under Benito Mussolini or the chaotic conditions brought about by the leaders of Labor, they preferred Mussolini as the lesser of the two evils. And when Italy became an out-and-out Fascist state, no one was either greatly surprised or showed any profound signs of indignation.

As for the majority of our fellow citizens, they did not care a straw. The tourists who came back from the Mediterranean holiday reported that all the beggars had disappeared from the streets of Naples, that Italy was a good deal safer for lonely travelers than Chicago, and that the trains ran on time and that the banks no longer cheated the customer who presented a letter of credit. America expressed the opinion that the fellow who had been able to bring about such a miracle must have something to him and went about its own business, occasionally looking with awe at the magnificent Italian ships which began to visit our harbors and which, in the matter of service and comfort, were far superior to our own with their ruffian crews of ill-trained stewards and arrogant sailors.

That this new Fascist government was a completely reactionary setup was a detail which seems to have escaped our attention. Some of our people heartily approved of Mussolini's desire to relegate women back to the position they had until recently held in all Mediterranean countries as breeders of children, managers of households, and the obedient slaveys of their lords and masters, only thinly disguised as husbands. Napoleon himself (who despised women almost as much as the Duce) could not have been more thorough in reducing the women to the ignominious rank they came to hold in Fascist Italy. Nor could the French usurper have been more efficient in the way in which the universities were once more converted into mere propaganda schools for the prevailing political opinions.

As for the press, it ceased to be a vehicle for the expression of public opinion and became a shabby mouthpiece for the government. And the less said about Parliament, the better. It is true that the Italian Parliament had long since ceased to have any influence upon national life. It had (as I already said) become a debating society in which the cheapest kind of politicians belabored each other with words without (with a very few noble exceptions) giving a thought to the country as a whole and restricting its activities exclusively to whatever village and hamlets these honorable gentlemen happened to represent. But we again felt that all this was none of our affair and our businessmen rejoiced at the idea that there was at least one country in which Labor had been taught its place. And so nothing was done and the Duce was given our cordial blessings and bade to go ahead as he pleased, provided he occasionally give American capital a chance to get its share of the fat contracts which until then had usually gone to its British rivals.

Then there was France. Poor France! The best of its children lay dead on the field of battle. The parliamentary manipulators who had grabbed hold of the power in the state were about as contemptible a lot as were ever honored by the name of "statesmen." They allowed France to hasten from one crisis to the next. They plundered the nation and each other and finally they even bought up the judiciary. But the American tourists, getting handfuls of francs for their dollars, returned with glowing accounts of the free life in this happy nation of realists, and America paid no heed.

I might as well skip the rest of the European nations. The Scandinavian lands, Switzerland, Holland and Finland gave an example of how countries could be run for the benefit of all their citizens if politics were encouraged to become part of a regular science of government and reason was substituted for emotion and tradition. But the leaders in those countries were known to be Socialists and anything that smacked of Socialism was highly suspicious in the eyes of most Americans. We paid lip service to the economic and social achievements of these Socialistic communities but we were very careful not to follow their example or let our enthusiasm reach out beyond the Smörgasbord table at which the polite Swedes used to entertain those congressional committees which had traveled to the land of the midnight sun to find out how those Scandinavians managed to do so many things (and without the firing of a single shot or the creation of any noticeable amount of ill-feeling) which we ourselves were completely unable to do.

As for the Balkan nations, we conveniently forgot about them except when we were honored with the visit of one of their royal rulers, in which case we were usually treated to an amount of scandal which might have shown us (but failed to do so) that any money we might sink into those countries was lost the moment it had left our shores.

There remained our former enemy, the hopelessly defeated people of Germany. We were surprisingly lenient to them. They had been licked and they knew it. Now give them a chance to get back on their feet and do their share in the work of world rehabilitation. That the leading German businessmen had learned nothing from their recent experience and had not in the least been humbled by their defeat but were just as rapacious for power as ever was conveniently overlooked while we entrusted them with hundreds of millions of dollars (most of which proved a complete loss) which they claimed to be necessary if Germany were to reach that point of prosperity at which it could begin to dream of repaying part of the astronomical sums for reparation money which the Old Men of Versailles had loaded upon the backs of the German people.

Most of you who read this, without remembering any of the harrowing details, will remember that those reparations became a steady part of our daily diet of news. Few of us were able to imagine (even remotely) the sums of money that were being discussed and even smaller was the number of those who thought that more than a thousandth part of these billions would ever find its way to either London or Paris. To us over here, the whole transaction seemed rather silly and we thanked a kind Providence which had saved us from becoming a partner in that famous League of Nations which had been the life ambition of our great war-time President, and our gratitude increased as we observed that all the European shilly-shallying led up to no practical result whatsoever, but only made chaos more chaotic, if it is possible for such a thing to happen.

Then came the era of the great conferences. A hundred and twenty years before, Metternich had maintained the European *status quo* by his endless conferences. The diplomats, with his example still before them, decided to do likewise. After all, I have decided not to give you the detailed lists of these meetings which toward the end were held almost every six months, at which vast armies of experts endlessly discussed "solutions" which were doomed to failure before they had even been incorporated into a formal "protocol" and which benefited nobody except the local hotel managers and the railroad companies.

During this period of the great conferences, America was kept informed about what was happening in Europe by a group of newspaper correspondents who have never been rivaled for the intelligence and the devotion with which they approached their difficult task of giving a free democracy such a comprehensive picture of the situation that every man and woman in our Republic was given the chance to formulate his or her own opinion upon the issues at stake. Unfortunately, all these events took place at the exact moment when we over here were so busy acquiring paper millions that we had no time left for anything else, least of all for the job of watching over our own future. To the average American, Europe was almost as far away as the moon. We felt that no matter what the outcome over there should be of these endless quarrels, we ourselves were safe. The ocean was still three thousand miles wide, only half a dozen German U-boats had been able to approach our shores during the last war and a man who had actually flown across the ocean was a nine days' wonder, to be welcomed here with the freedom of the city and a public reception up Broadway.

As for Asia, it was an even more remote entity than Europe and when an author (who knew his business) wrote a book prophesying a Japanese attack upon the United States in the not far distant future, he was merrily laughed out of court and treated as contemptuously as that unfortunate general who predicted that within another dozen years our cities would have to take measures to protect themselves against the attacks of German bombers.

Here and there a few organizations of honest patriots (of both sexes) tried to make the American people understand that they were now an integral part of the world at large, but their influence did not reach very far. The average citizen was content to leave his safety to the width of the ocean and to that kind Providence which was supposed to love and protect democracies and to see to it that Right should always prevail over Might. Therefore when Japan suddenly went upon the warpath, broke all treaties, attacked China, and occupied Manchuria, nobody was seriously worried. It is true that our State Department tried to prevail upon the Department of Foreign Affairs in London to bring about some sort of joint action and bid Japan observe her duly sworn obligations. But when the Tories, who then ruled over the destinies of the British Empire and who feared only one enemy (the wicked revolutionaries of the Kremlin), bluntly refused to participate in such a step, no one on this side of the ocean took the matter very seriously. Let the Chinese and the

Japanese stew in their own juices and let us make a handsome profit selling the funny little Japs all the scrap iron they needed. Eventually they would use it against the Bolsheviks and that would be grist to our mill. And so we left Europe and Asia to their own devices and continued to pile up profits until that very uncomfortable day when it was suddenly made clear that we had indulged just a little too long in our pleasant daydreams and that because Europe and Asia had caved in, we, too, were on the brink of ruin. And on that day we told Hitler that now was the time for him to try his coup. It was still several years before the outbreak of the second World War but because we had failed to realize that we were all fellow passengers on a small planet and that the weal and woe of every single individual affected that of all others, we deliberately played into the hands of that strange megalomaniac Adolf Hitler, who was inspired by but one single ambition—to make the German people the master race of the whole world.

Does all this sound more like a philosophical treatise than a serious discussion of historical facts? I am sorry if it does, but in an emergency like the present one, when each of us is fighting for his own life and freedom, the philosopher is in a much better position to explain the inevitable sequence of events than the historian, for he looks at them from the angle of eternity and that is the only point of view that can provide us with that insight which we will need if we are to bring this war to a victorious end. And let it be said to the everlasting credit of those philosophers, many of them disguised as plain, ordinary newspaper men and newspaper women, that they did their utmost best to awaken our people to the perils which awaited them.

Our diplomats seemed to have been stricken with the same color-blindness as their British colleagues and the men of Big Business in both countries, who declared that the whole world was steeped in red and who therefore failed to notice that there was as much brown and black (perhaps even more) as there was pink and red.

Of course, the economic catastrophe at home, where a

whole community had now switched over from the trusted ancestral system of paying cash to the easier but infinitely more dangerous method of living on credit—the widespread misery which was depriving millions of our fellow citizens of even the barest necessities of life and was condemning them to live like pariahs in an Indian jungle —that, too, made it practically impossible for us to devote the whole of our attention to the terrible task of preparing ourselves for the task of protecting our shores against the imminent onslaught that might come at any moment from the side of either the Nazis or the Japanese or from both at the same time.

And that was the beginning of the tragedy which now has overtaken us. The exigencies of the moment were so great that America was still too much occupied with its own affairs to devote any spare time to the affairs of a world to which it preferred not to belong. Washington had become a beehive of social and economic activities. It was impossible to let hundreds of thousands of people continue to sleep in hallways and on park benches. It was urgently necessary to take care of millions of young men who in the strictest sense of the word had been thrown on the community. And the nation at large, although it had been brought up on the strict maxims of "individual effort," now began to suspect that the time had gone by when one could go gaily ahead with one's own private affairs and leave those who had fallen by the wayside (for no reasons of their own) or who had grown too old to labor any longer to the mercies of the poorhouse or proverbial charity. As a result of which there now arose a number of new federal organizations which had never been tolerated before (being until then considered as completely un-American) which made the lot of the average citizen a great deal happier by relieving him of that most dreadful of all his nightmares—the ever-besetting fear of the future.

All this, of course, was not accomplished without considerable opposition from those classes of society which until then had profited so generously from the older arrangement of "each one for himself and the devil take the hindmost," that they now anticipated the immediate collapse and downfall of the Republic. But as the years went by and nothing very serious happened—as the majority of the populace continued to live very much as it had always done—eating three meals a day, wearing shoes and collars, and spending a great part of every day in little automobiles moving to and from the movies—these changes did not lead up to that revolution which had been so eagerly foretold by many of the enemies of the New Deal and they became so thoroughly incorporated into the general fabric of the nation at large that they will never again be struck off the statute books. And we might have continued quietly along the peaceful path of progress if it had not been for the everlasting rumbling that came to us from across the ocean and which proved that the thunder clouds were piling up and that any time now the storm might break loose.

But again we failed to take serious notice, these events still seemed very far away from us and all the unhappy recollections from the last war once more began to spook around in our heads. And all the racial elements which for one reason or another had not yet been amalgamated and had become truly American in their feelings, tried to use this most welcome opportunity to do a little fishing in muddled waters and to settle some old scores of their own without (I fear me) very much regard or consideration for the well-being of the nation as a whole. With the result that we easily fell prey to the most dangerous weakness that lies inherent in a democratic form of government and once more wasted valuable time (at a moment when every hour might mean life or death to thousands of our young men) debating, discussing, slinging mud, calling names, and in the name of "free speech" allowing a large number of citizens, not remarkable for their ability to think either logically or constructively, or even patriotically, to prevent those preparations that were absolutely necessary if our nation wished to hold its own when Armageddon should overtake it.

Until that fateful Sunday morning when the treacherous bombs of Japan blew all further hope for peace to pieces and we were suddenly made to realize that, whether we liked it or not, we were a part of the world at large.

And that, I think, is the most important item in the history of our nation during the last twenty years. We had been fighting against the inevitable. We had so thoroughly enjoyed ourselves during the first century and a half of our national existence, during which we had fallen heir to the riches of a virgin continent, and had been protected from foreign attack by a couple of wide oceans, that we had come to accept our blessings as something to which we were entitled—as something which was ours by decree of Providence itself so that we had forgotten that greatest of all lessons of history—that liberty of thought and action are not the result of high-sounding oratory and wishful thinking—that they can only be achieved by those willing to fight for them, work for them, live for them, and, if necessary, die for them, and finally that they can only be preserved by those eager and able to tend them and cherish them with unrelenting watchfulness as the highest good after which a civilized human being can hope to strive during his short residence on this tiny planet which he calls home.

That is the lesson which America is learning while this is being set in type. We have made many and grievous mistakes during the last twenty years and we shall have to pay for them as dearly as individuals must do when they are guilty of an error of judgment. But now that we have come to realize the situation in which we find ourselves, we have settled down to the business in hand and being a people which likes to finish a job, once we have made up our minds that the job is worth while, there can be no doubt about the outcome of the conflict. We cannot possibly hope to live in a world, one part of which is inhabited by people of good will and with at least some semblance of respect for the teachings of the great Nazarene prophet, and the rest of which is populated by savages who have gone the law of the jungle one better by decreeing that even children in arms shall not be excluded from wholesale murder and execution.

But our greatest opportunity will come once this war is over and the dreadful scourge of Nazi-ism shall have been stamped out, as we have stamped out cholera and smallpox and other hideous epidemics of loathsome diseases. For then it will be America which will have to show the rest of the world the road to a newer and happier form of civilization in which all of us (each to the best of his or her ability) shall in truth co-operate with the best of our fellow men for the greatest good of that nation which is our noblest heritage and the source of our greatest pride, the free and independent Republic of the United States of America.

"The hard condition of the historian is that if he speaks the truth he provokes the anger of men; but if he commits falsehoods to writing he will be unacceptable to God who will distinguish in his judgments between Truth and Adulation."—*The Venerable Bede.*

# NOTE

HENDRIK VAN LOON died in 1944, and *The Story of America* was finished shortly before his death. In the text there are references, in the present tense, to certain "current" events that have now become history. The editors of this Dell Edition have not tried to disguise this fact.

One does not tamper with a classic. *The Story of America* stands as the monument to a profound, far-seeing intelligence; to alter van Loon's material, to attempt to "up-date" it would be a bold and foolish presumption. All great writers are ahead of their time, and van Loon's remarks about the condition of our modern world are as significant today as they were a dozen years ago. We have felt it totally unnecessary to burden them, or the reader, with the listing of additional facts familiar to all. For them one may review the newspapers, even his own memory; but for history with the ring of timeless immediacy, and of truth, *The Story of America* must stand as it was written.

# INDEX

## A

Adams, Charles Francis, 303
Adams, Henry, 326
Adams, John, 131-132, 137, 145,
    147-148, 172, 177, 178, 187, 191,
    197, 199, 200, 205, 228, 239, 277
Adams, John Quincy, 239, 242
Adams, Mrs. John, 200
Adams, Samuel, 131-132, 134
Africa, 344
Alaska, 231
Alien Law, 203
Allen, Ethan, 140
Amazon River, 33
America, Discovery of, 25
American Revolution, 103, 124,
    128ff, 134ff
Amherst, General Jeffry, 27
Amsterdam, Holland, 62
Anderson, Major, 291, 292
André, Major, 174
Annapolis Convention, 181-182
Anti-Federalists. *See* Republicans.
Aristocracy, 277
Armada, 48-49
Arnold, Benedict, 140, 174
Articles of Confederation, 180
Arts and Sciences, 249ff, 274, 324,
    327
Asia, 11, 344
Atlantic Charter, 355, 361
Austria, 14, 82, 215, 245, 346
Azores, 21, 24

## B

Balboa, 33
Barre, Colonel, 115

de Beaumarchais, Pierre, 163, 164,
    165
Beauregard, General, 292
von Bismarck, Otto, 344
Bladensburg race, 297
Blanchard, 262
Block, Adriaen, 75
Blockade, British, 216
Blockade, Northern, 299, 305, 307
Bloody Mary, 68
Bolivar, Simon, 225, 227-228, 254
Booth, 316
Boston, 70, 121, 135, 140, 154, 176,
    192
Boston tea party, 121
Bowie, Jim, 256
Boycott, 132-133
Brandenburg, 82
British Muscovy Company, 74
de Brouage, Samuel de Champlain. *See* Champlain.
Brown, John, 287
Brownites. *See* Puritans.
Bull Run, Battle of, 300
Bunker Hill, 136
Buonaparte, General. *See* Napoleon.
Burgoyne, John, 155, 165, 176
Burke, Edmund, 151-152, 193
Burr, Aaron, 212-213, 240, 317
Bush, Sarah, 284
Buzzards Bay, Massachusetts, 55

## C

Caesar, 71
Calvert, George, 85
Calvin, Dr. John, 40-41, 52, 72,
    209, 248

377